SEARCHING FOR SAFETY

SOCIAL
PHILOSOPHY
& POLICY CENTER

SEARCHING FOR SAFETY

Aaron Wildavsky

transaction

Transaction Books
New Brunswick (USA) and London (UK)

Published by the Social Philosophy and Policy Center
and by Transaction Publishers 1988

Copyright © by the Social Philosophy and Policy Center

Library of Congress Cataloging-in-Publication Data

Wildavsky, Aaron B.
    Searching for safety / Aaron Wildavsky.
        p.   cm. — (Studies in social philosophy & policy; no. 10)
    At head of title: Social Philosophy & Policy Center.
    Bibliography: p.
    ISBN 0-912051-17-5. ISBN 0-912051-18-3 (pbk.)
    1. Risk. 2. Uncertainty. 3. Safety regulations. 4. Health. 5. Policy
sciences. I. Bowling Green State University. Social Philosophy & Policy
Center. II. Title. III. Series: Studies in social philosophy & policy; no. 10.
H91.W56 1988
303—dc19   87-37659
                                                                CIP

Cover Design: Jacky Ahrens

To the memory of my friend, Bill Havender.

Contents

Acknowledgments

Learning about (and keeping up with) the literature on risk is a monumental task. Even if one excludes the political and social aspects of the subject, arguably its most important, and concentrates, as I do in this book, on the consequences of technology for health and safety, keeping up with risk, where a new hazard is seemingly a daily discovery and views about old ones are continuously revised, has become a full-time occupation. But not, as a political scientist and policy analyst, for me.

In order to broaden greatly the range of phenomena that could be treated, as well as to make up for my lack of knowledge, I sought collaborators. After drafts of the first four chapters were completed, I asked four people—Dennis Coyle, a graduate student in the Political Science Department; William Havender, a geneticist and consultant on risk; Elizabeth Nichols, a graduate student in the Sociology Department; and Dan Polisar, an undergraduate at Princeton—to work with me respectively on how the human body defends itself, on how measures designed to reduce risk go wrong, on whether adding safety measures improves safety, and on why the law of personal injury harms people. I have been extremely fortunate in my collaborators. All of them have made my work better than it otherwise would have been. (Elizabeth Nichols, with whom I continue to work on the inspection of nuclear power plants, also prepared material for me on natural disasters.) Because of the special expertise required, I asked Bob Budnitz, a nuclear physicist and former head of research for the Nuclear Regulatory Commission, to write a section on substituting performance standards for detailed specification in regulation of nuclear power plants. Without them, this book would have been much poorer.

I am also grateful to a number of expert critics who gave valuable advice on parts of the manuscript: Eugene Bardach, Robert Budnitz, Dennis Coyle, Douglas Easterling, Amitai Etzioni, Robert Goodin, Peter Huber, Robert H. Nelson, Emory Roe, Michael Tartar, and Michael Thompson. The editor of the series in which this volume appears, Ellen Paul, also made helpful suggestions. Responding to their comments has led to considerable improvement.

I have left the special contribution of William Havender for last so it will stand first and foremost. Bill and I met five years ago when I organized a seminar on risk for the Survey Research Center. For most of that time, until illness overtook him, we met every two or three weeks to discuss risk. I learned more about risk from him than from any single person. His detailed critique of the entire manuscript is the toughest and most useful of any I have ever received.

A geneticist by training, a social scientist by avocation, Bill Havender was far too sophisticated to believe that "the facts" interpreted themselves or that the preponderance of evidence would necessarily prevail in the political system. Nevertheless, now that he is gone (Bill died in April 1987), his passion for truth remains with me. Our first game was to take unfolding events about this or that substance or event (How soon before the latest sweetener was alleged to be worse than saccharin or cyclamates?), and place our bets on what the evidence would show after further studies had been reported. (Would Chernobyl also turn out to be a consequence of trying to improve safety?) He was right, so far as I could see, more often than anyone whose opinions appeared in the public prints. Our last game—trying to figure out why safety measures so often produced the opposite result—appears in Chapter 9. There the argument has been formalized, but I hope some of the fun shines through. Dedicating *Searching for Safety* to Bill is my way of saying that his search will live on.

Financial support for this book has come from three sources: The National Science Foundation, grant No. PRA-8412418; the Survey Research Center; and the Smith Richardson Foundation, through the Institute for Educational Affairs. As always, Joshua Menkes at NSF and Director Percy Tannenbaum and Assistant Director James Wiley at the SRC facilitated my efforts. Doris Patton, my secretary, bore with numerous revisions and names of creatures and substances not found in ordinary parlance, let alone polite company. I try but do not always succeed in doing my job as well as she does hers.

The Jogger's Dilemma
or
What Should We do When the Safe and the Dangerous are Inextricably Intertwined?

...Consider...the publicity over the death of James Fixx this summer. Mr. Fixx, an ardent runner and author of several popular books on running, died of a heart attack while running. His death stirred considerable controversy in both the lay and the medical press on the risks and benefits of exercise.

—(*Wall Street Journal*, October 4, 1984, article by Jerry E. Bidrop)

Were I asked why anyone would want to read this book, I would answer that it offers a theory accounting for the considerable degree of safety achieved in contemporary society, as well as the danger introduced by technological development. Almost all books on risk treat it as a bad thing to be avoided or diminished, rather than as an inevitably mixed phenomenon from which considerable good, as well as harm, is derived.

Since there can be no safety without risk, as I shall show, the importance of thinking about better and worse ways of searching for safety gives this subject an open-ended quality that is in danger of being foreclosed by thinking in terms of "all good" or "all bad." For if, as I will further show, both good and bad inhere in the same objects, strategies, and processes—albeit in different degrees and in uncertain combinations—the only way to discover how to achieve more "good" is to search for safety—which, by my way of thinking, involves risk.

To those who see safety as a goal we know how to achieve, the task of decision making is simple: choose the safer path. There is no need to look further, since we already know what to do; no act designed to secure safety could have the opposite effect. Imagine instead, however, safety as largely an unknown for which society has to search. An act might help achieve that objective, or it might not. Often, we would not know which, safety or danger, had in fact been achieved until afterwards. Given this uncertainty, we would always have to be as concerned that the existing level of safety not be lowered as that it might be raised.

The most important part of the safety enterprise is thinking about how to think (and, therefore, how to act) about risk. As things stand, the dangers of new things are viewed in isolation from, and with no attention to, potential advantages. Yet playing it safe, doing nothing, means reducing possible opportunities to benefit from chances taken, and can hurt people. Just as the unknown consequences of technological advance have to become part of our safety calculus, so must "safety risks"—possible damage resulting from measures designed to improve safety—enter into our considerations.

Thinking about risk, I contend, has been one-sided: safety has been over-identified with keeping things from happening. My aim is to redress this imbalance by emphasizing the increases in safety due to entrepreneurial activity. If this essay in persuasion achieves its purpose, the focus of the risk debate will shift from the passive prevention of harm to a more active search for safety.

This book is about how risk and safety are produced, about the fact that they are intertwined, and about what, therefore, should be done to make the search for better combinations both efficient—devoting resources to the worst hazards—and effective—actually improving safety. Because safety must be discovered, and cannot be merely chosen, I shall argue that trial-and-error risk taking, rather than risk aversion, is the preferable strategy for securing safety. Encouraging trial and error promotes resilience—learning from adversity how to do better—while avoiding restrictions that encourage the continuation of existing hazards. Increasing the pool of general resources, such as wealth and knowledge, secures safety for more people than using up resources in a vain effort to protect against unperceivable, hypothetical dangers. Wealth adds to health.

Objective Risk

My subject is the objective aspects of safety and of danger (popularly known as "risk"). By "objective" I do not mean to assert my own particular respect for facts. Nor would I suggest that all people see eye to eye about what risks under which circumstances should or should not be taken. Nevertheless, almost all participants in the risk debate do claim a respect for facts and attempt to legitimate their policy preferences by reference to canons of scientific inquiry. Citing ghosts or gremlins would not do. Assuming that the common objective is to secure safety, let us all try to see what sort of actions would best achieve that goal.

By objective aspects of risk, therefore, I mean both observable dangers as well as the observable consequences of actions undertaken for the ostensible purpose of increasing safety. Do, or do not, actions undertaken in the name of risk reduction achieve safety? In the end, to be sure, evaluation of strategies is done by human beings, like myself, who bring biases to bear on their perceptions. Though I shall try to be persuasive, I make no claim to some transcendental objectivity. It is the certainty of the question—How best to secure safety?—not the uncertainty of the answers that leads me to talk about objective risk. Except in passing, therefore, I shall not deal with the subjective aspects of safety: What sorts of people are risk-taking or risk-averse for which reasons in regard to different matters (say nuclear energy or acquired immune deficiency syndrome). Nor shall I emphasize the overtly political aspects of the controversies over risk, though mobilizing support is indeed a vital and often decisive activity. In this book I shall concentrate instead on what ought to be done to improve safety regardless of its immediate political feasibility.[1]

That this book is not overtly concerned with political action does not signify that it is devoid of political ideas. On the contrary, I have deliberately set out to redress existing risk-averse biases by countering them with my own risk-taking bias. Nor does the undoubted fact that all positions in the risk debate reflect views of the good life imply that all are equally correct, i.e., that all would result in the same consequences for safety. Not so. What sort of strategies work best in securing safety remains a problem subject to investigation. A good place to start is with the multiple meanings of risk.

"Safety," E. Siddall writes, "is the degree to which (a) temporary ill health or injury, (b) chronic or permanent ill health or injury, or (c) death are controlled, avoided, prevented, made less frequent or less probable in a group of people."[2] The reference to a particular group rather than to an entire society makes us aware that risk may have distributive consequences. "Safety for whom?" is always a good question.[3]

Following current usage, William Rowe defines risk as "the potential for harm."[4] According to this conception, risk is the probability of encountering negatively-valued events. This definition has the virtue of being clear, concise, and general. Because it views risks as never carrying associated benefits, however, it also has the disadvantage of prejudging the conclusion of inquiries. To take risks thus stands condemned as being bad, the only question being, how bad. Yet, in ordinary usage, we often speak of taking risks in order (hopefully) to secure gains. If and when we succeed, risk taking can help improve safety. Altering the definition to refer to "the potential for harm and/or for safety" complicates matters. I favor this definition, however, because it compares gains as well as losses, accepting the possibility that a single act or thing can cause both positive and negative safety consequences.[5]

Consider the case of the "rational" potato. Like all growing things, it could not survive the process of evolution unless it was able to ward off predators. Unable to run away or fight directly, the homely potato has evolved chemical defenses. When mother told us that the potato's vitamins were concentrated in the jacket, she was right. What she did not know, however, was that the poisons the potato uses to ward off predators also were in the jacket. Under unusual conditions, these poisons accumulate and can be dangerous to human life. Nevertheless, when we are urged to eat potato jackets because it is healthy, I concur, providing only we understand that the potato's poisons and its nutrients are largely in the same place.

The Principle of Uncertainty, the Axiom of Connectedness, and the Rule of Sacrifice

Once we stop thinking of health and safety as qualities we already know how to achieve—and government's task being simply to choose what it confidently knows is life-enhancing, while rejecting what it already knows is life-denying—the question of how to search for safety becomes paramount. Which set of principles, axioms, and rules, I ask, helps us discover how to reduce risk overall so that society as a whole becomes safer? Though no one can say for sure, my candidates in opening up the inquiry on risk and safety are: the principle of uncertainty, the axiom of connectedness, and the rule of sacrifice.

Dangers will arise; everyone agrees on that. Uncertainty about the consequences of present acts and about others as yet unforeseen cannot be reduced to zero. The principle of irreducible uncertainty is based not only on the self-evident premise that no one knows it all, but also on the slightly less obvious consideration that even as human beings act on their environment they are creating consequences of which they are as yet not fully aware. Although some uncertainties may be reduced under some circumstances, a modicum of uncertainty is a universal condition. Hence Kenneth Boulding writes about "irreducible uncertainties."[6]

To the principle of uncertainty I wish to add another—the axiom of connectedness. This states that the good and the bad (safety and harm) are intertwined in the same acts and objects.[7] There may be unalloyed goods (though I doubt it) but, if so, they are few and far between. Take the two principles together—uncertainty cannot be eliminated and damage cannot be avoided. This combination stipulates the conditions (old risks cannot be reduced without incurring new ones) under which the question of how to increase safety should be considered.

Suppose the things of this world, and the practices people follow, were all good or all bad in terms of securing safety. Then nothing would matter except to discover and choose the safe, and reject the dangerous. The end—securing safety—is given, and a decision rule exists for choosing among available means.

But life is not so straightforward. For the most part, safety and danger coexist in the same objects and practices. Under the right (or wrong) conditions, everything we need for life can also maim or kill: water can drown, food can poison, air can choke. Babies cannot be born without risk to the mother, nor can they grow to adulthood without facing innumerable dangers.

The trick is to discover not how to avoid risk, for this is impossible, but how to use risk to get more of the good and less of the bad. The search for safety is a balancing act. For if the axiom of connectedness holds, there is no choice that results in no harm. Merely minimizing danger to some people would not meet the safety criterion if it resulted in less safety for a larger number of other people than there otherwise would have been. If every act and every thing has harm for someone somewhere, indeed, if the safety we seek is ineluctably bound up with the danger that accompanies it, more harm than good may be done by efforts to avoid risk.

The principle of uncertainty and the axiom of connectedness can be generalized to all (including human) systems: each part of every system cannot be stable at the same time. Economist Burton Klein expresses the thought well:

> It is true, of course, that in an imaginary, unchanging world economies can be predictable both in the small and in the large: that is, they can survive simply by taking the classical law of supply and demand as a given. However, if an economic system is to make smooth adjustments in dealing with new circumstances—if it is to remain predictable in the large, so to speak—it must be able to adapt itself to new circumstances. In fact, what I mean by "dynamic" *is the ability of a person, a firm or an economy to adapt itself to new circumstances by generating new alternatives.* But, it should be apparent that if predictability in the small is defined as "microstability" and predictability in the large as "macrostability" neither an individual firm nor an entire economy can simultaneously conserve its micro and macrostability. Only in heaven can microstability be equated to macrostability. Here on earth, the greater the insistence on microstability—the greater the insistence on preserving a way of life—the lower will be its macrostability. Conversely, if a system is to enjoy a high degree of macrostability it must enjoy the ability to generate new alternatives, when confronted by necessity.[8]

I will call this—the safety or macrostability of the whole being dependent upon the risk taking or instability of the parts—the "rule of sacrifice."

Does risk in the human context mean that specific individuals must give up their lives or limbs for a collective entity? No. It does mean that if the parts of a system are prevented from facing risks, the whole will become unable to adapt to new dangers. The concern with harming individuals for the benefit of the collective is warranted (see Chapter 10 for discussion) but misapplied. For harm is being done anyway; existing hazards are already taking their toll. The only real alternatives involve understanding the balance among those helped and hurt. Since there is no way of avoiding harm for everyone, the search for safety has to proceed on the understanding that the rule of sacrifice is inexorable: there can be no stable whole without some unstable parts.[9]

Rival Strategies for Securing Safety

Assertions about risk should be treated as hypotheses. That is why I have decided to focus on the agreed objective—securing safety—rather than the disputed means. Is "taking no chances," for instance, conducive to safety? In the first chapter, "Trial and Error Versus Trial Without Error," I argue that it is not. Many predicted dangers have turned out to be exaggerated or nonexistent. Others are real, but the policies invoked merely shifted dangers from one place or people to another. Still other, worse dangers resulted because the products or practices protested against were replaced by more harmful substitutes. There are, to be sure, unanticipated consequences of technology that do more harm than good. But there are also, as Michael Thompson calls them, "unconsequent anticipations," i.e., predictions of unsafe events that never come to pass. When government acts to prevent all imaginable dangers, the costs associated with such predictions are no longer cheap. The cost is counted not only in money but also in damage done by those very preventive measures, and in harm that might have been mitigated had resources not been used up on unrealized risks.

Acting safely, it is said, requires rejection of risky things—chemicals, processes, apparatus—that could cause grave damage. Instead of making progress by trial and error, some proponents of safety propose a rule of allowing no trials without prior guarantees against harm. This across-the-board risk aversion actually increases danger, I shall argue, because in thus achieving "safety" the harm avoided is part and parcel of even larger, as yet unknown, benefits that will be forgone. By taking a narrow view—a certain thing does harm—instead of a broad perspective—what is the balance of harm and help here compared to alternatives—measures designed to increase safety can lead to an overall decrease. When a strategy of "no trials without prior guarantees against error" replaces "trial and error," the opportunity to take risks in order to achieve beneficial consequences is lost.

This is the theme of the second chapter, "Opportunity Benefits Versus Opportunity Risks."

The risks stemming from trial and error should also be discounted by the "safety risks" that flow from trying to prevent damage. For if all things are potentially dangerous, merely giving a measure a safety label is no guarantee that it will not do harm. Rem Khokhlov, an eminent mountain climber and scientist, for instance, was also part of the Soviet political elite. When he suffered a pulmonary embolism during a training mission at 20,000 feet, a helicopter was sent for him, after which he was taken to Moscow for treatment. "It has been suggested to me by several Soviet friends," Peter Franken wrote in *Science*, "that Khokhlov's seniority in the Soviet system was partly responsible for his death in that it led to his being treated by physicians who were less familiar with this particular illness than was the medical community nearer the site of the accident."[10]

Overwhelming evidence shows that the economic growth and technological advance arising from market competition have in the past two centuries been accompanied by dramatic improvements in health—large increases in longevity and decreases in sickness. One might expect a focus on profit to have led to neglect or even disregard of safety. Why, then, does society nevertheless usually end up healthier? Economists, so far as I know, have not turned their attention to the relationship between markets and safety: Does economic competition increase or decrease safety?

The positive association between market processes and economic wealth is well documented. "Richer Is Sicker Versus Richer Is Safer," the third chapter, begins by postulating another truth, just as well-established, though less well-publicized: human health is a function of economic wealth. Whether comparisons are made between nations or among people within them, wealthier is healthier. Why this is so, however, is not self-evident.

Disputes over the moral implications of economic costs as a consideration in regulation of risk (Should life be sacrificed to material gain?) do not make sense if health and wealth are positively related. In a wealth-health analysis, I ask whether a regulation or device or practice adds more to human safety than its cost subtracts from that safety.

The common wisdom is captured in the proverb "an ounce of prevention is worth a pound of cure." As is usually true with proverbs, however (he who hesitates is lost, but, look before you leap), they do not state the conditions of applicability. Cure may well be better than prevention if the former is feasible and the latter is not or if cure increases flexibility in dealing with future dangers while prevention induces rigidity.

Is it better, I ask in Chapter 4, to attempt to anticipate dangers before they occur or to inculcate a capacity to respond resiliently, i.e., to learn from experience to cope with untoward events? If seeking to anticipate dangers saps a system's energies without enabling it to guess right, for instance, then the system might end up without the benefits of either anticipation or resilience. And, further, if anticipation works well enough to suggest that stability is permanent, unexpected challenges may yet overwhelm the system. How, then, can society protect itself against unknown dangers?

Human beings can engage in prevention. They can plan. But how well? Planning depends on prediction, which presumes the elimination (or, at least, reduction) of surprise. I am not talking about minor (a small change in probabilities) but about major surprise, a change in kind, a change like acquired immune deficiency syndrome that central decision makers could not imagine might occur. Confusing quantitative surprise (where we surmise what might happen but not its probability) with qualitative surprise (where we have no idea of the kind of event) trivializes the problem of unexpected danger. If only "expected surprise" existed, there would be a lot less to worry about. Fire drills may protect against expected surprises, but not against the qualitatively unexpected.

How, then, might members of society develop defenses without knowing what might be in store for them? How might a society sample the unknown so as to get hints about future dangers before they become massive? One good question deserves another. Who has both the capacity and the incentive to undertake this strange sort of task? Who might so benefit from outguessing the future as to be willing to absorb the losses from what might be a high rate of failure? The larger and more centralized the organization that seeks to predict the future, the longer it will take to get agreement, the fewer hypotheses it can try, and the more costly each probe is likely to be. Instead of assuming that anticipation must be centralized, therefore, I would like to open up the possibility that safety might be improved by spreading the anticipatory function more widely throughout society.

Decentralized anticipation (numerous independent probes of an uncertain future) can achieve a greater degree of safety. Since innovations are introduced piecemeal as a result of these independent probes, a larger proportion of emergent dangers can be perceived early while each hazard is still localized and small. The ability of market competition to interrogate the unknown at a low cost to society, while simultaneously encouraging individuals to overcome adversity, has been underappreciated.

Anticipation and resilience, the broadest strategic alternatives for attempting to secure safety, subsume other strategies. Decentralized, rapidly moving trial and error contributes to a strategy of resilience. Centralized, slow-moving regulation of trials to prevent errors is essential to a strategy of anticipation. Are these strategies mutually exclusive, or can they be combined?

Why, the reader may well ask, are these strategies dichotomized into extremes instead of joined together? Obviously, the intelligent person would want to combine anticipation with resilience. Even though, in the end, a mixed strategy should be adopted, I think these large questions, with their polar-opposite alternatives, are good to ask.

Each extreme alternative has real advocates. The strategy of "no trials without prior guarantees against error" has substantial support; as the second chapter shows, it is written into law. The debate about whether the "no threshold effect" (a single molecule of a carcinogenic substance, some say, is enough to kill) should be used as the major criterion of regulatory choice is instructive in this regard.

But if we suppose, following Ronald Heiner's seminal essay on "The Origin of Predictable Behavior," that human uncertainty is deeper and more pervasive than has heretofore been thought,[11] reliance on simple rules of thumb makes more sense. Has the individual on the verge of decision reached the right conclusion about both his objectives (or preferences) and/or the means for obtaining them? Perhaps he has the right preferences, but at the wrong time or for different conditions. Since the consequences of actions are so entangled—undoubtedly the product of diverse causes, some recent, the others long past—our decision maker cannot be at all certain about whether past solutions have worked or to what degree. Evolution proves survival, to be sure, but survival alone is hardly convincing evidence that the strategy itself was beneficial. The doctrine of "adverse selection"[12] reminds us that organisms or practices may be selected because they inhere in desirable objects despite the fact that the item selected, were the truth known, is actually harmful.

Torn by uncertainty, decision makers place a high premium on reliability, i.e., on increasing the likelihood that a choice will work reasonably well under most conditions, though not necessarily exceptionally well under any. The chance that a given objective can be perfectly realized, Heiner argues, is exceedingly low compared to the probability of missing by so wide a margin that nothing is attained. Blame is reduced by reasonable success, not by failing to achieve perfection. The need for reassurance in an uncertain world, therefore, may lead to adopting a polar strategy—resilience or anticipation—even though neither is expected to work supremely well in every instance.

Also, mixed strategies are not always feasible; when a decision maker must choose a single strategy, therefore, it is desirable to estimate which one would yield the best overall results. It may be advantageous to start with one possible strategy, modifying it as circumstances warrant. The danger is less in beginning than in ending with a single strategy. Polarizing proposed solutions is largely a device that ultimately enables us to devise mixed strategies.

Diverse Arenas for Studying Risk

The first four chapters in Section I contain examples drawn from current controversies over risk—regulation of chemical carcinogens, efforts to reduce pollution of different kinds, safety on the job, and so on—that appear to have reached an impasse in terms of productive thinking. Wishing as I do to alter how we view risk and safety, I have sought new areas in which to study rival efforts to reduce risk. Hence, the rather unusual subject matter in Section II—nonhuman life forms, the inspection of nuclear power plants, the human body, and the law of personal injuries—deserves a word of explanation.

I want to show that resilience and anticipation are universal strategies. One way to do this is to pick an area of life remote from current concerns, an area which contains both sets of strategies, fairly evenly matched, operating under different conditions. The safety (ecologists speak of systemic or species stability) of plants, animals, and insects is well-suited for this purpose. Also, I want to see what happens when a strategy of anticipation is used far more frequently than a strategy of resilience. The inspection of nuclear power plants, where one safety measure after another is used in an effort to ward off danger, meets the criterion of predominant anticipation. The other side of the risk coin—more resilience than anticipation—is exemplified by the human body. Though the body tries to anticipate by building some barriers against certain dangers, most of its rather economical defenses work toward mitigating harms as, and after, they occur. A fourth arena for studying risk illustrates the worst of the two worlds, in which there is neither much resilience nor much anticipation. The law of torts is avowedly a form of resilience; people cannot sue for damage arising from personal injuries unless they first show that there has been injury. Nevertheless, the tort law has been applied so as to cause the worst consequences of anticipatory regulation with almost none of the benefits of resilience.

Anticipation and resilience are generic strategies, capable of being employed by diverse life forms under many different circumstances. These strategies are useful in classifying the ways in which "Nonhuman Life Forms Cope With Danger" (Chapter 5). The efforts of plants, insects, and animals to protect themselves have much to tell us about diverse approaches to safety.

Consider, for instance, a principle enunciated by Gerald Rosenthal: "No defense is inviolate."[13] The emerging discipline of chemical ecology studies the interaction between plants and their enemies. In certain desert areas the hairs or trichomes of plants store natural toxins, some of which cause allergic reactions that deter herbivores from feeding on them. Other defensive mechanisms are more indirect. Some plants produce analogues to juvenile hormones that keep the insect in perpetual youth, so that it cannot metamorphose and become a pupa. But juvenoids, which resemble juvenile hormones, must also kill their predators, for otherwise they merely prolong its larval stage, which happens to be the most destructive stage of the insect.[14]

Defenses may be counteracted. Even safety alarm systems can be used against an organism. When attacked by a predator, the aphid *Myzus persicae* secretes an alarm pheromone that informs other aphids of the coming danger. This aphid also preys on wild, tuberous potatoes. In apparent response, the wild potato releases a substance that mimics the aphid's alarm signal.[15] Organisms, we may conclude, have to live with incomplete defenses.

Are human beings so different? Can *Homo sapiens* devise foolproof defenses? Is safety always secured by multiplying the number of safety measures? The problem is not only whether measures purporting to increase safety always accomplish that purpose but, less obviously, whether measures that, taken singly, do increase safety have the same positive effect if deployed one on top of the other. A study of inspection and inspectors in nuclear power plants, the sixth chapter, reveals a curvilinear relationship: introducing a few devices tends to increase safety, but multiplying them decreases safety—they get in each other's way; the devices themselves become the causes of new failures.

If relying on anticipation has its drawbacks, what can we say about a preponderant strategy of resilience? "How the Human Body Defends Itself," the seventh chapter, is largely a story of resilience. Rather than evolving systems that never or rarely break down, biological processes are accompanied by a variety of repair mechanisms. The most important body strategies, so to speak, appear to be "search and destroy" and "redundant repair"; they are based on learning how to bounce back from insults. Some dangers are anticipated, but most are left to learning through trial and error. Sometimes, however, a safety mechanism such as the immune system turns against the body it is designed to protect; in the body as in society, the axiom of connectedness holds, for the sources of life and death are intertwined.

The eighth chapter looks at the evolution of the law of torts, concerned with personal injury, from a mode of resilience to one of anticipation.

Consequently, tort law now operates (read your local newspaper) as if defendants were subject to regulation—i.e., to enforceable prohibitions in advance of action.

The concluding chapters, comprising Section III, seek to set out principles that reduce harm and increase safety. The ninth chapter—"Why Less is More: A Taxonomy of Error"—accentuates the negative by developing principles specifying what not to do to improve safety. The normal revulsion to risk is misleading. Paradoxically, overconcentration on danger has led to neglect of safety: measures to increase safety often end up decreasing it, while courting danger may reduce it. In the same spirit, Michael Novak suggests that we pay less attention to the causes of poverty, which we do not wish to produce, and more to the causes of wealth.[16] An overwhelming concern with large consequence, low probability events screens out strategies that have probability of accumulating small, health enhancing benefits. To the degree that securing safety is our ultimate concern, principles guiding thought and action—the objective aspects to which I referred earlier—should be reconsidered and redirected, from risk aversion to risk taking.

By seeking to eliminate all but infinitesimal sources of risk, conformity to the single best safety strategy is sought. Thus, organizations in society become fewer and larger, and, in order to prove that products do no harm, much more capital is required. Consequently, small organizations are driven out. Diversity among organizations declines as they are subject to the same regulations. Hence the available responses to unexpected adversity diminish. The growth of knowledge slows down because fewer hypotheses are tested. Increases in wealth are held to a minimum, both because resources are devoted to anticipation and because of regulatory restrictions on market transactions. Because earlier efforts at prevention lead to less experience in coping with unanticipated risk, resilience declines. Eventually there is also less ability to prevent damage through such anticipatory measures because past efforts to ward off innumerable dangers, most of which do not materialize, have led to internal exhaustion. Just as the effort to mobilize too many resources against threats can lead the body's defenses to turn on the body itself, destroying healthy cells and tissue, so, too, society, while preoccupied with eliminating harm, can inadvertently destroy its sources of safety. What understanding of risk and safety, I ask, would lead to better strategies for securing safety?

If all things are potentially risky, losses here may be made up by gains there. Advantages in one place may be given up in another. There is no problem in protecting a part (of an apparatus, a person, a group, a society). The difficulty lies in advancing the whole so that more people are gaining than losing at any one time, most people are safer over a period of time, and almost all people are better off than they would have been in decades past. Steady improvements in safety, I hypothesize, depend upon enlarging society's overall resource capacity so as to increase its resilience.

General and Global Resources

On the global level, safety is a function of general resources in a given society at a certain time. By general resources I mean knowledge, education, wealth, energy, communication, and any other resource that can be shifted around. General resources can be converted into other things. These are not just food crops, for example, but the capacity to grow food and to alter what one grows according to the conditions of the time. The global level stands for overall resource capacity—the ability to mobilize and to redeploy general resources.

Conceivably there could be a limit on global resources, a limit not only at an instant in time but for all time thereafter. While the materials out of which energy is transformed should last for eons, for instance, it is possible that at some time their cost will become prohibitive. While physical resources may be limited (a topic covered under the elusive subject of entropy), however, the true currency of human ingenuity is information, and I am not aware that it faces exhaustion.

Since my subject here is objective risk, assertions about limits have to be treated as subject to empirical inquiry. No limits are in sight, I think, even though one day they may reveal themselves. In this book, I shall assume, in accord with the evidence of the last several hundred years, that global resources can and do grow. If this assumption is unwarranted, if mankind is on a declining resource curve, then drastic, perhaps desperate, measures might be indicated; for allowing things to go on as they are might be worse than using up resources in trying preventive measures that have very low probability of success. But I doubt it.

Hypotheses about global resource potential do not dispose of the question of how safety might best be achieved at any stipulated level of global resources. Whether an act or a program designed to increase safety actually works as intended cannot be determined in advance. Every act must be treated as a potential source of harm as well as help. Just as abuses are committed in the name of liberty, so measures taken in the name of health can still make us sick. Purported safety measures, in addition to local consequences—their effectiveness against the specific hazard at which they are aimed—may also affect the global level of resources. Since I hypothesize that this global level determines the safety of society overall, it follows that safety measures that cause a decline in general resources will decrease the net safety of society.

While acts designed to secure safety may have the opposite effect, so, too, acts that do not intentionally consider safety at all may actually increase it. When the global level of resources grows, so my hypothesis suggests, safety grows with it whether intended or not. "Richer is Safer" not necessarily because of good safety intentions, but rather because the global resource level has gone up, thereby increasing the capacity to undertake both anticipatory and resilient strategies. Conversely, measures intended to secure safety actually may increase harm—not only because they may be misguided, but also (and, for my thesis, more important, since mistakes are inherent in life) because they reduce the amount of global resources. In the tenth and final chapter ("The Secret of Safety Lies in Danger") I shall try to explain how and why citizens of nations in which there has been technological progress through trial and error have become healthier and safer than they or their forebearers used to be.

The jogger's dilemma brings us full circle to the essence of the relationship between courting danger and securing safety, for the two are different sides of the same coin. Too much or too strenuous exercise too soon is unsafe. Too little, too infrequently is also bad. So far, so simple. The complication is that during the limited time devoted to the most strenuous exercise, the risk of heart attack rises. That's the bad news. The good news is that for the rest of the day, as well as the days in between regular exercise, the body is safer. "Although the risk of primary cardiac arrest is transiently increased during vigorous exercise," a study in *The New England Journal of Medicine* reports, "habitual vigorous exercise is associated with an overall decreased risk of primary cardiac arrest."[17] You cannot have the one—a safer organism—without the other—expanding its resilience by allowing it to face risks. As the experience of joggers shows, safety is the other side of risk.

SECTION I:
STRATEGIES

1

Trial and Error Versus
Trial Without Error

There are two bedrock approaches to managing risk—trial and error, and trial without error. According to the doctrine of "trial without error," no change whatsoever will be allowed unless there is solid proof that the proposed substance or action will do no harm. All doubts, uncertainties, and conflicting interpretations will thus be resolved by disallowing trials. Taking "error" here to mean damage to life, this—prohibiting new products unless they can be proven in advance to be harmless—is an extraordinarily stringent prohibition. Surely no scientist (or businessman or politician or citizen) can guarantee in the present that future generations will be better off because of any individual action.

True, without trials there can be no new errors; but without these errors, there is also less new learning. Science, its historians say, is more about rejecting than accepting hypotheses. Knowledge grows through critical appraisal of the failure of existing theory to explain or predict events. Learning by criticizing implies that existing theory is in error—not necessarily absolutely, but relative to better knowledge. Rules for democracy say little about what one does in office, but much more about getting officials out of office. "Throwing the rascals out" is the essence of democracy. Similarly, in social life it is not the ability to avoid error entirely (even Goncharov's *Oblomov*, who spends his life in bed, cannot do that), but learning how to overcome it that is precious. As Joseph Marone and Edward Woodhouse say: "This is the classic trial-and-error strategy for dealing with complex problems: (1) establish a policy, (2) observe the effects, (3) correct for undesired effects, (4) observe the effects of the correction, and (5) correct again."[1]

The current debate on risk, however, which proposes a radical revision of this strategy, results in the opposite doctrine: no trials without prior guarantees against error. I do not mean to imply that proponents of trial without error would never permit error. They see "no errors" as the goal (albeit one that cannot be fully realized) only for certain classes of situations. In this perspective, trial and error is all right in its circumscribed place. But that place would be limited to conditions in which possible consequences are quite modest (as distinguished from catastrophic) and where feedback is fast. This limitation implies a certain foreseeability of the possible sorts of error and the extent of their consequences. Yet this presumption itself may be erroneous; that is, it ignores the most dangerous source of error, namely, the unexpected. When large adverse consequences probably will occur, and when preventive measures are likely to make things better (without, in other ways, making them worse), of course no one disputes that trials should be regulated. The difficulty, as usual, lies in reaching agreement about whether and when a catastrophe is coming. One side wants special reasons to stop experimentation, and the other wants special conditions to start. Which bias, the question is, is safest?

The outcome of analysis depends in large part on how the criterion of choice is defined. Some prominent environmental economists, such as Allen Kneese, would opt for the standard of efficiency called *Pareto optimality*, under which actions are justified if they make some people better off without harming others. But this criterion assumes, erroneously, that it is possible to separate harmful from beneficial effects. Thus, a vaccine that saves millions but kills a few would not be justified, even though the health of society as a whole, and of almost all of its members, would be improved. Indeed, the pursuit of Pareto optimality can strangle growth and change, because any new developments are likely to hurt someone, somewhere, sometime. Lindblom's criticism is justified:

> Economists often blunder into the conclusion that policy makers should choose Pareto efficient solutions because they help some persons and hurt no others. Not so. If, as is typically the case—and perhaps always the case—there are still other solutions that bring substantial advantages to large numbers of persons and these advantages are worth seeking even at loss to other persons—for example, protecting civil liberties of minorities even if doing so is greatly irritating and obstructive to others—then, there remains a conflict as to what is to be done. The Pareto efficient solution is not necessarily the best choice.[2]

In discussing trial without error with participants in the risk debate, I often sense an air of disbelief, as if no reasonable person would support such a practice. But people do; I shall show that trial without error is indeed the prevailing doctrine among the risk-averse and that in important respects it is government policy. For illustrative purposes, I have deliberately chosen the most persuasive exponents of this doctrine.

No Trials Without Prior Guarantees Against Error

Trial without error is proposed as a criterion of choice by David W. Pearce, who wishes to prevent technologies from being introduced "without first having solved the problems they create. This 'reverse solution' phenomenon characterizes the use of nuclear power, where waste disposal problems remain to be solved even though the source of the waste, the power stations themselves, forms part of whole energy programs."[3] There is nothing unusual today about this way of introducing new technologies. In the past, however, it was common practice to solve the problems associated with novelty as they surfaced following adoption of the innovation. One could well ask whether any technology, including the most benign, would ever have been established if it had first been forced to demonstrate that it would do no harm.

In 1865, to take but a single instance, a million cubic feet of gas exploded at the London Gas-Works, killing ten people and burning twenty. The newspapers screamed that the metropolis faced disaster.

> If half London would be blown to pieces by the explosion of the comparatively small quantity of gas stored at Blackfriars, it might be feared that if all the gasholders in the metropolis were to 'go off,' half the towns in the kingdom would suffer, and to be perfectly secure, the source of danger must be removed to the Land's End.[4]

Could anyone who planned to introduce gas heating or lighting have certified in advance that there would be no explosions, no danger of blowing up the city? I think not. Nonetheless, the gas industry, without such guarantees, did flourish.

But Pearce sees otherwise. In order to guard against potential harm from new technology, he suggests amassing information from experts on both sides, with attention being paid to the possibility of refusing to go ahead with a particular technology. By funding the opposition and by bringing in wider publics, Pearce hopes to insure that "surveillance of new technology is carried out in such a way that no new venture is embarked upon without the means of control being 'reasonably' assured in advance."[5] This, I say, is not trial and error but a new doctrine: no trials without prior guarantees against error.

The most persuasive and most common argument is that trial and error should not be used unless the consequences of worst-case errors are knowable in advance to be sufficiently benign to permit new trials. For if irreversible damage to large populations resulted, no one might be around to take on the next trial. A strong statement of this view comes from Robert E. Goodin:

> Trial and error and learning by doing are appropriate, either for...discovering what the risks are or for the adaptive task of overcoming them only under very special conditions. These are conspicuously lacking in the case of nuclear power. First, we must have good reasons for believing that the errors, if they occur, will be small. Otherwise the lessons may be far too costly. Some nuclear mishaps will no doubt be modest. But for the same reasons small accidents are possible so too are large ones and some of the errors resulting in failure of nuclear reactor safeguards may be very costly indeed. This makes trial and error inappropriate in that setting. Second, errors must be immediately recognizable and correctable. The impact of radioactive emissions from operating plants or of leaks of radioactive waste products from storage sites upon human populations or the natural environment may well be a 'sleeper' effect that does not appear in time for us to revise our original policy accordingly.[6]

Past practice had encouraged people to act unless there were good reasons for not doing so. Goodin reverses that criterion, explicitly replacing it with a requirement for "very special conditions" before trying anything new. His justification, like Pearce's, is the potential danger of nuclear energy, or of any other technology that might lead to irreversible damage.

Yet the argument against taking any irreversible actions is not as broadly applicable as it may appear. On this ground many policies and practices that make up the warp and woof of daily life would actually have to be abandoned. Maurice Richter makes the case well:

> Our legal system makes it relatively easy for people to commit themselves to specified courses of action "irreversibly" through the signing of contracts; a contractual agreement that is too easily reversible may thereby lose much of its value. The movement away from irreversibility in marriage is widely regarded as a social problem. Why, then, should irreversibility, which is sought in so many other contexts, be considered a defect when it appears in material technology? There may be a good reason, but the burden of proof falls on those who insist that reversibility in technology is a valid general principle, and they have hardly proved their case.[7]

Put a little differently, we might want reversibility in some areas of life (say, alternation in political office), but not in others (say, diversion of social security funds to other purposes).

Returning to the effects of nuclear radiation, there are extraordinarily sensitive means available for measuring radiation, down to the decay of single atoms. Moreover, human exposure (consider Hiroshima and Nagasaki) has been so intensively studied that it is possible to accurately estimate the health risk of exposure to a given dose, including long-range risk. This comparatively great understanding of radiation notwithstanding, however, no reasonable person could say with complete certainty that any particular dose—for given individuals, or, still more remote, large populations—would never produce irreversible consequences. And there is still doubt about the long-term effects of very small doses. Even when the best estimates of risk (the magnitude of the hazard/error times the probability of occurrence) approach zero, one can always imagine some concatenation of events that make it impossible (viz., Chernobyl) to rule out potential catastrophe. Presumably, then, the only safe action, according to the "trial-without-error" school, is no trials at all.

Though agreeing that there has been useful learning about nuclear energy, Goodin draws a pessimistic conclusion:

> Sometimes, once we have found out what is going wrong and why, we can even arrange to prevent it from recurring. Precisely this sort of learning by doing has been shown to be responsible for dramatic improvements in the operating efficiency of nuclear reactors. That finding, however, is as much a cause for concern as for hope. It is shocking that there is any room at all left for learning in an operational nuclear reactor, given the magnitude of the disaster that might result from ignorance or error in that setting.[8]

Heads, I win; tails, you lose. Here (as elsewhere) correcting error actually did prove to be an effective route to increased safety. So, since trial and error is exactly what Goodin wishes to prevent, he needs a stronger argument for its inadvisability.

Goodin does argue that nuclear power plants are different because "we would be living not merely with risk but also with *irresolvable* uncertainties."[9] But I hold that this is not good enough; after all, every technology, viewed in advance, has "irresolvable" uncertainties. Only experience can tell us which among all imaginable hazards will in fact materialize and hence justify measures to reduce them. "Irresolvable" uncertainty about the future is a condition of human life. One thing no one can have for sure is a guarantee that things will always turn out all right in the future.

Turning to the only recent and comprehensive study of trial and error as a strategy for securing safety (it covers toxic chemicals, nuclear power, the greenhouse effect, genetic engineering, and threats to the ozone layer), Morone and Woodhouse "...were pleasantly surprised to find how much learning from error has occurred. In part because the ecosystem (so far) has been more forgiving than reasonably might have been expected, trial-and-error has been an important component of the system for averting catastrophe."[10] They conclude:

> For years, regulation of toxic substances proceeded by trial and error. Chemi-

cals were regulated only after negative consequences became apparent. This type of decision process is a well-known, thoroughly analyzed strategy for coping with complex problems. But we had assumed that long delays before obtaining feedback, coupled with severe consequences of error, would make trial and error inappropriate in managing hazardous chemicals. Contrary to our expectations, there proved to be numerous channels for feedback about the effects of chemicals, as demonstrated in detail for pesticides. Regulators were able to take repeated corrective actions in response to the feedback.[11]

There are many historical examples also of feedback from affected citizens that led to corrective measures after the fact. When beekeepers began to complain that inorganic pesticides were harming bees (allegations supported by early entomologists, for instance), agricultural extension agents in the 1890s urged that spraying be delayed until the bees had departed. Again, as it became clear that London Purple (which had supplanted "Paris Green" as the favorite American insecticide, to choose another of many examples) burned plants, and as substitutes existed that did not have this harmful quality, market and governmental action moved toward a different approach to insect control.[12]

Despite such evidence, the "no error" criterion has much support. In the Environmental Protection Agency (EPA), Melnick concludes, this criterion represents the governing principle of the organization.[13] Strong elements in Congress also favor this form of risk aversion. In December 1985, for instance, Senators David Durenberger and Max Bacus introduced a bill to replace voluntary oversight with mandatory regulation of engineered organisms. Any firm that sought to release or use such a product "must be able to prove that no adverse effect to the environment will occur as a result of its actions."[14] This is a "conservative" criterion that is widespread among academics, and it is presented as the epitome of rationality. Peter Nemetz and Aiden Vining concluded that "...conservative standard setting procedures is the most desirable course of action. In fact, it can be argued that the maintenance of such an approach is not to err at all, but to adopt the only rational approach to public policy."[15]

It is instructive here to look at the approach that over decades has been in use for determining the allowable level of poisons in food: set up a dose study in animals; determine the dose where "no effect" is observed; divide this level by 100 (10 times to allow for possible differences in species sensitivity, and another factor of 10 to allow for greater human variability); and declare this level "acceptable" for anyone to eat during a lifetime. This method has worked well for at least 50 years (as far as anyone knows); yet it lacks all theoretical elegance. It is merely a rule of thumb. Possibly a chemical might turn up to which rats and mice were resistant but that could poison half the human population. Also, the "no effect" levels are determined in animal tests of limited scope; maybe one really should test many more than just 50 or 100 animals (as usually is done) to exclude "rare" effects. Were Goodin's criteria (immediate recognizability and correctability) followed in this instance, something as common as salt—or pepper or sugar or Vitamin D—could never be added to prepared foods. After all, any of these might be carcinogens to which everyone is unavoidably exposed; the last three have in fact been shown to cause cancer in at least one animal test. And, because of the long latency of carcinogens, we could not hope to detect their effects in humans before several decades had passed.[16]

Turning to actual policy, the final cancer-exposure regulation prepared by the Occupational Safety and Health Administration (some 300 pages long in the Federal Register) contained assumptions, the agency promised, that would err on the side of identifying noncarcinogens as carcinogens rather than the reverse. This is no risk with a vengeance. Even epidemiological studies that failed to show that carcinogens were present or caused harm would be ignored unless:

> (i) The epidemiologic study involved at least 20 years' exposure of a group of subjects to the substance and at least 30 years' observation of the subjects after initial exposure; (ii) Documented reasons are provided for predicting the site(s) at which the substance would induce cancer if it were carcinogenic in humans; and (iii) The group of exposed subjects was large enough for an increase in cancer incidence of 50% above that in unexposed controls to have been detected at any of the predicted sites.[17]

Studies showing positive results (i.e., the presence of carcinogens) were exempt from these criteria. As Mendeloff concludes, "Extremely few epidemiological studies can meet these criteria."[18]

The risk averse position—no trials without prior guarantees against error—has lately infiltrated the whole arena of public life. What consequences, we may ask, would result from adopting a criterion of choice that would restrict new technologies to those few that might be able to provide such extraordinary advance reassurance?

The No-Safe-Dose Argument

Risk aversion is sometimes justified on grounds that the smallest probability of irreversible disaster overwhelms all other considerations. "If the extinction of mankind is evaluated at minus infinity," Jon Elster writes, "then it swamps all disasters of finite size. We must, of course, have some precise probability attached to this event: mere logical possibility is not sufficient. It does not matter, however, if this probability is extremely small, for an infinite number multiplied by a positive number remains infinite."[19] So what do we have? Terribly low probabilities of awfully terrible events. Infinitesimal amounts of strontium 90 may accumulate in enough bodies to kill off entire peoples. Why, just imagine—if everything else is held constant, an increase in goat's milk projected to infinity could drown the earth and everyone on it! "The weakness of this argument," Elster continues, "is that it may turn out that most actions have such total disasters associated with them, at an extremely unlikely but still quantifiable probability. I believe, therefore, that one should be very cautious in arguing along these lines."[20] One should indeed be cautious, but many are not, because it is hard to resist the temptation to present a case against which there appears to be no reasonable reply.

Under the designation of the "no threshold" theory, it is said (and, I add immediately, sufficiently supported to form the basis of governmental policy) that a single mutagenic event can cause cancer. "The 'predisposition,' if one can call it that, to cancer builds up over a period of time, perhaps from constant exposures to carcinogens along with individual susceptibility," Jacqueline Verrett of the Food and Drug Administration wrote, "and there may come the day when that extra molecule of a carcinogen may overload the system and cancer begins to grow." Reasoning on that "last straw" basis, researchers from the National Cancer Institute assured congressmen that a single molecule of DES (in the 340 trillion or so molecules present) in a quarter of a pound of beef liver might well be enough to trigger human cancer.[21] Should no trials of possibly carcinogenic chemicals be allowed because every error might well kill someone? Let us study this "one-hit" theory, because it offers insight into what one would have to believe in order to justify a policy of no trials without prior guarantees.

The "one-molecule" or "no-threshold" or "no-safe-dose" theory of carcinogenesis holds that exposure to the very smallest amount of cancer-producing material may over time have some chance of causing a deadly change in the affected cell such that the malignancy multiplies out of control. But, as Marvin Schneiderman of the National Cancer Institute asked, why is it "prudent...to assume no threshold for a carcinogen...?"[22] In the field of toxicology, the traditional method had been to develop empirically a "dose-response" curve so that exposure below a certain level, called the "threshold," to all intents and purposes was safe, while higher doses would be (increasingly) harmful. This method of dealing with hazards is not appropriate for carcinogens, some scientists might say to Schneiderman, because of fundamental differences in mechanism between toxins and carcinogens; also, there are inherent uncertainties in the task of carcinogenic risk assessment. Further, given the difficulty of using large numbers of animals in research, very large doses must be given to small numbers of animals; this makes it hard to say what would happen at the low doses that are more typical of human exposure. Since human variability is so great, moreover, a threshold (or "safe dose") for one person might be quite different for another. So little is known about mixing carcinogens and noncarcinogens that their interaction might turn out to produce cancer, even at very low levels.[23] The no-dose-is-safe theory claims either that the last infinitesimal dose will break the camel's back of cancer resistance (increments can kill), or that through evolution "nature" has learned how to deal with natural but not with industrial carcinogens (technology can kill).[24]

Yet we all know that virtually everything human beings breathe or eat or drink brings them into contact with carcinogens. Poisons are an integral part of nature. So is chemical warfare among plants, animals, and insects. To ban carcinogenic substances, therefore, is to ban life. Remember that the idea is to develop a rationale for regulating the products of industrial technology, not for ending all life.

Viewed as rhetoric, the no-safe-dose argument is superb. If it is accepted, it creates a convincing rationale for forbidding any trials of new chemical substances on the grounds that errors (assuming a large number of people were affected) could be catastrophic. Think of it: a single molecule can kill. Were that not enough, we are to be persuaded that the most sensitive person in a population—running into hundreds of millions of people who have wide variations in susceptibility—should set the standard for regulatory decisions about safety. The ancient tale, "for want of a nail..." ending "the battle [in this case, for life] was lost" is trotted out as grounds for banning any innovation, however small. And all change one does not like may be prevented merely by claiming that the tiniest part can be catastophic to some segment of the population. That sounds like a conclusive argument.

Incrementalism as Risk Aversion

At this point in the discussion, some students of decision making may experience *deja vu*. They have been there before. The criteria suggested for political and social decisions—errors should be small, recognizable, and reversible—are those usually attributed to the method for making decisions called incrementalism that was popularized in the decades following the Second World War. According to this doctrine, which Karl Popper once called "piecemeal social engineering,"[25] alternatives should (1) be small in size, (2) limited in number, and (3) follow a consistent pattern of relationships. The benefits presumed to follow from incrementalism include an ability to enhance learning because errors, being small, are easier to correct. Political agreement is to be promoted, in addition, by narrowing the range of dispute to a few alternatives, which differ only marginally from existing policy.[26]

Although the validity of incrementalism as a description of some (but by no means all) decision processes has been recognized, the normative status of the method has been hotly disputed. In a word, incrementalism has been criticized as an ideology that rationalizes conservatism, and defined as adherence to the status quo.[27] These critics would, in stipulated instances, prefer radical—i.e., fundamental, wholesale, large-scale—policy or political change. In response, defenders of incrementalism have argued that "it [the conservatism of incrementalism] ain't necessarily so." Runners can get as far by taking many small steps as by a few larger ones.[28] Moreover, had they known about the "one-hit" theory of cancer causation, the defenders of incrementalist doctrine might have been able to point out their more progressive posture.

Incrementalism was also part of the doctrine of the positive, interventionist state. The idea of incrementalist doctrine was not to do nothing; it was emphatically to do something.[29] If incrementalism were designed to justify inaction, its supporting doctrine would have stressed the unacceptability, not the desirability, of trying out small moves.

Incrementalism as Trial With Small Errors

Observe that the old incrementalism is conservative, *not* reactionary. The doctrine does provide a positive justification for change in the form of repeated trials. Errors are welcomed so long as they are small and diverse—i.e., not cumulative. The extent of change may be small and (if knowledge or consent are lacking) slow, but the sign, the direction, is positive. Incrementalism was conceived as a strategy for action, however moderate, not inaction.

This warm, if cautious, welcome to change in areas of public policy has not been extended by everyone to technological development. On the contrary, incrementalism has now been recast as a reactionary doctrine in which the tiniest conceivable increment of error or harm (recall the single molecule test) can halt all change.

Like the strategy of trial and error it resembles, incrementalism (using small doses of experience to discover uncertainties unpredictable in advance) has been attacked as inappropriate for certain risky realms of decisions. Trying out a nuclear exchange or experimenting with a little plague are inadvisable. "Since incrementalism is a reactive strategy," Jack Knott sums up the prevailing critique, "it cannot anticipate sharp discontinuities; because the strategy relies on successive comparisons, it receives no guidance when responses to actions are long term."[30] Decision makers who face such conditions, the argument goes, should not go for the incremental approach. What approach, then, should they use? The major contender as a strategy for decision making was one known as synoptic choice (centralized control of means and ends through prediction of long-term effects). Through comprehensive, large-scale planning, bad things would be prevented and good accomplished. Yet Knott recalls that:

> Earlier efforts to study decision strategies generally concluded that longer feedback loops, ...complexities, and sharp discontinuities were precisely the kinds of problems for which incremental strategies had a decided advantage over more synoptic [big change] approaches. Martin Landau has argued, for example, that task environments *not* characterized by sharp discontinuities are most suitable for synoptic decisions, while environments characterized by uncertainty require experimental, open-ended approaches.[31]

Synoptic decisions, based on the assumption of being able to predict and control large-scale change, it was then argued, worked best in situations without discontinuities, i.e., in more readily predictable environments. The greater the uncertainty, therefore, the more reason to adopt the incremental approach of successive, limited comparisons.[32] When theory was powerful and discriminating, so was prediction, and hence control of consequences. Problems, therefore, could be prevented by large-scale intervention. When knowledge was weak, however, and better decisions had to be discovered because they could not be figured out analytically in advance, the incremental search procedure called trial and error better fit the circumstances.[33]

It would be better to work with powerful and discriminating theories. But when these are unavailable, task environments usually display high degrees of uncertainty. Under such circumstances, vigorous trial and error seemed the best way to proceed—so that there could be mutual adjustment among different sorts of experiences and problems. And, because error was both expected and valued as an aid to learning, decisions (and, hopefully, consequences) were deliberately kept small; this reduced risk and increased the chances of learning from mistakes. Taking fewer risks may ultimately decrease safety, but, as Lewis Dexter advises, "going slow frequently" may improve our prospects.[34] Large numbers of small moves, frequently adjusted, permitted tests of new phenomena before they became big enough to do massive harm.

Playing It Safe

That was another era. Nowadays we find ourselves in a world in which the ancient verities have been turned inside out. Except under improbable conditions—theoretical or laboratory proof that the next move will do no harm—resort to experience has been ruled out on the self-reinforcing grounds that trials permit errors.[35]

The most seductive form of playing it safe is prudential conservatism: Why be half safe? When in doubt, add margins of safety. Allow nothing new unless preguaranteed as harmless. Such fields as toxicology and engineering do present honorable examples of conservatism. A structure or a substance would be estimated to carry a certain load, or to cause a certain degree of difficulty. Concerned that future conditions might lead to change far beyond the parameters of their models, engineers and toxicologists would, as a matter of ordinary procedure, design structures to carry far heavier loads than expected, and decrease allowable exposure to substances far below expected dangerous levels. So far, so good.

But beyond these prudential safety factors, however, there has grown up a tendency to add other levels. Safety margins will be increased on "worst case" considerations, and then again increased on the grounds that it doesn't hurt to be even more careful. That is, one first estimates the dangers of a product or practice according to existing knowledge. Then at every step decisions are made as to where uncertainty can be resolved. Prudence, presumably, is the byword. Having arrived at an estimate (or range of estimates), one chooses the upper bound of danger, then multiplies it by a safety factor of, say, ten to a hundred. But observe what has occurred. As uncertainties are resolved by exaggeration, estimates of potential damage also may be increased thousands of times over. So what? Is there anything wrong with being supercautious? What is wrong is that there is no inherent stopping point. If supercaution is the one guiding principle, there is no reason why estimates should not be exaggerated again and again. "Conservatism" can be pursued to infinity. And since virtually everything contains some harm, the inescapable conclusion is to decide that the activity in question should be disallowed altogether.

In an important paper, H.W. Lewis distinguishes between conservatism that tries to compensate for inherent uncertainties and conservatism for its own sake. "In the design of bridges and buildings, for example," he writes, "a value for the breaking strength of steel is commonly used that is far below its actual breaking strength, but one would obviously not want to use the same value to calculate the real probability that the structure will collapse." Yet often regulators compensate for uncertainty as though it were as accurate as the best calculation of risk.[36] Suppose, however, that an actual situation of technological uncertainty exists. How should a regulatory agency behave? Lewis makes the essential distinction:

One is not dealing here with a situation in which one knows the correct answer for the damage probability, and uses conservatism to set it low enough to be tolerable, but is rather using conservatism to mask ignorance. It is common under such conditions to proceed through the calculation of the risk, dealing with each point at which there is scientific uncertainty by deliberately erring in the direction of overestimating the risk. There is an essential difference between calculating a risk carefully, and then deliberately choosing a conservative design in such a way as to reduce the risk to a desired level, and deliberately erring in a conservative direction in the calculation of risk. An error in the conservative direction is nonetheless an error.[37]

It is not, however, an error from which one can learn because, since the error is deliberate and far out of bounds, the magnitude of its excess remains unknown.

The imposition of safety factors is sensible, but only if two considerations are observed: first, the best known probabilities are calculated, and then the adverse effects of increasing the margin of error are taken into account. One could hardly find a better example than Lewis's use of aircraft wings:

The penalty for a conservative design which makes the wing too strong is a heavier airplane, with a negative impact on all the other virtues of flight. The result is that the safety factors on aircraft wings have always been much lower than the factors of five or ten which are common for civil structures, and are in fact substantially lower than a factor of two. This author's experience has been that many engineers are shocked when they learn this fact, since they are accustomed to larger factors of safety. However, in this case, there would be a recognizable penalty for excessive conservatism, and experience with aircraft wings has enabled the designers to reduce the safety margin to the minimum possible. Even in the early days of aviation, when the accumulated experience was not large, the fact that heavy airplanes can not fly was sufficient to reduce the safety factors, and aircraft design has always involved the conflict between weight and structural integrity.[38]

Making flight impossible or causing crashes is not usually recommended as a conservative measure to increase safety.

Albert Nichols and Richard Zeckhauser claim, correctly I think, that the practice of "conservatism" confuses risk assessment (estimating hazards) with risk management (policies to control hazards). They would prefer to estimate hazards as close as existing knowledge will permit and then, as a matter of management, decide how much risk to take. Otherwise, they write, "Conservatism can lead to less rather than more safety by misdirecting public concern and scarce agency resources."[39]

Perhaps this account of risk aversion is a caricature. Quite possibly, advocates of risk aversion wish to be prudent, but not extreme; for that to be so, in a given study, they must establish supportable limits to the number of times conservative estimates ought to be multiplied in subsequent calculation. Also, they must allow estimates of the safety benefits of the product or substance being evaluated to weigh in the balance. The result would be a return to the useful practice of cost-benefit analysis (efforts to compare the gains and losses from proposed projects so as to assess their relative desirability)—from which the emphasis on conservative calculation is intended to depart.

This exact issue is at the root of a current conflict between the Environmental Protection Agency and the Office of Management and Budget (OMB). The question concerns standards for allowable amounts of carcinogenic substances in ground water. OMB objects to the way EPA makes cascading conservative projections, so that it is impossible to judge the protection provided; instead, OMB feels that EPA should try to calculate the risks and then add a reasonable margin of safety. OMB claims that an individual would face a cancer risk 4,000 times higher from drinking a diet soda with saccharin than from the amounts of solvents and dioxins in the ground water.[40] Does this comparison, assuming that it is roughly accurate, tell us anything? Or should the faintest prospect of harm dictate regulation to eliminate the offending substance? Are we to reject any new substances that are not risk free? What, then, will be the effects of the attendant decline in innovations for our society?

Safety Comes from Use

So far as safety is concerned, old dogs can learn new tricks, for older products do not necessarily have to remain as unsafe as they are. Relative safety is not static, but is rather a dynamic product of learning from error over time. By "dynamic" I mean not only that new products may be safer than their forerunners, but also that those older products may be successfully modified in certain aspects.

Pioneers suffer the costs of premature development. But if development is allowed to continue into succeeding generations, the costs of error detection and correction would be shared to some extent with the next generation of future innovators; and the resulting benefits likewise would be passed back down to the now "old" originators. Needless to say, however, a second generation of products cannot learn from the first if there isn't one.

Technology, as Nathan Rosenberg observes, is not merely the application of theory: "Technology is itself a body of knowledge...of techniques, methods and designs that work...even when one cannot explain exactly why." But people who do not "know why" may yet "know how." This "know how" is responsible for much progress. "Indeed," Rosenberg concludes, "if the human race had been confined to technologies that were understood in a scientific sense, it would have passed from the scene long ago."[41]

Existing knowledge may be incomplete. Indeed, in the sense that new and more powerful theories potentially will replace or alter the now known, knowledge is always incomplete. The presenting problem, moreover, may contain combinations of factors that are new—in this proportion, or that sequence, or the other location. As Fredrich Hayek tells us in his essay on "The Use of Knowledge in Society," the relevant factors may occur only in local combinations.[42] The task of decision making in a complex society, therefore, may not be so much to create general theory but more to be in touch with, and apply, knowledge that is attuned to local conditions.[43] An important component of innovation entails applying knowledge to a product even though the consequences cannot be known (i.e., specified in all details) in advance.

How can one make use of this unarticulated "know-how"? Learning by doing is one way. Kenneth Arrow locates learning as part of the process of production. His argument will set the stage for our consideration of learning how to do better, in terms of health and safety as well as economic productivity. According to Arrow:

> Knowledge has to be acquired.... The acquisition of knowledge is what is usually termed "learning".... I do not think that the picture of technical change as a vast and prolonged process of learning about the environment in which we operate is in any way a far-fetched analogy; exactly the same phenomenon of improvement in performance over time is involved.

> Of course...there are sharp differences of opinion about the processes of learning. But one empirical generalization is so clear that all schools of thought must accept it, although they interpret it in different fashions: Learning is the product of experience. Learning can only take place through the attempt to solve a problem and therefore only takes place during activity.... A second generalization that can be gleaned from many of the classic learning experiments is that learning associated with repetition of essentially the same problem is subject to sharply diminishing returns.... To have steadily increasing performance, then, implies that the stimulus situations must themselves be steadily evolving rather than merely repeating.... I advance the hypothesis here that technical change in general can be ascribed to experience, that it is the very activity of production which gives rise to problems for which favorable responses are selected over time.[44]

No trials, no new errors—but also no new experience and hence no new learning.

We all know the old adage, "experience is the best teacher"; well, an appropriate, if wordy, interpretation would be to say that error correction through trials increases reliability and efficiency. Think for a moment about the inspection of nuclear power plants by government regulators. Since inspectors differ, and because rules are not always codified or applicable, the thousands of change-orders at each facility may lead power plants—though built from the same or similar designs—to differ considerably. Talking to engineers reveals that the situations of plants can be so different that local experience is essential for controlling their performance. Only a few nuclear power plants, for instance, are on sites containing four or more reactors. Experience reveals that single reactors alone on a site are more likely to break down than reactors on sites with multiple units. "A reactor seems to 'learn' significantly faster," Alvin Weinberg notes, "when it is next to 'older brothers,' than when it is an 'only child.'"[45] This family aspect of safety extends also to consumers (users) as well as producers of products (doers).

The distinction between learning by doing[46] and learning by using, introduced by Nathan Rosenberg,[47] is essential for understanding innovation and how innovation relates to safety. After a product has been designed, learning by doing (that is, confined to manufacturing) refers to the process of increasing skill and efficiency in production. Now, whereas cumulative gains in production involve "doing," advantages that occur from utilization have to do with "using." Manufacturers "do" while consumers "use." These two types of learning differ, Rosenberg argues, because "...many significant characteristics of...products are revealed only after intensive or, more significantly, prolonged use."[48]

A vital aspect of the competitive position of a product is its maintenance cost, which is in part a function of reliability. And reliability is often determined by user-sponsored changes.[49] Reliability and safety are closely connected. Where equipment is difficult to reach, for instance, as in underwater cables or space satellites, extending the time period between maintenance checks and replacements is both cheaper for the user and safer for the fixer. As anyone acquainted with a computer product knows, "...the optimal design of software depends upon a flow of information from its customers."[50]

Much technological innovation is accomplished by users who modify products, not merely by designers who originate them. A crucial test of this hypothesis is to measure the rate of discovery by research units in large organizations who specialize in new applications by comparison with feedback from the customers who use these products. On an anecdotal level, Thomas J. Peters reports that:

> After 25 years of studying IBM, GE, Polaroid, Xerox, Bell Labs, and the like, he [Brian Quinn] concluded of one of them: "Not a single major product has come from the formal product planning process." The offender of rationality:

IBM. In two years of using Quinn's line with hundreds of audiences (virtually all with past or present IBMers in attendance), I've only once heard a demurring voice. It came from a Bell operating company vice-president, who said: "Nonsense. That statement is probably not true for IBM, and I *know* it's not true for the [Bell] Labs." He pointed to a very respected Labs vice-president and said, "You tell him." The Labs man scratched his chin for ten seconds or so (as my heart skipped beats) and replied: "Well, I've only been at the Labs for a bit over 30 years, but I can't *think* of anything that ever came directly from the new product planning process."[51]

A substantial majority of major twentieth-century inventions—from the continuous casting of steel to ballpoint pens—as John Jewkes demonstrates in his book on *The Sources of Invention*, came from people outside the then-existing industry.[52] The special role of early users is developed by James Utterback, who concludes that the initial intended use for a new product is rarely the one that catches on.[53] After reviewing some 80 studies of the emergence of new products, Peters concludes that "The great majority of the ideas...come from the users."[54] This view is supported by Eric Von Hippel's study of 160 innovations in scientific instruments. Users made not only 60 percent of minor modifications and 25 percent of the major ones, but also originated all "first of type" innovations. To qualify for inclusion in the study, users had not only to come up with the idea but also to make a working prototype.[55] In the field of pharmaceutical drugs, I should add, there is good reason to believe that the bulk of benefits have come not only from the original discovery, however brilliant, but from innumerable variants produced by a sort of rough-and-ready empiricism, where incremental changes are tried out to see if they would suit a particular class of potential users. Reducing the number and variety of new products, while it may indeed diminish the errors (say, damage to the body) associated with these trials, also can eliminate unsuspected health-giving potential.

Thought of in another way, the user is always right, for the value of a product does not inhere in the producer but in the ultimate judges of utility, the users. Users are more numerous and more diverse than producers. Their number and diversity suggest that more tests by users be made under more varied conditions. The larger the number and the greater the variety of hypotheses tested ("Is this product satisfactory under my conditions?"), the greater the probability of learning about good and bad impacts and the conditions under which they apply. The more unsatisfactory, that is, error-like, experiences that come about, the greater the likelihood that efforts to overcome the bad will lead to useful innovation.

Surveying the advantages of a strategy of trial and error makes it difficult to believe that it would be subject to wholesale rejection. Perhaps all that is meant is the unexceptional view that trial and error is not suitable for every sort of situation. Such a conclusion would indeed appear reasonable, but would it be factually correct?

Not so fast. Do proponents of trial without error ("institutions that anticipate the risks," as Page put it) actually exist in real life? Maybe it is wrong to claim not only that a viable doctrine of taking no new chances exists, but also that there are serious people who believe it. I think this usage has become quite common. "I shall consider only the dangers and costs of biomedical advance," Leon Kass tells us. "As the benefits are well known, there is no need to dwell on them here." Perhaps Kass is exceptional in alerting the reader to his premise—*"My discussion is, in this regard, deliberately partial."*[56] Philosophers are one thing, however, and those who make the law of the land are another. Have I, out of the scribblings of deranged philosophers and madcap activists, created a straw man just for the pleasure of knocking it down? Well, let us look at public policy and see whether this straw man is alive and kicking.

"Trial Without Error" as Public Policy

In an article aptly entitled "Exorcists versus Gatekeepers," Peter Huber demonstrates that the doctrine we have been discussing—no trial without prior guarantees against error—is embodied in current regulatory practice. Producers of old products and substances still operate on a trial-and-error basis, in that the burden of proof (in justifying any regulation) is lodged with the government; but innovations must function under the rule of "no trials without prior guarantees against error"; here, producers must be able to prove beforehand that their product will do no harm.[57]

Regulation, Huber observes, has two, sometimes contradictory, purposes: One is to reduce existing, older risks (such as bad air quality or in digging for coal), and the other is "to impede technological changes that threaten to introduce new hazards into our lives"—new toxic chemicals, nuclear power, and so on. Attached to old risks is the mode of regulation called standard setting; here, producers are left alone until the federal government forces them to meet a revised standard. New risks, however, are handled by screening procedures under which advance licensing applies. Permission is required both before and after a new thing is done or produced. The Food and Drug Administration (FDA) and the Nuclear Regulatory Commission (NRC) screen or license; the Occupational Health and Safety Administration (OHSA) sets standards.

Sometimes the same agency does both; EPA, for example, screens new pesticides and also sets production standards for old ones.[58] There is a wide gap between "it can't be allowed to come into existence" and "let's make it better." As David Foster wrote, responding (as he says, for himself, not for EPA) to Huber's article, the bias against new sources threatens to create

> ...some negative environmental consequences. As Huber notes, the most effective means of reducing risk may be to encourage the introduction of competitors that impose a lower level of risk. Ironically, our "gatekeeper" regulations may do just the opposite. Regulations that impose significantly greater costs on new sources than on existing ones may discourage industry from replacing older heavy-polluting facilities with newer and cleaner ones. Rigorous screening of new pesticides and chemicals may unintentionally delay the entry of potentially safer substitutes for existing risky products.... The new-source bias affects not only consumer goods and services, but also the equipment and technology used in pollution control. Approval for innovative pollution-control equipment takes longer and is more uncertain than for traditional devices. That can make polluters reluctant to take a chance on buying innovative control equipment even if they expect it to be more effective and less costly than more traditional devices.[59]

These are the practical differences between setting standards for the old, and screening development of the new: "A screening system admits only the 'acceptably safe', while a standard-setting system excludes only the 'unacceptably hazardous'...."[60] Since old dangers are systematically treated more leniently than new hazards, Huber asks, quite rightly, "What accounts for the double standard?"[61]

The common view that old dangers are treated less strictly because they are well understood, Huber believes, is fallacious. "Those in the business know that informational problems are pervasive even for hazards as old as asbestos and wood fires." Exactly so. He is also properly skeptical about the psychological view that since people are inured to "common killers," the rarer kind should be subject to harsher measures. After all, "Rare catastrophes are caused by old sources of risk every bit as by new ones." True. In the end, Huber is convinced that "Congress thinks that it is much more expensive to regulate old risks than new ones." To wipe out tangible benefits people already enjoy—familiar products, traditional jobs, with their "identifiable and self-aware constituencies"—is politically more difficult to do than to stop something new that is not yet surrounded with a self-protective belt of interest.[62] "Legislators care more about *political* costs than about economic ones," in Huber's estimation. "Consumers lose, of course [in being denied the benefits of new products] but—here's the political kicker—they don't know it."[63] Why not?

"Statutes," Huber observes, "almost never explicitly address the lost opportunity costs of screening out a product."[64] The producer of a new product might go to court and succeed in overturning a ban by showing that the agency wrongly estimated the dangers, "but he will get nowhere by arguing that the decision incorrectly evaluated the potential benefits of the product."[65] Ignoring the good, even if it might exceed the bad, does not optimize safety for society, though it may be palatable for the polity. The clamoring constituency is worried about safety now. Proponents of safety now, like the planners they resemble, can talk of specific measures on behalf of tangible people. Proponents of trial and error can speak only of safety later, a safety, moreover, not for this or that specific group but— because they cannot predict or control what will happen (their very reason for advocating trial and error)—for society in general. "You'll be better off in the 'by-and-by'" has never been noted as a politically potent appeal. The benefits lost because of rejected opportunities are seen as inferior political goods.

A Question of Proportion

In his characteristically inventive, "The Principle of the Hiding Hand," Albert Hirschman sees negativism rather than overenthusiasm as the prevailing vice in considering the establishment of development projects in poor countries. Therefore, he wants to bias consideration in favor of action, even (or especially) if that means ignoring possible negative consequences. Hirschman's reasoning is instructive:

> ...each project comes into the world accompanied by two sets of partially or wholly offsetting potential developments: (1) a set of possible and unsuspected threats to its profitability and existence, and (2) a set of unsuspected remedial actions which can be taken whenever any of these threats materializes.... 1) If the project planners had known in advance all the difficulties and troubles that were lying in store for the project, they probably would never have touched it, because a gloomy view would have been taken of the country's ability to overcome these difficulties by calling into play political, administrative, or technical creativity. 2) In some, though not all, of these cases advance knowledge of these difficulties would therefore have been unfortunate, for the difficulties and the ensuing search for solutions set in motion a train of events which not only rescued the project, but often made it particularly valuable.... Or, put differently: since we necessarily underestimate our creativity, it is desirable that we underestimate to a roughly similar extent the difficulties of the tasks we face, so as to be tricked by these two offsetting underestimates into undertaking tasks which we can, but otherwise would not dare, tackle.... Language itself conspires toward this sort of asymmetry: we fall into error, but do not usually speak of falling into truth.[66]

The disinclination to consider the ability to respond to risks (anticipated or unanticipated) thus creates a bias towards technological inaction.

Trial and error is not a doctrine one would like to see applied to engaging in nuclear war. But at the same time, "no trial without prior guarantees against error" is unsuitable for everyday life. The question, as always, is one of proportion (How much of each strategy?) and relevance (What kinds of dangers deserve the different strategies?), and ultimately, given uncertainty, of bias (When in doubt, which strategy should receive priority?).

Trial and error is a device for courting small dangers in order to avoid or lessen the damage from big ones. Sequential trials by dispersed decision makers reduce the size of that unknown world to bite-sized, and hence manageable, chunks. An advantage of trial and error, therefore, is that it renders visible hitherto unforeseen errors. Because it is a discovery process that discloses latent errors so we can learn how to deal with them, trial and error also lowers risk by reducing the scope of unforeseen dangers. Trial and error samples the world of as yet unknown risks; by learning to cope with risks that become evident as the result of small-scale trial and error, we develop skills for dealing with whatever may come our way from the world of unknown risks.

Now if these small advances and big disasters are independent of one another, incrementalism works, and search is hardly necessary. But if the two are interdependent, in that you cannot have one—an overall increase in safety by small advances—without the other—occasional disasters—search becomes more complex. For then we have to figure out how to cut down on big losses without simultaneously reducing incremental gains to such a degree that net safety declines.

If the incremental road led to disaster, society already should have suffered substantial losses. Instead, we find that morbidity is way down and life expectancy way up. We would be well advised to ask how these large numbers of small moves have led to our extraordinary improvement in health and safety.

We are faced with an anomaly in studying safety: large-scale disasters (flood, fire, earthquake, explosion, food poisoning) are a fairly frequent occurrence (see the next chapter); yet decade by decade, people are living longer and experiencing fewer serious accidents, and are healthier at corresponding ages. How is it that safety improves amidst disasters? Incremental advance offers a possible explanation. Large numbers of small improvements in safety may add up sufficiently to overcome a much smaller number of severely damaging episodes.

Just as most accidents occur in or near home,[67] and most foods contain carcinogens[68] (as the axiom of connectedness suggests), so there is some degree of danger getting out of bed or taking a shower or eating a meal or walking across the street—or, need I say, in making love as well as war. Risking and living are inseparable (hospitals make people sick, exercise can hurt you, herb tea is laden with carcinogens); even breathing, according to a prominent theory in which cancer is caused by oxygen radicals created through the burning of fat, can kill.

The direct implication of trial without error is obvious: If you can do nothing without knowing first how it will turn out, you cannot do anything at all. An indirect implication of trial without error is that if trying new things is made more costly, there will be fewer departures from past practice; this very lack of change may itself be dangerous in forgoing chances to reduce existing hazards. Of course, the devil you know may be preferred over the one(s) you don't know. Existing dangers do have an advantage: they are bounded by past experience. If they are not too large, they may be tolerable and indeed preferable to novelty, whose dangers, being uncertain, may be unbounded. Nevertheless, existing hazards will continue to cause harm if we fail to reduce them by taking advantage of the opportunity to benefit from repeated trials.

By reducing still-existing dangers, not merely by avoiding new ones, risk taking becomes socially desirable; old hazards can be eliminated or alleviated in ways that improve human life. These, the "opportunity benefits" that are lost without a strategy of trial and error, will be discussed in the next chapter.

2

Opportunity Benefits Versus
Opportunity Risks

*[I]t is not enough to count the hidden costs of saying
yes to new enterprises. We must also learn to count
the hidden costs of saying* no.

—Freeman Dyson[1]

Can't we have both safety and technological progress? If we plan ahead
and consult the best people, if we work from the most recent information
about science, technology, and human behavior, can't we avoid most danger by slowing down progress a little? Isn't it better to prevent disasters
from occurring than to suffer the ravages and only then do something
about it? In this chapter I shall try to explain that it is dangerous to take
this seemingly prudent approach to reducing risk—that is, to take few
chances, and thus avoid new harm—because the sources of safety and risk
are so intimately connected.

To go beyond the simplistic idea that safety means merely avoiding
danger, a few concepts deserve long-overdue consideration. The opportunity cost of a given expenditure, as economists define it, is those different
goods that otherwise might have been purchased with the same resources.
Opportunity benefits, as defined here, are those opportunities to reduce
existing harms that society forgoes when it decides to delay or deny the
introduction of a new substance or technology.

A recent opportunity benefit comes from methyl tert-butyl ether
(MTBE), a chemical included in gasoline to prevent knocking, which has
been found to dissolve human gallstones. The process is quicker and
cheaper than surgery; so far, no adverse side effects have been discovered.[2]

Benefits defined thus have come to be overlooked as a matter of course so
that in the now dominant discourse on risk, the very act of comparing risks
to benefits is considered corrupt. For comparison suggests that we might be
trading health for money. No present good should be sacrificed for a greater

future benefit; only acts that promise to do good without doing harm can be tolerated in decisions about new technology. But then we lose opportunity benefits.

A possible opportunity benefit, which we are now being denied, would come from lifting prohibitions against genetic engineering. Since many such organisms are already widespread in the environment, the prospects of them "taking over" are minimal. Among the many foreseeable benefits, in addition to economic growth, are microorganisms that would detoxify many dangerous chemicals.[3] Wise decision making should consider the benefits lost from foregone opportunities. The dangers from risk taking and from risk aversion should be considered together. For if we do away with the risks, according to the axiom of connectedness, we may also eliminate even greater health benefits.

Why Aren't We All Dead?
Incrementalism and the Importance of Connectedness

We have Jeryl Mumpower to thank for making us aware of how far one can carry the argument for a world without risk. In "An Analysis of the *de minimus* Strategy for Risk Management," Mumpower takes issue with those who argue that tiny dangers (say, 10^{-5} or 10^{-6}) should be ignored when choosing which risks to do something about. He agrees that a de minimus strategy is almost always reasonable in eliminating consideration of trivial risks. When a portfolio of de minimus risks is considered together over a period of time, however, Mumpower believes that the cumulative effect might well justify governmental intervention to prevent even the smallest harm from occurring. Because it makes explicit a (perhaps the) major argument in favor of trying to control tiny dangers, his line of reasoning is instructive.

Mumpower reasons that:

> A level of risk that is not of concern in any single instance may be viewed quite differently if it is part of an ongoing cumulative series. While no single risk in such a series may be large, over time a high overall level of risk will eventually result. Cox has dubbed this the *incremental effect.*[4]

This incremental effect is illustrated by a table (below) in which what appear to be very small risks turn out to be very large when compounded over time. Thus 12 monthly 10^{-5} risks add up to a 39-to-1 danger of dying. When the de minimus strategy is applied to old hazards that we already live with, Mumpower concludes, it reasonably separates large from small dangers. But, "Risks from multiple new hazards falling under the *de minimus* level may collectively result in a total level of risk substantially greater than the nominal *de minimus* level." Consequently, Mumpower recommends:

> To ensure that the total level of risk for society would not increase as a consequence of accepting new hazards under this scheme, a constraint could be introduced requiring that any time a new risk is accepted, an old one of equal or greater magnitude would have to be eliminated.[5]

Here we have a more refined notion of the strategy I have called "trial without error," in which the risk of damage may be accepted provided that government takes action immediately to offset it by securing an equivalent gain in safety.

TABLE 1
Lifetime Odds of Mortality

Nominal *de minimus*	Condition 1 (single risk)	Condition 2 (one new risk/year)	Condition 3 (one new risk/month)
Annual 10^{-5}	1,429 to 1	40.7 to 1	3.9 to 1
Annual 10^{-6}	14,288 to 1	403. to 1	34.3 to 1
Lifetime 10^{-6}	1,000,000 to 1	28,169. to 1	2,378. to 1

The power of Mumpower's hypothetical analysis depends critically upon accepting certain assumptions; to make these critical assumptions explicit will help us see the risk debate in a larger perspective.

Let us stipulate that new substances indeed create numerous small hazards—far more than merely one per month. Indeed, it would not take many more than 12 to reduce the probability of annual death to unity. Why, then, given the utter reasonableness of these assumptions, aren't we all dead? Now. Many times over.

Mumpower suggests that:

> If one believed, however, as the actuarial data suggest, that the overall level of risk to society is declining, then a different view might be taken.... Even the potential for large incremental accumulations from *de minimus* risks might be dismissed if the rate of risk reduction from other sources were sufficiently great.[6]

There is an explanation for increased safety through economic growth or scientific advance, but these "other sources" apparently run on a different track, i.e., they are treated as if the sources of safety were quite separate from the sources of harm. In that case, harm might be diminished while not decreasing safety. But this is going about seeking safety backwards.

Do we explain why machines can fly, or why they can't? Although some airplanes crash, we explain what exists—flying machines—not what doesn't—crashes every time. On the same grounds, presumably, we ought to be interested in explaining the growth in life expectancy, which has occurred, not an increase in early deaths, which hasn't. Yet there is no denying that new hazards are continuously being introduced into human life. How, then, can we explain why new hazards of all kinds do not lead to our extinction? A key assumption of the trial without error school is that the sources of safety and the sources of hazard are separate and separable; predicting *independent causation,* all that remains is to choose the safe and reject the unsafe. Then (and only then) would it make sense to refuse even tiny hazards, because such hazards could not be connected to anything good.

If we assume a state of *interdependent causation,* however, safety must be searched for indirectly, through processes that will lead to more good (and less bad) health effects. If the principle of uncertainty applies, in most instances we will not be able to figure out in advance the second, third, and umpteenth effects of new things. Hence, we are as likely to rule out the good as to reject the bad. And if, as I claim, the axiom of connectedness applies, so that good and bad effects are bound up in the same objects, we cannot achieve the advances in safety recorded in those actuarial tables without accepting unwanted hazards. Since this combination of the principle of uncertainty and the axiom of connectedness actually explains what we observe—namely, that society gets safer despite the continuous introduction of new hazards—it must be that the safety benefits of the new outweigh their associated dangers.

Opportunity Benefits and Natural Disaster

The study of opportunity benefits—safety improvements that result from trial-and-error risk taking—is fraught with difficulty. When things proceed according to a regulatory plan, predictions of specific benefits to be achieved (by following the program indicated) may be compared with actual outcomes. Without such a program, however, when, according to the theory of opportunity benefits, we cannot know in advance which new advances may mitigate old risks, then there is no adequate research design. The problem is one of comparing outcomes to intentions in self-regulating versus command systems. Like others before me, I cannot provide a way to measure effects without having a plan specifically designed to produce them. That we do not and cannot know about many present and future dangers is the very basis for preferring trial and error to a strategy of trial without error.

What I can do is ask whether it is possible to improve the safety of people who now live with lower levels of technology by preventing technological development from taking place. Two gross comparisons are feasible: the United States and other industrial nations in the present, compared to earlier times; and industrial societies versus less industrial ones, today. Natural disasters, and how they are managed, offer obvious objects for comparison because these happen everywhere and in all eras. The question is whether the severity of outcomes is greater or less in nations with lower or higher levels of technology.

Many people concerned with the dangers of modern society assume that most spring from technical innovation. Danger appears largely to be man-made, to come less from nature than from an urge to bend the natural environment to human purpose. The security of our present existence is illusory, people believe, since we are constantly introduced to new dangers such as industrial accidents, pollution, toxic waste, and various new technologies. Where does the balance lie between damage done by nature and man, and damage mitigated by technology?

The belief that danger comes from man, not nature, has some basis in fact. Very few Americans die from lightning, earthquakes, floods, or venomous snakes. But, in studying the relationship between technology and safety, several important factors go unrecognized. One of the most important is the degree to which better living conditions may have raised overall safety levels in the United States. The health of Americans has been consistently improved through better housing, sanitation, and nutrition. We have also developed the ability to mitigate many consequences of natural disasters. Tornadoes and hurricanes still threaten us; due to improved radar tracking and communications, however, far fewer lives are lost. Floods still wreak havoc in many areas but, thanks to improved dams and levees, less damage is done and fewer people die.

It is certainly true that in the past hundred years many people have perished in accidents involving new technology; and others also have died in industries supporting the new technical wonders. The worst accidents involved boiler explosions and other types of ship fires. Catastrophic fires and major explosions in coal mines also killed large numbers in the early twentieth century. The worst of these accidents was in a West Virginia mine in December 1907, where an explosion killed 361 miners.[7]

Boiler technology has been superseded or improved, and boiler accidents are now rare; only 71 people were killed by boiler explosions in 1980.[8] Mine, marine, and railroad safety have improved also, even if not to the same degree. Although accidents involving technology are still common, relatively few people are killed.

The Metropolitan Life Insurance Company provides data on catastrophic accidents in the United States by type of accident for years after

1950. A catastrophic accident is defined as one in which five or more people were killed.[9]

TABLE 2
Catastrophic Accidents

	Accidents	Deaths
1951-60	1,483	13,790
1961-70	1,340	12,530
1971-80	924	10,090
1981-82	141	1,492
1983	59	484

Source: Metropolitan Life Insurance Co. data published in Statistical Abstract of the U.S., 1985 Edition.

What is most striking about these statistics is that during that thirty-three-year period, a total of only 38,000 people died in such accidents. Given an annual death rate of about 1.7 million per year for this period, catastrophic deaths constituted an extremely small proportion of the total; and, even in absolute number, accidental deaths have continued to decline.

Transport accidents account for a large number of catastrophic accidents. As air travel has become more common over the past three decades, the contribution of airplane accidents to the total has understandably risen. Although the absolute numbers of accidents declined, air transport accounted for 16 percent of catastrophic accident deaths in the 1950s, 24 percent in the 1960s and 70s, and 27 percent in the 1980s. Motor vehicle accidents accounted for 45 percent of catastrophic accidents between 1951 and 1960, and about 30 percent of the deaths. By 1981, motor vehicles accounted for less than 20 percent of the accidents and only 11.5 percent of the deaths. Statistics indicate that although technology (cars, airplanes, industry) does play a major role in catastrophic accidents, it seems proportionally no more today than in 1950.[10]

Many advances in technology have allowed much greater control over the consequences of potentially disasterous natural events. The United States—with its leveed rivers and flood controls, warning systems, and emergency plans—can count the consequences of natural disasters in the tens and hundreds. Economic damage to the nation may often be tremendous, but not the loss of human life. In 1982, floods that killed only 155 people did $3.5 billion in damages.[11] In less industrialized parts of the world, by contrast, natural disasters often kill thousands, sometimes tens of thousands. For example, flood waves generated by offshore storms often push their way up the unleveed rivers of coastal India, burying whole villages and their populations under tons of mud. Hurricanes sweeping across Puerto Rico and Haiti have killed thousands who might have been saved by early-warning systems or better shelter.

Although the total number of tornadoes sighted and recorded in the U.S. has increased enormously over the past seventy years, the overall pattern of death and injury has shown a very marked downward trend. In 1982, 1,046 tornadoes were recorded; 92 of these did more than half a million dollars damage. Yet, in large part due to improved detection and warning systems, only 64 people died.[12]

On a single day, May 31, 1985, 27 tornadoes killed 91 people in 4 states and Canada, injured over 800, and left thousands more homeless. A study by the Center for Disease Control tried to differentiate between those killed and injured and those who escaped; the chief difference was the amount of warning time. Where communication systems reach the majority of people, safety is greatly enhanced. When communication falls short, the danger to human life remains high.

In September 1985, hurricanes Elena and Gloria struck the Gulf of Mexico and the Atlantic Coast. Before each storm, municipal and county governments (with coordination by civil-defense and emergency-management agencies) evacuated low-lying areas. Gloria weakened greatly just before coming ashore in New England but still knocked out power to about 70 percent of those living in Connecticut and Rhode Island. The U.S. Public Health Service tracked the results of the storms, fearing that, in addition to any trauma inflicted directly by high wind and water, towns in the hurricane's path might suffer outbreaks of gastroenteritis due to damaged water systems. Research turned up only seven fatalities for both storms—two of them due to a lack of electricity, but none because of increased disease levels.[13]

These few fatalities contrast sharply with the toll taken by hurricanes in previous decades. The lack of tracking and warning systems before the mid-1950s made the few hurricanes striking the U.S. very dangerous. Over 6,000 were killed at Galveston, Texas in September 1900, when a hurricane sent a huge storm wave over the city. In 1935 a hurricane struck a government relief camp in the Florida Keys; a train sent from the mainland to rescue 700 veterans at the camp was swept off the tracks and about 400 died. Three years later another hurricane that swept across Long Island and several New England states killed over 600.[14]

In order to survive such storms, one needs three things: sufficient warning, safe shelter, and transportation to get there. People in the Caribbean nations suffer far less today than in earlier times because of improved warning systems. In the past decade, only one hurricane (August 30–September 7, 1979) has killed large numbers of people (a total of 1,100 in the Caribbean and eastern U.S.). Not all areas yet have the benefit of such technology. Take Bangladesh: the terrible windstorms that hit Bangladesh in the mid-1960s killed over 57,000; over 300,000 died in the cyclone of May 1970; and even the smaller storm that came ashore in May 1985 killed 10,000.[15]

Countries lacking a strong economy and a well-developed infrastructure suffer far more from such natural disasters because they have fewer ways of protecting their population. As a United Nations report on disaster prevention and mitigation points out, the most disaster-prone areas coincide with the rapidly urbanizing tropical and subtropical areas of Latin America, Asia, and Africa. These areas attract far more people than can possibly be protected. People in slums and squatter areas are far more apt to be injured or killed—not only by fires, but also by earthquakes, floods, and landslides—than are people living in better housing and supported by adequate emergency communication and transportation networks.[16]

Where knowledge of the coming danger is obtainable beforehand, prediction, followed by warning and evacuation, undoubtedly are of great use in establishing a greater level of safety. But these particular strategies are not always effective. The 1980 El Asnam quake comes as close as any to bearing out a successful prediction. As far back as 1978, experts had said that this region of seismically-active Iran was the most likely area to experience an earthquake in the near future, and yet 5,000 people were killed. On the other hand, the 6.5 earthquake at Coalinga, California in 1983 came as a complete surprise to experts. It received much attention because it happened in an area where seismic knowledge was thought to be most complete, but where no quake was expected. The 7.7 quake at Akita, Japan, which killed 105 that same year, also had been totally unexpected despite a record of detailed seismic studies.

Charles Richter, developer of the scale by which earthquakes are commonly measured, has expressed strong doubts about safety strategies that rely too greatly on limited predictive ability: "I regret the pervasive emphasis on prediction. It directs attention away from the known risks and the known measures that could be taken to remove them. We know where the dangers are and which structures in those areas are unsafe."[17]

The greatest earthquake disaster of modern times came on the morning of July 28, 1976. A 7.8 earthquake struck directly under the city of Tangshan, China. The entire city of 1,000,000 was leveled, and 243,000 people died. The quake and its aftershocks collapsed bridges, twisted railroad tracks, and overturned trains. All four hospitals in the city were destroyed. Property damage totaled over $2 billion.[18]

Why so much damage and so many deaths? The Tangshan example illustrates the earthquake engineering argument that "Earthquakes don't kill people, buildings do." Before the quake the most common construction method used in the city had been unreinforced brick walls, even for multistoried buildings. When the quake struck, walls gave way and tens of thousands were killed outright or trapped beneath the rubble.

In the history of the world's most destructive seismic events, China has suffered often. A large earthquake in Ningxia Province (December 1920) caused landslides that buried several villages and towns and killed over 200,000; 3 years later, 5,000 were killed in Sichuan; and in Gansu in 1927, another 41,000 died. Only 2 years before the Tangshan disaster 20,000 had died in a 7.1 earthquake in Yunnan Province.

The city of Tangshan is being rebuilt at great cost. But throughout China buildings continue to be made with similar unreinforced brick walls. To completely replace these buildings is beyond the country's current means. Some earthquake specialists have urged a major effort at strengthening existing buildings by tying them to external concrete frames. Certainly this seems a more direct route to safety than waiting for improved predictions. Yet even the attempt to reinforce existing structures drains significant resources from other projects.[19]

In the face of so many dramatic destructive events, it is easy to forget that a great deal of our everyday safety derives from far more prosaic types of technology. Much of the world's population lives with constant exposure to parasitic and infectious disease. This day-to-day struggle is made more difficult by the lack of regular clean water supplies and adequate facilities for disposing of human waste. The World Health Organization's annual report includes estimates of what percentage of the population in each area has current access to water and sanitation systems. Clean water is available on a regular basis to only about 60 percent of the urban population of Africa; in rural areas this drops to 25 percent. Conditions are only slightly better for those living in Southeast Asia. In the Middle East, clean water is available to about 80 percent of those living in cities, but less than a third of the rural population is supplied with water.

Sanitation presents an even more difficult problem. Urbanized areas in Africa have sewage and sanitation systems for about 55 percent of the population, but rural Africa furnishes adequate sanitation for only about 21 percent. Southeast Asia provides but 30 percent of its urban population, and a mere 6 percent of the rural population, with sanitary facilities. The Middle East, though it has the least provision for sanitation in rural areas, does manage to furnish adequate facilities for more than half of those in urban areas. Most countries, even the poorest, report plans to extend clean water supplies to much of their remaining urban population before 1990, but given the limited resources, rural areas will have to wait.[20]

Some of the dangers of modern society certainly are byproducts of technical innovation. While enjoying the benefits of modern industrial power, we have simultaneously increased air and water pollution and created concentrations of toxic waste that may be difficult to eliminate. But the image of complex technologies as a major threat to safety needs to be balanced against the grim reality of living without such technologies. Our own life expectancy has increased due to better housing and nutrition, cleaner drinking water, and the elimination of common sources of infectious diseases. Natural disasters have not been eliminated, but we have learned to escape many of their worse effects. Industrialization has made resources abundant, and these can be used to provide protection against any number of destructive forces, including those we do not now expect. Today we are safe enough to debate the merits of abandoning development of certain technologies that seem to have undesirable side effects.

Safety Risks:
Seeking Safety May Increase Danger

> *Don't play for safety. It's the most dangerous thing in the world.*
>
> Hugh Walpole[21]

My purpose here is not to deny the importance of taking steps to lessen technological dangers but, rather, to put these dangers into perspective. No safety measure comes without a price. Sometimes the price, going beyond effort and money, includes increased danger in other areas or from other sources. If an overall increase in safety is the goal, then the full range of everyday dangers (natural and man-made), including side effects, must be explicitly recognized.

If every actor, act, and object is potentially hazardous under some conditions, then measures intended to increase safety actually may decrease it. By enforcing its Earthquake Hazardous Reduction Ordinance, for example, Los Angeles encouraged owners to tear buildings down—depriving 17,000 low-income residents of housing and disrupting thriving commercial areas. Though officials believe they are protecting people, the city is not providing replacement housing. The result is that residents now are more at risk in their higher-priced but still substandard housing than they were before.[22]

In a study of whether San Francisco, in its Chinatown, should adopt the Los Angeles approach to decaying buildings, Mary Comerio argues that the desire to rehabilitate unreinforced masonry buildings must be tempered by a consideration of alternatives facing the tenants. In her view, "for low-income residents, surviving day-to-day has a much higher priority than surviving a disaster." As Comerio tells it:

> If protecting residents from risk means driving people out of their homes and out of their neighborhoods, then the definition of risk needs to be re-evaluated. When tenants are forced out of unsafe buildings because the cost of renovation is too great, they will move into another unsafe building in another ghetto. Upgrading their building(s)...will have done nothing to improve their safety.[23]

Under these circumstances, the supposed protection from earthquakes may indeed turn out to be hazardous to health.

When certain drugs become popular with doctors and patients because they work, a predictable consequence may be observed: the absolute (though often very small) number of deaths or injuries attributed to the medicine itself rises. Since many medicines do have side effects, increasing the size of the population taking them necessarily increases the number of people who are harmed. Hence, public authorities are pressured to withdraw the drug on grounds that it is unsafe. This deprives much larger numbers of people who otherwise could have benefited. When such large damage overwhelms such relatively small risk, as William H. W. Inman argues, overall health declines. Inman gives examples of two anti-arthritis drugs in Britain where the death rate from different types of that disease varied from one per hundred to one per thousand. Fifty-four cases of renal failure or jaundice, with twenty-two deaths, had been attributed to "opren" (benoxaprosen) by 1982, when it was banned. Reanalysis eliminated half of the suspected cases as due to other causes. The risk of serious injury actually was around one per twenty-five thousand. Again, after zomax (zomepirac) was banned, due to reports of anaphylactic shock among a few patients out of two million, it turned out that more lives had been saved by an unintended benefit: reduction of thrombosis. Taking drugs off the market may appear to be a prudent act to increase safety, but whether or not there are overall benefits—safety and injury compared—is another matter and should be considered.[24]

It is true also that energy production is dangerous; but so is energy conservation. Small cars, by and large, are less crashworthy than big cars; less lighting may increase crime. Use of hydropower means construction of dams—dangerous in itself as well as creating a future risk of rupture after lightning floods.[25]

Or look at another area: biochemist Bruce Ames calculates that natural pesticides from our ordinary daily food (the poison plants use to ward off predators) leave residues more than 10,000 times greater than those that derive from industry. Concentration on man-made substances is understandable. But if these are, in bulk, relatively trivial, the danger is that we will spend time, energy, and resources worrying about such comparatively less-important influences on health and safety. Most man-made residues in food (around 100 parts per billion) are not carcinogenic. But, although DDT and its metabolite DDE are carcinogenic in certain animals, the daily DDT–DDE human intake would be no more than the (carcinogenic) chloroform that comes from chlorination of a glass of tap water. Far more substantial contamination, say at 100 times the average level from a contaminated fish, would still amount to no more than eating a peanut butter sandwich with its aflatoxin. Beer, wine, and diet soda all have more carcinogenic residue than comes on average from industrial pesticides. The moral of the story, according to Ames, is that

> we must ignore the trivia if we are to deal effectively with the important causes of cancer. We might possibly eliminate every trace of man-made carcinogens from our water or food supply, but it would cost an enormous amount, be of minimal relevance to the causes of human cancer and distract health workers from real, more important cancer risks.[26]

The harm to health from safety measures may outweigh the help.

Risky Safety:
Accepting Risks May Increase Safety

Because dangers and benefits are intertwined in any product or technology, steps toward safety actually may make life more hazardous. Conversely, technologies with obvious risks may turn out to improve the safety of society. But if "no risk" is the criterion of choice, such benefits will go undiscovered and unused. Many aspects of life that we take for granted as safe enough under current standards could yet be ruled out as too dangerous. Flammable gases in industry require special "intrinsically safe" circuits so that sparks will not lead to explosions. Yet the gas gauge in our cars works by means of an unadorned thermostat in contact with the gas. Theoretically, there ought to be a large number of explosions. In what might be conceived of as a huge experiment that has lasted some 75 years and has included millions of cars, nothing of the sort has happened. That is why we still get away with cheap gauges.

Let us go on to the London underground: painted yellow lines effectively keep people from falling beneath train wheels. Given use by tens of millions of passengers, and with even conservative estimates of pushes and stumbles, much potential loss of life and limb might be predicted. Following today's standard calculations, guardrails, automatic gates, and very close platform tolerances for trains could well be mandated. But, for all we know, in addition to the expense, these devices could malfunction and themselves cause harm. Next we go to the humble table lamp. Absent a light bulb, the empty socket of this lamp might well be expected to electrocute large numbers of people. But experience shows that it does not. "Yet, who, nowadays," H. S. Eisner (who provided these examples) writes "imbued with both the letter and the spirit of codes of personal safety, would offer this design for sale for the first time to a public, many of whom know an electric shock only as a demonstration in a school laboratory?"[27]

Fortunately, light bulbs and gas engines came along before technologies were presumed guilty until proven immaculate. Development of nuclear power, however, has coincided with the regulatory pursuit of absolute safety, and that development has been stymied by arguments that no benefits of nuclear power may be considered so long as risks remain.

There are, of course, counterarguments. Robert Goodin describes economists who contend that while it may be all right for individuals to be risk averse, there is no reason for society to follow suit. These economists reason that while some projects turn out badly, others do well; over time, therefore, society can select the good ones, and end up better off. But in rebuttal, Goodin contends that:

> This argument crucially presupposes that the risky venture is symmetrical in its payoff structure, admitting of both the possibility of worse-than-expected and better-than-expected payoffs. This seems to be missing in the case of nuclear power: what unexpected windfall might we imagine that would balance out the giant costs associated with a meltdown breaching containment walls? It is of course difficult to say for certain, but it seems extraordinarily likely that all the good that can ever come from nuclear power we can anticipate ahead of time, leaving only the evil to surprise us. Thus society should, contrary to economic advice, display the same aversion to large and uncertain risks of nuclear power as do individuals.[28]

Goodin is ignoring probabilities, tacitly arguing that any worst case, no matter how remote, overwhelms any best case, no matter how much more probable. Astounding as is the view implied here—that mankind can anticipate all the good or bad of anything new (I am reminded of a gentleman early in this century who wanted the patent office closed down "Because everything that could be invented has been invented")[29]—it lies at the heart of objections to trial and error.

Let us try to help Goodin think of symmetrical payoffs from nuclear energy, unexpected windfalls that might overbalance its dangers. He rejects, wrongly I think, the suggestion that a partial switch to nuclear energy will decrease the cost of conventional fuels, thus improving living standards for poorer people. Many people might be saved from early death by the mitigation of malnutrition or starvation through the effects of lower energy prices on the costs of food—perhaps many more than would be lost in nuclear accidents. The January 1986 issue of *Discover* discusses the possible death of the earth from the CO_2 generated from fossil fuel plants. Would not avoidance of this catastrophe through the timely use of nuclear energy be an unforeseen but worthwhile benefit? Moreover, Goodin totally ignores political hazards in presenting his balance sheet. During the crisis surrounding the fall of the Shah of Iran, the United States Government, under President Jimmy Carter, went on a nuclear alert, implying that the nation might use nuclear weapons to prevent a loss of Persian Gulf oil. Is it too much to suggest that enhanced use of nuclear power might decrease the danger of waging a nuclear war over oil supplies?

Seeking safety in energy policy should mean not having to rely exclusively on any single source or mode of generation, so that whatever unanticipated event threatened supplies or technology, society could respond with effective alternatives. A social order ready to react resiliently against risk through redundancy would rely on several sources of energy—including nuclear—each with different advantages and disadvantages; consequently, we could shift among them if one or two faced unexpected difficulties. Solar electric technologies, with their small size and independence from central coordination, may be advantageous because they are less likely to be knocked out all at once. Yet solar plants might prove vulnerable to climatic change or unable to meet an unforeseen demand for continuous high bursts—capabilities better met at the present time by nuclear power. As for burning fossil fuels, some scientists claim that this results in increased carbon dioxide in the atmosphere, thereby warming the earth so that polar ice will melt. Others fear "volcanic winters" that would greatly diminish food supplies.[30] At such a time we might wish (too late?) that we had nuclear power to substitute for fossil fuels—now the greater danger. Whatever the negative aspects, at least no one suspects nuclear power plants of causing acid rain.

Moreover, is Goodin correct to suggest that the benefits of nuclear power are already largely predictable? Hardly. Its future benefits are at least as unpredictable as are the future hazards of greater reliance on other fuels. When the one sure thing is that we cannot predict important future difficulties, the best defenses are to develop diversity and flexibility, rather than just to stick with what we have.

Developing a sense of the unexpected requires a corresponding feeling for the expected—a feeling, that is, for the probability of events. Yet, we do not hear about probabilities from the Goodins, and for good reason: because this would lead them to a different conclusion. A good general rule is that the danger, the horror, if you prefer, of a worst-case event can be discounted by the smaller probability of its occurring. Goodin counters this logic of expectations with the assertion that "only the evil," not the desirable, can be left to "surprise us."[31] Though Goodin speaks more bluntly than most, he is only supplying the rationale required to support strict risk aversion.

To disentangle the logic of expectations takes a bit of time, but I think the results in clarifying thinking about risk will be worthwhile. Consider the connection between the logic of expectation and Zeno's paradox.[32] One can hold that if the time is now 1:45 p.m., it can never become 2:00 because the minute hand must travel half the distance, and then half again and half again to infinity, never reaching 2:00. But, clearly, 2:00 always comes; the answer is that the time it takes to pass through each of a series of intervals is also decreasing in steps; hence, you have two infinite series decreasing at the same time and canceling each other.

The connection of this paradox to risk is that while the potential catastrophe itself may be large, the product of this loss times its probability of occurrence might be very small; and these offset each other. It is fallacious to focus on only one side of risk—the catastrophic size of the event, if it were to occur—while ignoring everything we can do to make the probability of its occurrence vanishingly small. And, if you have already lowered the risk of the catastrophic event by making it highly improbable, it is unnecessary to predicate a windfall of immense dimensions for "symmetry" or balance. The windfalls need not be immense if their probabilities are fairly substantial. A highly probable windfall of only modest size may well swamp a remotely probable catastrophe. All of us adore a wood fire on a cold winter's eve (a modest windfall, but with a high probability of enjoyment), while managing to ignore the incremental contribution our CO_2 production might make to the heat death of the earth—a true catastrophe but of low probability.

Another more important and more subtle connection is that we do not need a huge "windfall" to counterbalance the effects of a possible meltdown.[33] What we do need is a steady yield of high probability, low-value gains. Although the benefits of sanitation may not be as spectacular as the catastrophe of a ruptured dam, for instance, the safety effects of the former may well outweigh the damage done by the latter. To forbid trials on the grounds of risk might mean ruling out many small improvements whose cumulative benefits could be substantial.

"All the good that can ever come from nuclear power," Goodin says, "we can anticipate ahead of time...."[34] But how could he, or anyone, be sure that they had anticipated all or most of the possible consequences? The unanticipated, by definition, cannot be known in advance. How can one distinguish a situation in which such consequences might exist, latent in previous actions—but one does not know that they will occur, or what they would be like—from a situation in which one has successfully anticipated all possible consequences? Ahead of time, both situations will seem alike. The coming into being of unanticipated consequences can be known only after, or during, the fact by virtue of their actual occurrence.

I have argued, then, that risk taking can improve safety, and that "safety risks" can be damaging. Society can benefit by taking risks as well as by not trying to prevent them. If risk can increase safety, and if safety measures can increase risk, what criterion of choice can guide us through these apparent contradictions?

Net Benefit

It may be that life expectancy goes up and accident rates go down for the same reasons—say, better nutrition—and yet that for other reasons—say, cancerous pollutants—we may suffer ill health beyond what otherwise might have taken place. The best test of something's effect is to hold everything as constant as possible, varying only the item in question. "The important question...," Paul Ehrlich states, "is not what the index [of health] is doing but what it would be doing if everything else were held constant and only levels of pollution varied."[35] I agree. One could only wish that net benefit consistently stood as the criterion of choice. For then health-enhancing could be compared to health-diminishing effects in order to arrive at an overall appraisal of health consequence.

A lot of misplaced nostalgia goes into the (mis)perception that all old, handcrafted items are safer than the new and mass-produced. Yet we now know that wood stoves, private wells, and yard sprayers pose, on average, greater danger than do the area-wide water systems, generating plants, and commercial or governmental pest sprayers that have replaced them.[36] It follows, therefore, that we should focus our attention on net benefit—the difference between dangers reduced and dangers created. If the damage done is considered alone, more people may suffer needless harm from being forced to do without, than from using, the offending product. A letter to the editor of *The Economist* makes the point bluntly:

> After going to dermatologists for over half of my life with little success, I was successfully treated for acne with Accutane. Each of the dermatologists from whom I received treatment warned me that Accutane did cause birth defects and that I would be required to take oral contraceptives concurrently with the drug. If I became pregnant anyway, each doctor insisted that I undergo an abortion. I have never received such stern instructions when using any other medication.... It would be a tragedy for this drug to be denied to the many people it can help, because of the idiocy of some people who have used it. You can't make something foolproof, because fools are so ingenious.[37]

Regulators and juries who ignore opportunity benefits thus deny responsible use of such products by people in need. There are two vaccines against polio. One helps those who receive it and hurts no one while the other, also effective, badly hurts a tiny proportion of users. The case in favor of the harmless Salk vaccine would appear to be overwhelming. But it isn't. For although the rival Sabine vaccine harms a few people, it also does a lot more good by conferring immunity upon those who come into contact with users (unlike Salk vaccine). Consequently, after Sabine the number of new cases of polio declined dramatically.[38]

Keeping to the net benefit principle, safety is not necessarily served by requiring products to build in additional safeguards. Safety measures are inputs, but the payoff comes from outputs—safety achieved. When substitutes for dangerous substances are deemed essential, a difficulty arises if no one knows what the risks of these replacements will be compared to those imposed by substances given up.[39] If the consumer demands red foods, for instance, red dye number two (long in use as a food additive but now alleged to be a potential human carcinogen and hence forbidden) may merely be replaced by other dyes about which much less is known. Replacement substances or devices are often viewed as safer only because they have been tested less extensively than the substance being replaced. Many different flavoring agents added to cigarettes when the tar was removed have not been tested to see if they too produce carcinogenic substances when burning. Several different solvents in succession have been used in decaffeinating coffee, only to be shown, each in turn, to be carcinogenic. Saccharin, which came into wider use after cyclamates were banned, now is known to be the more carcinogenically hazardous of the two. The replacement phenomenon reveals once again that the accent must be on net benefit. This is so because, as we have discussed, goods and bads may coexist in the same substance.

A substance or a device may be chosen as the best compromise among several risk considerations that are inherent in the same activity. Lead dichromate, for instance, is the yellow paint used for street markings, such as center lines. Its overwhelming advantage is that because it lasts longer than other paints, it need not be replaced so often. This is a substantial safety consideration for those driving in fog or a storm, where the only guide to the road's twists and turns is that comforting yellow stripe. Banning lead dichromate (as has been proposed) because of a presumed cancer hazard (based only on animal tests and without any human data) would trade off this advantage for a hypothetical lowering of cancer risk to the painters. Even those workers, also drivers, presumably (and who alone run the supposed cancer risk), may risk accidents less often if the yellow lines last longer.

If all risks were proscribed, no hospital in the world could stay open. Since some people actually get sick from being in hospitals—a phenomenon called iatrogenic (doctor-caused, hospital-related) disease—these institutions would have to be closed (despite the net good hospitals obviously do), on the undeniable ground that they also do harm. Only since the beginning of this century (estimates vary but are in the same ballpark) has medicine (doctors, drugs, hospitals) been estimated to do more good than harm. Permitting an enterprise to continue for centuries, although a risk-benefit analysis made at any given moment in time would have been negative, is a strong vote of confidence for trial and error.

Public health measures are responsible for vast improvements in the safety of large populations. Among these health-enhancing activities, vaccination figures prominently. Yet, in the United States, the availability of vaccines at a low price is now being threatened by the growing cost of damage suits. Though the vaccines themselves are manufactured properly, serious damage befalls a tiny proportion of people treated. The vaccines against diphtheria, pertussis (whooping cough), and tetanus (DPT), for instance, are given to about three and one-half million children annually. Unfortunately, 25,000 get high fevers, 9,000 collapse in some way, 50 are brain damaged, and between 5 and 20 die. Other vaccines—approximately eight children per year get polio after vaccination—also leave a tiny fraction of users badly off. Yet when vaccine use drops precipitously, far more children die or suffer other severe disabilities from the diseases thus unprevented.[40] To the children afflicted as a consequence of receiving a vaccine, and to their parents who know only pain, banning the vaccines might have avoided grief. But to society at large, health gains outweigh the losses. The current problem stems from the high cost and uncertainties in compensating victims, as a result of which several companies have stopped making vaccines. Some firms have begun to focus research attention on developing vaccines that might result in fewer lawsuits. The price of whooping cough vaccine has risen from 12 cents to $2.80 a dose, almost wholly due to the increase in liability costs.[41] One could take the position that substantial harm to a single uninvolved or innocent person should be sufficient to damn a new thing. Objection by a single person would be enough to stop anything. Zero risk—as in the Polish Diet (its old parliament), which required unanimity to make decisions—is veto power with a vengeance. Many people may be hurt in future years by a ban on products that threaten the health of even a few.

When a beneficial product yields harmful effects, immediate proscription is understandable, but may be self-defeating. Whether the replacement will be a hero or a demon depends not on speculative predictions, but on learning through trial and error. Only through experience can the net benefits of substitutable goods—such as saccharin and cyclamates—be compared. Hazards such as carcinogenicity are so widespread that there is no avoiding them entirely.

In the absence of certain knowledge about the future, the only way to achieve long-term net reduction in risk may well be to run a short-term risk, i.e., during the testing period of a new drug. Taking one risk to lower prospects of running an even greater one is, more often than not, the usual situation in society. It is known that early innoculation against mild diseases protects against much more serious illness, such as, for example, the abnormal babies born to pregnant women who contract German measles. The small risk of getting a disease from "dead" or weakened vaccines must be compared to the larger danger of coming down with a serious illness if one is not innoculated. When few people are treated, the probability of many getting seriously ill is huge. To ignore opportunity benefits, as I have been saying, is to raise risk.

Reprise

Where should we draw the line—at fewer trials (in order to reduce dangers), or at more trials (so as to experience errors that can teach us how to proceed more safely)? There ought to be more than a negative finding of actual, or potential, harm from an activity. In addition, the good that is done should be allowed to counterbalance the bad. "Net benefit," not "no harm," should be the criterion of choice. For if we impede the discovery of new arrangements that are superior to those that now exist, future increments to safety will be foregone.

When I said that "without trial there can be no new errors," I should have emphasized the "new." For, in regard to such matters as curing a disease we do not know how to cure, or using a manufacturing process that demands far more effort than an (as yet undiscovered) alternative, we are already making mistakes. Everything we do not yet know how to do could, in the broad sense, be called error; so, to be denied trials means that we forgo the opportunity of reducing existing defects. More important, methods to limit or adjust to danger can be developed only through experimentation. The sections on "safety comes from use" and "learning by doing" illustrate this point. The emphasis in trial and error is on discovering *dangerous errors* and *correcting* them.

Benefits also (like errors or catastrophes) cannot be fully anticipated in advance. Even newly discovered dangers that cannot be eliminated through trial and error may be tolerated if benefits turn out to outweigh hazards. And benefits will never be discovered unless risk is tolerated.

Discovery procedures that consider benefits are thus a subset of trial and error.

A particularly interesting situation is one in which clashing consequences (i.e., both safety and hazard) for the body and for the natural environment coexist in the same technology; for with good and bad intertwined, it is impossible to measure one without considering the other. Yet if no new risks are assumed, no new benefits can be gained. Since mankind is unable to select only consequences that enhance health, the question is how best to balance the competing considerations so that, over time, safety does improve.

The global objective of reducing risk, as I have been arguing, cannot be realized by a narrow strategy of avoiding predictable harm. A jogger's dilemma—allowing some increased danger to health (muscular damage, heart attacks, etc.) in order to decrease it as a whole—should not be resolved by staying in bed—not, at least, if you want to be healthier overall.

Is there a better way than trial and error? Why is society collectively unable to anticipate errors, and prevent them from occurring or greatly reduce their severity? There are several reasons: one is the inherent uncertainty about future low-probability events, coupled with the need for some of society's limited resources to be kept in reserve for dealing with surprises. A second is that often we must accept initial risk in order to secure long-term safety. Third, much vital knowledge can be developed only as a result of trials and use. Fourth, one must sample the unknown in small doses in order to keep in tune the coping mechanisms that are needed for dealing with surprises. Fifth, given the uncertainties, collective judgment is not only likely to be wrong but also to be wrong in a massive way. Putting more effort into avoiding risk in order to try to become safer is much more likely to render society poorer than it would otherwise have been. Richer is safer and poorer is sicker, as I hope to demonstrate in the next chapter, because wealth increases the global level of general resources upon which our safety mostly depends.

3

Richer Is Sicker Versus
Richer Is Safer*

The proverbial man from Mars, observing the debate over risk, could not help but conclude that Americans must be dropping in the streets like flies; therefore, he might well conclude that the United States Government was justifiably engaged in a desperate multi-billion dollar effort to restrain technology in order to increase an unnecessarily brief life expectancy. Looking more closely, however, the Martian chronicler of safety from 1880 to 1980 would see that almost every increase in industrialization and wealth during that century had been accompanied by a corresponding increase in personal safety, as measured by statistics on morbidity and longevity. Since personal safety and economic growth had advanced together, our man from Mars must wonder, why is present policy based precisely on severing that link by decreasing wealth in order to improve health?

Unbridled economic growth, the standard argument says, has hurt the natural and human environment. The land has been despoiled, the seas polluted, the people diseased. Some advantages of quantitative growth, therefore, must be sacrificed to improve the quality of life. The usual question is to ask how much wealth should be sacrificed for how much health. Answers vary, but none are enlightening because that is the wrong question.

Discussion on the subject of risk is about costs and benefits. Some say that human life is priceless and should not be contaminated by discussing it in vulgar terms of money. Others say that citizens would not willingly reduce their standard of living a lot in order to reduce risk a little. Immediately, as everyone knows, comes the objection that life and nature are being bought and sold like soap; the whole exercise, therefore, is branded as

*An early and, in some respects, different version of this chapter, was published in *The Public Interest,* no. 60 (Summer 1980), pp. 23-29.

immoral.[1] As Representative James J. Florio recently put it, the Office of Management and Budget has been "ghoulishly insisting that the value of a human life be calculated on a discounted present value basis."[2]

Tired of what appears to be an irrational argument, because "income" also stands for all sorts of nonmonetary things that might improve peoples' lives, proponents of cost-benefit analysis would convert the currency of discourse to a common denominator other than money, such as lives saved or accidents prevented. They then rename this activity "risk-benefit" analysis. They try to show that more efficient alternative uses of the same amount of society's resources could save many more lives or prevent accidents. Having done the same sort of thing, I can testify that this soft answer does indeed turn away wrath. For the moment, at least, an argument about who is most morally monstrous may be turned into one about which means work best to reach the same or similar ends.

Ultimately, however, the argument neither satisfies nor suffices. It does not suffice because the opponent of risk-benefit analysis comes back with what appears to be a conclusive rejoinder, namely, that the choice is illusory because no one is proposing to spend money on safety per se. There is, in fact, no safety budget from which such sums might be allocated to higher order uses.

The argument that expenditures on safety should be compared across the board for their efficacy, including their potential harmful effects, fails to satisfy as well because its proponents really do not know how to explain why. Consuming the entire national product to reduce risk (in the most efficient way, of course) is not exactly what they have in mind.

The radical reorientation of cost-or-risk-benefit analysis I am advocating calls for an enormous expansion of the classic concept of opportunity cost. On one side, opportunity benefits that correct old faults should, in a sensible system of decision making, be compared to the possible damage done by new technology. This I have tried to do in Chapter 2. On the other side, risk assessment should also be used to ask what the total of all expenditures to reduce risk (i.e., in terms of increasing safety) would be worth, compared to the net benefits for human health of economic growth. This I propose to do here.

Existing public policy is based on the belief that the way to reduce risk is to do so directly for each group of people adversely affected. What are believed to be excessive risks are to be identified and policies then are to be proposed to reduce such risks by direct government action. Requiring special car seats for children is an example of regulation that works. Yet this particularistic view, reasonable as it may appear, is sometimes mistaken. Though efforts to reduce risk in individual instances may be successful, the very same actions, I shall argue, often increase risk for other people. While direct expenditures may reduce certain dangers, this improvement may be outweighed by the resulting reduction in global resources. Applying the concept of opportunity benefits suggests that not to spend the funds thus, but allowing them to be used for other purposes, might in the end produce a greater reduction in existing hazards. To the current conventional wisdom that the way to reduce risk is to take actions that end up making the nation poorer than it would have been, I counterpose the perception of our parents that, having tried the alternative, poverty, "richer is better"— and, as I will show, safer too.

Health and Wealth

Consider the condition of poor countries. Death rates are higher; income is lower. Though considerable improvement does result from the introduction of inexpensive public health measures, they still lag behind richer countries. Increases in wealth over time within a single country also produce increases in safety.

In a study of some five countries in 1953, Adelman found the usual "negative long run association between death rates and economic conditions." She goes on to state what everyone then took for granted: "For it stands to reason that such factors as better nutrition, improved housing, healthier and more humane working conditions, and a somewhat more secure and less careworn mode of life, all of which accompany economic growth, must contribute to improvements in life expectancy."[3]

The classic study of England and Wales in the 1920s by Daric led him to conclude that social class was a more powerful predictor of mortality rates than risk arising from work.[4] The more recent work by Antonovsky, summing up many prior studies on the effects of economic class, concludes that, "Despite the multiplicity of methods in the 30-odd studies cited, and despite variegated populations surveyed, the inescapable conclusion is that [economic] class influences one's chances of staying alive. Almost without exception, the evidence shows that classes differ on mortality rates."[5] By removing noneconomic influences such as sex, race, and age across a number of countries, thereby producing more refined hypotheses, Orcut and his colleagues found that lower death rates still were associated with higher incomes.[6]

Within the United States, Evelyn Kitagewa and Philip Hauser reach the same conclusion about "a strong inverse association between mortality and income." They write:

> Over the years mortality has declined by reason of a number of factors, including increased productivity, higher standards of living, decreased inter-

necine warfare, environmental sanitation, personal hygiene, public health measures, and modern medicine climaxed by the advent of the pesticides and chemotherapy. Programs aimed at the reduction of death rates have been primarily based on biomedical epidemiology and biomedical ameliorative programs. This analysis of socioeconomic differentials in mortality may be viewed as documentation of the need for increasing attention to socioeconomic epidemiology. The evidence indicates that further reductions in death rates in the United States may be achieved more readily through programs designed to improve the socioeconomic conditions of the disadvantaged elements of the population than through further advances in biomedical knowledge.[7]

The data on life expectancy and economic level for more recent times all point in the same direction: the lower the income, the higher the death rate at an earlier age. The two tables presented,[8] with data from quite different sources, show that in a large number of countries, life span increases along with the level of economic development (as measured by consumption of energy); and, within the United Kingdom, the poorer the people, the worse their chances of survival. As Ernest Siddall puts it, "It appears that the creation of wealth leads to the saving of lives in very large numbers at a net long-term cost which is zero or negative."[9] Increasing the income for countries or classes, as we shall see, increases their safety far more than all regulations to reduce risk.

The one important, specific estimate of the effects of income on mortality, based on U.S. counties, using detailed census data, comes from Hadley and Osei. Aside from the intriguing suggestion that good health in itself may lead to higher income, they present the income elasticity, that is, the change in mortality from all causes attributable to changes in income: "For both income variables considered [total family income and unearned income] a 1 percent change in income reduces mortality by about 0.05 percent on the average."[10] Hadley and Osei also note that there may well be adverse effects from higher incomes, such as lack of exercise, overeating, long working hours, and the like. If so, it should show up in the statistics.

TABLE 1
Average Life Span in Societies with Different Energy Consumption in 1950, 1960, and 1970

Average Energy Consumption (KG. Coal Equivalent Per Person)	Average Life Span (Years)		
	1950	1960	1970
10	45	52	56
100	48	53	57
1,000	64	66	65
10,000	67	71	72

TABLE 2
Effect of Relative Income on the Risk of Death from Various Causes Before Age 65
in the United Kingdom, 1970-72

Cause of Death and Age Group	Standardized Mortality Ratios For Five Social Groups[1]					
	(high) 1	2	3	4	5	(low)
Infant mortality and stillbirth (age 0-1)	66	77	89	111	174	
Childhood mortality (age 1-14)	82	82	96	116	159	
Adult male mortality (age 15-64)	77	81	103	114	137	
(circulatory disease)	(86)	(89)	(108)	(110)	(118)	
(cancer)	(75)	(80)	(102)	(116)	(131)	
(respiratory disease)	(37)	(53)	(93)	(123)	(187)	
(violent deaths)	(78)	(78)	(89)	(122)	(197)	

[1]Note: Where the income of the adult male varied from 44 pounds per week average in social group 1 to 20 pounds per week average in social group 5 in 1970-72. The average mortality ratio for all persons in each horizontal line is 100.

The point here, as in the rest of this book, is that good and bad are inextricably mixed. High incomes have some adverse effects, though most people would willingly exchange them for the opposite condition. It is the net balance between negative and positive, not the total preponderance of one or the other (I am told that some see a certain virtue in poverty) that matters.

To understand the importance of achieving a .05 percent reduction in mortality for a 1 percent increase in income, Peter Huber, using Hadley and Osei's findings, provides this illustration: "For a forty-five year old man working in manufacturing, a 15 percent increase in income has about the same risk-reducing value as eliminating *all* hazards—every one of them— from his workplace."[11] In short, modestly richer is markedly safer. Of course, this is a statistical statement meant to apply over large populations; I don't suppose that any increase in income would make up for being hit by a falling crane.

The common assumption that the costs involved in regulation are purely economic, not involving health, leads to divorcing wealth from health. According to this line of reasoning, if regulation is too stringent, perhaps a factory or two would have to close, but surely there would be no negative impact on health or safety. The debate, if costs are considered at all, becomes framed in terms of health versus corporate profits. In considering how stringent the Food and Drug Administration must be in evaluating the effectiveness of drugs, for instance, a judge reasoned that, "A timid approach can vitiate whatever protection Congress has created for the consumer. On the other hand, an overly zealous approach can ruin a drug manufacturer by destroying public confidence in its products."[12] On one side of the scales of justice is the protection of millions of American consumers, on the other is the financial well-being of one drug company. This is not making a balanced choice; this is rigging the scales. Accepted on these terms—health over wealth—strict regulation is always justified.

A more reasonable way to structure the "jobs vs. life" debate, however, is to point out that it is actually a "life vs. life" debate: i.e., the dispute is not over the objective—improving the quality of life (which, I take it, we all share)—but rather over how best to achieve it.

It matters not only how much is being spent, but by whom on whom. Phrasing the question from this redistributive perspective makes it clear that it is political as well as technical. Perhaps favoring poorer people in this regard will make up for their disfavor in others. From the standpoint of the subject pursued in this book—the overall level of safety or hazard—redistribution is irrelevant if more people's lives are lost than are saved. Indeed, given the huge disparities in public spending on risk reduction, it is possible (I think, probable) that a majority of all economic classes among those affected would be made worse off.

A cumulation of small costs from regulation can add up to a tidy sum. A neat example, which has been costed out, comes from the ban on using phosphates in detergents. The ban was deemed necessary because, being biodegradable, phosphates cause a rapid growth of algae; this, in turn, muddies the water so that oxygen levels drop and fish die. What could be wrong, then, as Viscusi phrases it, in banning phosphates so as to obtain "clearer water at no cost to the taxpayer?"[13]

For one thing, detergents account for only about 15 percent of phosphate discharges; the rest comes from farm fertilizers, human waste, and the like. For another, phosphates in detergents are there because they actually make clothes cleaner. The cost to the consumer of switching to the next most cost-effective cleaner (and having to use more of it) is estimated to be $38 per household per year. There are also other economic costs: around one-fifth of consumers raise water temperatures and increase use of bleaches and other additives in order to achieve the same level of cleanliness, which makes for more washing machine repairs and higher energy bills. The total cost, though well into the one-to-three billion dollar range,[14] is still less important than the demonstration that regulation is using up income that would otherwise increase the consumer's real purchasing power. To the extent that this power would work in ways that improve health, the cost of regulation must be counted in the currency of wealth as well as health.

Another sign of the relationship between being poorer and being sicker is that most of the world's disasters occur in countries of low income. As Jan Tinker, director of Earth Scan put it in a report on a joint worldwide disaster study (in collaboration with the Swedish Red Cross), "Modern disasters kill overwhelmingly poor people in poor countries. The scale of drought and deforestation defies comparison. Even when similar events occur, the consequences are vastly different. Thus the San Fernando, California earthquake of 1971 caused 62 deaths, while the Managua, Nicaragua quake of the following year, though of slightly less magnitude, killed tens of thousands."[15]

The conclusion stares us in the face: if health and wealth are positively related, then to sacrifice wealth for the direct improvement of safety may lead not only to less wealth but, indirectly, also to less health. The basic reason for these adverse health effects is that the safety losses from reduction of income can be larger than the gains from the safety measures adopted. How can this be? What specific mechanisms can underlie these correlations?

Poorer is Unhealthier

An effort to provide concepts for measuring the adverse health effects of environmental regulation has been made by Ralph Keeney and Detlof von Winterfeldt. They examine four paths through which health may be affected by these regulations. The first is simply the considerable construction activity (coal scrubbers, safety devices) involved in compliance, for in itself construction is known to be a dangerous activity—and likely to be more so than many other forms of employment. A second path is provided by the additional energy generation required both to construct the new facilities and to make up for the loss of efficiency due to the operation of pollution control equipment. Power plants of all kinds, whether involved in production, transportation, construction, or the acquisition of materials, can generate negative as well as positive health results. The third path—employment or unemployment—could either add to or detract from health, depending on whether regulatory processes add more jobs than are lost, from the higher equipment and personnel cost of producing and generating power. Unemployment, to emphasize what should now be obvious, has deleterious effects on health. The fourth and final path is the reduction of household income due to higher interest rates, lower wages, higher production and energy costs, and the like. Thus, there will be less income left for discretionary safety measures, such as fire alarms, and stress reduction (by hiring babysitters and household help or by going on vacation).[16]

Certain of the relationships between regulation and risk are well documented. These include construction accidents[17] and energy production.[18] More might be said about employment. Aside from experiencing lower self-esteem, depression, compulsiveness, and anxiety than employed people, as Linn, Sandifer, and Stein show, unemployed men visited doctors five times as often and spent five times as many days in bed.[19] Brenner estimates that a 1 percent increase in national unemployment over a 5-year period leads to an additional 19,000 heart attacks and about 1100 suicides.[20] Reviewing the same data, Tabor estimates an increase of 36,900 deaths.[21] "Assuming there are 100 million people in the labor force," Keeney and von Winterfeldt conclude, "this is equivalent to saying there is one death induced for every 27.1 individuals losing a job."[22]

There is always the possibility that suicidal tendencies cause unemployment rather than the other way around. Still, the correlation between the two rates is strong. When unemployment is between 3 and 10 percent, McMahon[23], bolstered by a host of other studies,[24] estimates that a 1 percent increase in unemployment among white middle-aged men is related to two suicides per 100,000, or something like 200 additional suicides per year.[25] Increased incidence of heart attacks,[26] alcoholism, crime,[27] and child abuse[28] are also positively connected to unemployment.

There is no need to try for spurious precision: neither the negative health effects of pollution nor the efforts to control it can be precisely set forth. Rather, I would say in general that measures designed to increase safety may have three bad effects on health: (a) the safety measures themselves may directly cause harm through their own designated mechanisms; (b) they may indirectly cause health to decline by reducing family income; and (c) they may reduce the wealth of society more broadly, thereby diminishing its resilience. These health reductions are in addition to the loss of opportunity benefits, discussed in Chapter 2, that might have been provided by a substance or practice that has been banned.

Medical Care Versus Income

There appears to be at least one straightforward explanation of why wealth and health move together: with wealth comes the capacity to spend more on medical care. So far as it goes, this is true. But expenditure on medicine, whether private or public, has so far been subject to definite limits. More is not necessarily better. Indeed, the phenomenon of iatrogenic (hospital related) disease, as well as other dangers of overindulgence, suggest that a little medicine goes a long way, but too much can do you in. Sources of safety are, by virtue of their potency, also sources of danger. Safety risks are real. Unless hospitalization promises to do so much good that it exceeds the considerable possibility of damage, it is better for one's health to stay home.

It is not generalized economic growth made possible by technological progress that improves health, one might argue, but medical progress that has left people better off. One might go further and contend that government expenditures on medical care, made possible by increasing wealth, has led to the major improvements in health. The direct connection between health and wealth is maintained, but its indirect contribution is weakened. Without denying the undoubted benefits of medical care, I believe that this direct effect is much less important than the indirect consequences of a general increase in the standard of living. It is possible, for instance, that overinvestment in medical personnel or technology leads to less healthy outcomes than spending the same money on food or vacations or some panoply of alternative uses.

"Fundamentally," Speigelman says, "health progress depends upon economic progress. By the rapid advance in their economies in the postwar period the highly developed countries have produced wealth for the development of health programs. Also, more efficient technologies in industry are releasing the manpower needed for an extension of medical care and public health services. The intangible contribution of economic progress to lower mortality is derived from the advantage of a high standard of living—abundant, better and more time for healthful recreation."[29] To the extent that access to medical care depends on expensive facilities—hospitals, doctors, drugs, devices—the direct connection between wealth and health is evident. Were it possible, nevertheless, to get health benefits from improvements in medical care alone, without "the intangible contribution of economic progress to lower mortality," the connection I have sought to establish would not be as strong.

The question of why health has become so much better is raised in the right way by Lewis Thomas:

> There is no question that our health has improved spectacularly in the past century, but there is a running argument over how this came to be. One thing seems certain: it did not happen because of medicine, or medical science, or the presence of doctors.... Medical care itself—the visits by doctors in the homes of the sick and the transport of patients to hospitals—could have had no more than marginal effects on either the prevention or reversal of disease during all the nineteenth century and the first third of the twentieth. Indeed, during most of the centuries before this one, doctors often made things worse whenever they did anything to treat disease.
>
> It was not until the early twentieth century that anything approaching rational therapy emerged for human disease, and it was not until the middle of the century that we came into possession of rational and powerful technologies for the treatment and prevention of infection on a large scale.[30]

Evidently, long before medical therapy was good enough to help most people, something else was going on. Wealthier is healthier in ways that are not immediately obvious.

If it wasn't medical science, at least until recently, what was it? Thomas surmises that:

> Much of the credit should go to the plumbers and engineers of the Western world. The contamination of drinking water by human feces was at one time the single greatest cause of human disease and death for us; it remains so, along with starvation and malaria, for the Third World.... Long before plumbing, something else happened to change our health prospects. Somehow, during the seventeenth and eighteenth centuries, we became richer people, here and in Europe; and were able to change the way we lived. The first and most important change was an improvement in agriculture and then in human nutrition, especially in the quantity and quality of food available to young children. As our standard of living improved, we built better shelters, with less crowding and more protection from the cold.[31]

Changes in society induced by growing wealth explain why Thomas believes the transfer of the entire panoply of modern medical technology to poor nations would have virtually no effect on the health of their general populations.[32]

In a study of longevity and birth covering 150 countries with some 99 percent of the world's population, Sagan and Afifi also find medical technology far less important than economic growth. Three variables—energy consumption (a surrogate for economic growth), literacy, and medical care—showed promise. By replacing cross-sectional with longitudinal analysis, so that change over time might emerge, availability of medical care becomes "insignificant in the longitudinal analysis."[33] The authors note that long before effective treatments for disease became available, European death rates fell substantially. The additional fact that death rates fell proportionately at all ages also makes it unlikely, in their opinion, that specific medical interventions could be responsible for such uniform change. They speculate that literacy, with its strong relationship to economic growth, might be responsible for changes in personal practices that improve health. This suggestion is strengthened by Orcutt and his colleagues who, using some two million death certificates coded by countries, discovered that "...independently of their own education, individuals generally live longer in county groups which have more educated citizens."[34] Apparently, health as well as disease is contagious.

"In summary," Sagan and Afifi conclude, "economic development has been shown to add approximately 30 years to life expectancy."[35] Why and how did this happen?

The "Hidden Hand" in Safety

How, we may well ask, did the United States become a safer place to live in the past century without anyone directly intending to achieve that result? Is it conceivable that risk may be reduced and increased by actions in no way intended to achieve that effect? With the important exception of the sanitation and public health movements, there was no department of safety, no one in charge of seeing that Americans lived safer lives. Whatever was done was done indirectly on the basis of other considerations, safety being a by-product or a consequence of decisions taken on other grounds.

Just as finding one thing when looking for another is common in science and technology ("Sloppy chemical synthesis by an illicit drug producer has led to important insights into the basic cause of Parkinson's disease," reads a headline in *Science*[36]), unintended consequences are a staple of social life. That individual action is based on intention does not necessarily signify, as Adam Ferguson, Friedrich Hayek, and others have argued, that society is a product of design. If we think of social life as an extraordinary chain of complex adjustments, each action fanning out in innumerable directions—bumping into others unforeseen, causing consequences described as sixth- and seventh- and 'umpteenth-' order effects, all the while adjusting to the latest development—it is not surprising that no one is fully in touch with what is happening. Admitting all of the limitations of inferring causality, it is possible to provide illustrations of how actions that did not have safety in mind nevertheless appear to have helped increase it.

So far as I am aware, the great industrial revolution that led to (or was produced by) the mechanization of agriculture was not designed by anyone for the purpose of improving the health and safety of the general population. Yet the extraordinary improvements in diet that resulted from cheaper and more plentiful food, which was a major consequence of mechanization, has done much to improve health and life expectancy. Since input affects output, it is perhaps not necessary to explain in detail why nutrition is related to health and life expectancy. Even overeating and other such abuses born of plentiful food do not impair health to anywhere near the extent that it has been improved for almost everyone in society. Better food, with more calories and protein, increases alertness, which helps prevent accidents. Good nutrition also improves education, which enables people to learn and, therefore, consciously avoid some of the more disagreeable situations that lead to premature death or unfortunate accidents.

The more capital, the less labor, the fewer the accidents per unit of production. The fewer laborers there are per unit of output, and the less hand manipulation in which they engage, the safer they are. Though machines are often dangerous, they are less dangerous to fewer workers than if similar efforts were engaged in under more primitive conditions by more people. The shorter the work day, moreover, the less tired the worker, the fewer the accidents, and the greater the longevity. While hard labor is no doubt good for all of us in moderation, extreme amounts over long periods of time are deleterious.

This is not to say that technology is invariably benign. Far from it. One has only to think of bloodletting, once thought to be beneficial, or of important inventions, like the steam engine, which often broke down or exploded, to realize that this cannot be so. These adverse safety consequences of the steam engine were undesirable. The relief of drudgery and the vastly increased capacity for work brought about by the steam engine, however, proved to outweigh the initial harm.

Entrepreneurs are not interested in exploring those parts of the unknown that do not appear to bring with them prospects of profit. Since they must be uncertain about where these parts are located, however, especially since what will be profitable depends on what other entrepreneurs are doing, they must perforce search more widely. With profits depending on consumer acceptance, moreover, the wealthier a society becomes, the greater the incentive to seek safety. The income elasticity of the demand for risk reduction, moreover, means that, as people get richer, they will demand safer products and safer jobs. If markets are responsive, greater safety will result. Market imperfections may prevent consumers and workers from gaining sufficient information about risks versus benefits. If markets were largely skewed against safety, however, health rates would be going down instead of up.

The higher the level of economic activity, the larger and more varied are the alternatives pursued. Diversity flourishes. Many more alternatives for doing things than would occur to any one person or any one organization are tried in different contexts. All of this trial is a discovery process leading to new learning about how to improve safety. Thus, there is a high probability that devices, processes, and practices will be tried that do in fact increase safety though they were not necessarily intended to do so.

Improvement in overall capability, i.e., a generalized capacity to investigate, to learn, and to act, without knowing in advance what one will be called to act upon, is a vital protection against unexpected hazards. An editorial in *Nature* observes that

> ...the understanding of AIDS that has now been wrung from a seemingly obdurate problem is striking proof of the value of the basic biomedical research on which people have for decades enthusiastically lavished their talents—and governments, less sure of themselves, their resources.

> In these terms, rapid demonstration that AIDS is indeed caused by a virus is

a triumph.... The triumph is that the research community has been able to respond so quickly to an unexpected development such as the emergence of AIDS. The explanation is again simple, exasperatingly so—the richness and diversity of the biomedical research enterprise in the United States in particular but also throughout the world.

More good luck? Almost certainly not. The chances are high that in the present pattern of medical research, there would have emerged some group of workers somewhere in the world able—and willing—to turn from its long-term interests to throw light on a medical emergency such as that which cropped up three years ago.... By means of large and costly social expenditures in research laboratories and clinics, the incidence of avoidable death is kept at a socially acceptable low level, but there is no avoiding the hazards still unknown. The best that can be done is to be prepared to deal with these hazards quickly, as they declare themselves.[37]

Dealing with unknown hazards "as they declare themselves" is another expression for resilience. And yet another way in which economic growth improves health is that being wealthier makes it easier to mobilize resources for dealing with specific hazards as they crop up.

The organism or the social system that has to maintain a full repertoire of responses to low probability future contingencies finds that its inventory of standard responses is costly and, quite likely, inadequate. Outguessing the future, like correctly anticipating the direction of the stock market, is rare. The organism or social system that can, from its supply of basic resources, synthesize what it needs whenever new dangers arise is, by contrast, in a much stronger position to cope with unexpected consequences or with hazards that only occasionally manifest themselves. Because it is not necessary to keep a repertory of all possible solutions on hand, such responsive systems are capable of converting available generalized resources, such as wealth, knowledge, and technical skill, into appropriately tailored solutions if, as, and when required.

It follows that reducing economic growth is likely to slow progress in improving health. Slowing economic growth reduces the rate of new trials, and hence of the discovery process; this, in turn, slows down the rate of reduction of existing hazards. Although no one can say in advance precisely what would have been discovered had economic growth not been slowed, society undoubtedly would have foregone considerable opportunity to reduce existing dangers, i.e., opportunity benefits would be lost. And that is what progress is about—making life better by, among other things, reducing risk to life and limb below what they are now.

I do *not* propose a general principle stating that societies are better off in every respect as they get wealthier. To say this would be to neglect human conflict—wealthier and more fanatic may be worse than being poorer and hostile—and human morality. Progress in moral behavior is far from inevitable; indeed, plausible arguments to the contrary (wealth as decadence) could be made. Other matters of the greatest importance to human life, from wars to terrorism to torture, either irrelevant to or made worse by modern technology, are entirely feasible. But that is another subject. Given my focus on the relationship between technology and health, however, it is more appropriate to inquire into the matter of whether regulating competition in the name of safety actually achieves that purpose.

Preventing Parts from Exploiting Wholes

Should each person be protected rather than the group—each group rather than the whole society? Do safer parts add up to a safer whole? Or is it the subordination of the parts to the whole that leads to greater overall safety? The rule of sacrifice states that whole systems cannot be stabilized unless the parts are destabilized in adapting to environmental change.

In a different era, John von Neumann postulated that the whole might be made more reliable than any of its parts. Though any particular part might fail, a sufficient number and variety of alternatives would give the system as a whole a higher probability of performing than would any of its constituent elements. Reliability is enhanced when, as in a submarine, there are numerous systems capable of replacing those that break down.[38] This duplication (a third, indirect mechanism by which "richer is safer") depends on having sufficient resources to add additional units so that overall safety increases over time. Redundancy works (as long, of course, as the failure of any single part is independent of the failure of its backups) because it divides risks; when each of three identical units has a one in a thousand chance of failing, the chance that all will fail at the same time will be one in a billion.[39]

The risk-averse position moves in the opposite direction by seeking to protect each part against failure. Would society be safer under non-von Neumann conditions—where the objective was to make each part as strong as possible?

The consequences of attempting to avoid failure in particular parts became manifest in the dilemma that faced Consolidated Edison before the New York City blackout of 1977. There were not one but two potential problems: reducing the risk that the entire city would be blacked out, compared to the risk that a single neighborhood would have to do without electric power. The greater the willingness to "dump" loads by blacking out one neighborhood, the less the likelihood the entire city would be overloaded. The safety of the whole was a function of the willingness to sacrifice a part—the particular part being unknown, and the occasion unforeseen. When there is unwillingness to risk a shutdown in any specific site, as events proved, the city system itself may be at stake. (Greater capacity, to be sure, might well have saved the entire system.)

People must take their chances; everyone can hope to share in general risk reduction; but no one can hope to protect himself without endangering others. Once risk reduction is up for grabs, however—a decision instead of a result—a process might be put into effect by which individual or group safety is bought at the expense of the whole.

The recent history of environmental impact statements may be understood to mean that the values being protected by each part of the ecological system should remain constant. The natural environment is to remain inviolable and the economy must vary to suit it. This is no problem, or at least not much of one, if taken in isolation. But when one adds health, safety, employment, inflation, urban, rural, and other impact statements, the world of public policy is in danger of becoming all constants and no variables. How will the costs of change be borne if everyone says "Not me"? The NIMBY reaction (Not In My Back Yard) of those faced with necessary but inconvenient facilities is a potent example.

Suppose some subgroups in society—farmers, workers, old people, youngsters, on and on—were guaranteed against risk. No matter what happened, their safety would have to be secure. Who, then, would take chances? Presumably, risks would have to be allocated over the remainder of the population. How would shocks of new developments or the delayed effects of old ones be absorbed? How could risks be run to increase health if no one could be assigned the losses? Since the social system would cease adapting, the evolutionary implications of removing risk would be horrendous.

The literature of organization has worked out the implications of protecting firms against decline: "We must consider...the anti-eugenic actions of the state in saving firms such as Lockheed from failure. This is a dramatic instance of the way in which large dominant organizations can create linkages with other large and powerful ones so as to reduce selection pressures. If such moves are effective, they alter the pattern of selection. In our view the selection pressure is bumped up to a higher level. So instead of individual organizations failing, entire networks fail."[40] The cost of keeping a part going now is the much larger dangers looming in the future.

Suppose life expectancy could be expressly funded by government: how much should be spent on all lives together? No doubt a huge amount. But since government must also serve other purposes, a form of resource allocation would be needed. If, then, the question were rephrased to ask how much should be spent on you or me, the only answer could be "everything," for to ourselves and our loved ones, we are precious and irreplaceable and of infinite worth. So long as we don't have to pay directly, we would be foolhardy not to demand all possible precautions, no matter how expensive; and each of us is likely to demand much more of government if we need not pay the full cost ourselves.

The system should be optimized, not the parts. If only certain parts were protected against failure, subsystem rationality (the reliability or productivity or safety of the parts) quite likely would be optimized to the detriment of the whole. Similarly, but in a quite different context, Charles L. Seitz of the California Institute of Technology, in his report on the feasibility of the Strategic Defense Initiative (SDI) (which depends crucially on the adequacy of software), argues strongly that the current conception of SDI is based on this same fallacy, namely, that perfecting every part of a system perfects the whole. In his view, "the hidden costs of that kind of optimization—in the tremendous load of communications and coordination required, in the rigidity and brittleness of the system—far outweigh the benefits."[41]

Competition Increases Safety

Left to its own devices, each element or subsystem may seek safety at the expense of others. So may individual entrepreneurs. Linked by competitive markets, however, firms cannot do this without chancing loss. Some will suffer but others better situated will carry on. This is how risk taking by entrepreneurs increases the safety of society over time. Instead of shifting dangers to others, there is a general advance.

Mancur Olson's historical, developmental theory asserts that "the longer a state has been settled and the longer the time it has had to accumulate special interest groups, the slower its rate of [economic] growth."[42] Japan and Germany reached record levels of growth after the Second World War, while Britain and the United States, among others, did not. Olson contends that this was so because losing the war destroyed the complex of interests that, by gaining excessive benefits, had slowed growth. He sees in the political organizational mechanisms of modern democracies—especially the desire of populations for goods available to all without the necessity of paying for them (an extension of his seminal *Logic of Collective Action*)—a gradual but pervasive cause of economic decline.[43] When the parts can win special benefits by limiting market competition, economic growth (and its corresponding, positive health effects) is reduced. Conversely, when war has destroyed past patterns of vested interests, new postwar competition will assure a resource flow to the most productive enterprises. Competition solves the problem of the parts beggaring the whole.

The joint stock company, the limited liability corporation, is the social invention that made (and makes) capitalism an engine of growth. Before that time, resources were subject to claim not only by other enterprises, but by the entire web of social relations in which the individual was implicated. By limiting liability, not merely creditors but family and friends were prevented from dissipating capital. It was the corporate forum that breathed institutional life into the old adage, "nothing ventured, nothing gained." In the terms of this chapter, the desire of each and every part to share in safety, without risking anything for it, is prevented by denying the entrepreneur the right to dissipate company capital.

Competition increases income; and that fosters people's well-being. The direct effects come from public health and medicine. The indirect effects operate through material advantages such as food, educational benefits, superior personal safety practices, and technological progress, which teach us how to do things better.

If there is merit in this line of argument—competition increases safety over time precisely because society need not respond to every subunit's demand for protection—the implications for decisions about risk are profound. Some protective decisions may be justified on the grounds that the safety of this or that part does enhance the health of the whole. But the bias in decision making ought to be against protecting the parts unless a strong case to the contrary has been made—not the other way around. Of course, here the "parts" are human beings who have rights; these are rights for individuals to take chances with the rest of us, however, not to gain personal protection without sharing in the risk.

In sum, market competition works to increase wealth so society can respond resiliently to dangers as they manifest themselves. Competition distributes the discovery process over the whole society (rather than concentrating it in a few hands). By engaging many independent minds in the discovery process, competition speeds the rate of innovation—and the perception of incipient dangers that could result from innovation—while hazards are still small and localized. Competition fosters efficient use of resources, hence maximizing wealth and, indirectly, health. By increasing wealth, competition fosters resilience. Whether society should mainly seek to increase its ability to respond to unexpected dangers by increasing its resilience, or whether it should seek to anticipate dangers to prevent them from doing harm, is what the risk debate is about.

4

Anticipation Versus Resilience

Anticipation is a mode of control by a central mind; efforts are made to predict and prevent potential dangers before damage is done. Forbidding the sale of certain medical drugs is an anticipatory measure. Resilience is the capacity to cope with unanticipated dangers after they have become manifest, learning to bounce back. An innovative biomedical industry that creates new drugs for new diseases is a resilient device. Are risks better managed, we may ask, by trying to anticipate and prevent bad outcomes before they occur, or by trying to mitigate such effects after they have shown up? What proportion of anticipation and of resilience (since we need both capacities) is desirable under which conditions?

Anticipation attempts to avoid hypothesized hazards; resilience is concerned with those that have been realized. If it were possible (1) always to predict efficiently with a high degree of accuracy, that is, to guess right often enough to make up for the costs of guessing wrong, and then (2) to react effectively—controlling the expected condition so as to leave life better off—anticipation would seem to be the preferred strategy. Why court unnecessary damage? Usually, however, the uncertainties are so substantial that we cannot tell in advance which, if any, among a multitude of hypothesized dangers will actually turn out to be the real ones. In focusing on a specific hazard that might have been averted, it is easy to lose sight of the many false predictions that were made at the same time. How, then, with the best will and the brightest thinkers in the world, can we know in advance which dangers will really come about? Wrong guesses are not merely a single person's error. Presumably, each "guesstimate" would be followed up with preventive (central) governmental measures. In addition to the cost of using up society's resources on false leads—that is, leaving insufficient resources to counter unexpected dangers—each preventive program contains its own pitfalls. Inoculations against disease or agricultural subsidies or regulation of industry can do injury: inoculations make some people sick; subsidies raise prices, thereby lowering the stand-

77

ard of living, and encourage overproduction, thereby driving farmers out of business; negative regulations deny people access to drugs that might help them. Each course of action also interacts with existing patterns and creates new developments that we do not yet understand but that may turn out to be harmful. All actions, including those that are intended to increase safety, are potential hazards.

I stress the counterintuitive implications of anticipation as a strategy for securing safety because this should guard us (and policy makers as well) against the facile conclusion that the best way to protect people is always to reduce in advance whatever hypothetical risk may be imagined, rather than enabling people to cope in a resilient fashion with dangers when, as, and if they manifest themselves. Are we better off doing nothing unless we are absolutely certain it is safe, or are we better off doing as much as we can, ruling out only high probability dangers that we can effectively prevent and relying otherwise on our ability to deal with harms as they arise?

Resilience

Ecologist C. S. Holling compares anticipation as a means of control of risk with the capacity to cope resiliently:

> Resilience determines the persistence of relationships within a system.... Stability on the other hand, is the ability of a system to return to an equilibrium state after a temporary disturbance.... With these definitions in mind a system can be very resilient and still fluctuate greatly, i.e., have low stability. I have touched above on examples like the spruce budworm forest community in which the very fact of low stability seems to introduce high resilience. Nor are such cases isolated ones, as Watt has shown in his analysis of thirty years of data collected for every major forest insect throughout Canada by the Insect Survey Program of the Canada Department of the Environment. This statistical analysis shows that in those areas subjected to extreme climatic conditions populations fluctuate widely but have a high capability of absorbing periodic extremes of fluctuation.... In more benign, less variable climatic regions the populations are much less able to absorb chance climatic extremes even though the populations tend to be more constant.[1]

To repeat: "low stability seems to introduce high resilience." Yet the very purpose of anticipatory measures is to maintain a high level of stability. Anticipation seeks to preserve stability: the less fluctuation, the better. Resilience accommodates variability; one may not do so well in good times but learns to persist in the bad. As Holling sums up:

> The very approach, therefore, that assures a stable maximum sustained yield of a renewable resource [say, a single variety of wheat or complete elimination

of predators or toxic substances] might so change these deterministic conditions that the resilience is lost or reduced so that a chance and rare event that
previously could be absorbed can trigger a sudden dramatic change and loss
of structural integrity of the system.[2]

Grass bends before wind but usually does not break; it is temporarily
unstable. Trees maintain strong stability under high winds but when they
break, they have no resilience. The damage is irreversible, even after the
wind has died down. There is a Darwinian explanation for this variation in
vulnerability. With a uniform environment (i.e., one that can be predicted
with high certainty), the best adapted genetic variants in the population
will quickly spread and dominate the rest, producing genetic uniformity;
then, when the environment does change in an unexpected way, the whole
population tends to die out at once. In a changing environment (i.e., one in
which any single prediction has a low probability of actually coming to
pass), by contrast, first one variant is favored, then another, and another, so
that all of them tend to be maintained in the population as a whole. When
a change occurs, therefore, several genetic variants are available, and some
will like the new environment.

Though the language of Holling's concept of resilience is abstract, it has
concrete policy implications: The experience of being able to overcome
unexpected danger may increase long-term safety; but maintaining a state
of continuous safety may be extremely dangerous in the long run to the
survival of living species, since it reduces the capacity to cope with unexpected hazards. Keeping "out of harm's way" (something Don Quixote
preached but never practiced, hence his longevity) may be harmful.

"We are not fully free," Friedrich Hayek warns, "to pick and choose
whatever combination of features we wish our society to possess, or
to...build a desirable social order like a mosaic by selecting whatever particular parts we like best...."[3] The good and the bad are inextricably mixed
says the axiom of connectedness; all we can do is try to choose a strategy
that over time will leave us better rather than worse off.

There is nothing inherently better in the one strategy over the other in all
situations. Rather, each—anticipation and resilience—is well-suited to different conditions. An environment with periodic extremes would correspond to a situation where uncertainties are large (i.e., trying to extrapolate
forward from the condition existing at any given moment usually turns out
to be wrong), while the condition of steady, unvarying stability would
correspond to a situation of low uncertainty about the future (i.e., projections forward from any given moment usually are right). Thus, under
considerable uncertainty, resilience is the preferable strategy. Under substantial certainty, anticipation (and hence protection of the system against
predictable forms of failure) does make sense. A strategy of anticipation

should be used judiciously, however, because the future is necessarily uncertain with respect to many types of hazards; thus, many hypothetical
hazards are always possible, though most probably will not materialize.
Hence, resources spent (anticipatorily) to guard against the majority of
them will turn out to be wasted.

Either strategy has its uses; the central problem in trying to determine
which is wisest for human societies is to examine the likeliest risk conditions we face. If our most serious risks come from unpredictable or low-
probability sources, then resilience (by conserving generalized resources
that may be shifted around and applied when and where they are needed) is
best. If danger will come from reliably foreseeable sources, then anticipation makes sense. Real human situations usually involve a mixture of the
known and unknown; hence, there is a tradeoff—the most likely large
dangers, if they are known and can be countered without making things
worse, can, and should be, prevented. One way of making things worse
would be to use up resources trying to prevent disasters, e.g., President
Carter's "energy crisis" or the rise in prices that was to have taken place
upon decontrol.

To show that anticipation is the best strategy in a particular situation,
therefore, one would first have to demonstrate that the worst risks we face
are in fact the ones we already can predict with high probability. We cannot
state in advance that no expected danger will materialize. But we could do
retrospective research on whether the worst dangers that have materialized
actually had been anticipated. We could look at damage faced over the past
fifty years, pick the worst, and ask if it could have been predicted, based on
the knowledge and information available at the time. Many of these risks,
like most of the benefits, I believe, will turn out to have been surprises.

Misprediction in military affairs is legendary. Failure to predict what has
occurred vies for honors with predictions that never came to pass. The
belief in the 1930s United States Navy that battleships would carry the
brunt of the battle—as aircraft carriers, escorted by submarines, scouted
for them—was about as wrong as could be. The battles of World War II
were forced by carriers, battleships bombarded shorelines, and submarines
raided commerce.[4] Jewkes and his colleagues observe that:

> Most of the outstanding technical features of modern life have crept upon us
> almost unaware. In 1906 the Engineering Editor of *The Times* was asserting
> that "all attempts at artificial aviation...are not only dangerous to human life
> but foredoomed to failure from an engineering point of view," and in 1910 the
> British Secretary of State for War could argue that "we do not consider that
> aeroplanes will be of any possible use for war purposes."[5]

In the light of this record, the prudent person is likely to avoid expressing too strongly convictions about what can or cannot occur. It is hard to think of anything important, such as the computer revolution or the rise of feminism, that was predicted. And no wonder. Stael von Holstein shows that people with better formal qualifications or deeper understanding of statistics make no better (and sometimes worse) predictions than others.[6] A study of "Long-Term Forecasts in International Economics," by William R. Cline reports one drastic misjudgment after another. A pertinent instance is the set of projections in the President's Materials Policy Commission (the Paley Commission), which overestimated requirements for a variety of materials in 1972 by some 46 percent, underestimated the growth of GNP 20 percent by 1975, and, in general, seriously underestimated technological change. Cline's general conclusion—"...long-term forecasts are rarely right"—is correct. His comments on policy implications are in line with the position taken here: "Policy forecasting should avoid at least two temptations: to corroborate the view of the established regime, and to err systematically on the side of optimism. Ideally, [there] should be...an assessment of the probabilities of alternative outcomes, and attention to the policy costs of premising action on the wrong one."[7] When people routinely say that prevention is better than amelioration, they neglect the "policy costs of premising action on the wrong" predictions.

A second requirement of anticipatory strategies is to make sure that such foresight as does exist actually is used in making policy—by no means a foregone conclusion. Is it true, for instance, that governmental activity is geared towards using the knowledge of modern science to create priorities among possible dangers, choosing to eliminate or mitigate those that promise to do the most harm? Since expenditures per accident or fatality averted vary from a few thousand to several hundred million, this claim can hardly be substantiated.[8] The billions spent to reduce water-borne pesticides, which have a trivial impact on human health, compares poorly with the tiny amounts that attempt to alleviate the far more serious problem of internal radiation (radon) in homes due to background factors in the soil.[9]

Assessing efforts to manage resources, ecologist William Clark concludes that:

> In each case, uncertainty or variability in the natural system was initially viewed as a source of risk/hazard. Without exception, it was assumed that removal of the variability would be an unmitigated good, resulting in reduced risk and improved performance of the resource system.... With that variability removed, [however] relationships shifted to accommodate the new reality: people settled the unflooded floodplain, budworms spread through the undefoliated forest, brush accumulated on the unburned understory, and so on. As a result, *the decreased frequency of variation in the system was*

accompanied by increased vulnerability to and cost of variation when it finally broke loose from managerial controls.[10]

Again, loss of variability due to anticipatory policies leads to decline of resilience. Does this syndrome, we may well ask, have to repeat itself?

Holling and his colleagues have concluded that the ecological system has a significant chance of breaking down from human action because two kinds of knowledge are lacking: how the nonhuman system works, and what kinds of human intervention there will be.[11] Their conclusion is that it is not only natural systems but the human efforts to control them that sometimes go wrong.

In discussing "myths of manageability," Holling and his coauthors describe the kind of syndrome they worry about:

> Consider the ostensible spraying policy in the budworm examples. Technical advisors insisted that decisions to spray in the past were determined by the tree-stress index. A monitoring program provided the data to develop maps of tree stress over the province and these maps were introduced to the committee that established yearly spraying programs. However, when we compared the approximately 20 years of field data of tree stress with the 20 years of actual spraying there was no significant correlation between the two. Moreover, there was little correlation with any other rule we could define using the basic information of insect density, defoliation, and amount of spraying and tree age. A purely random decision rule, within yearly constraints of costs, worked as well as anything. Why? Because the decisions were determined by values and by external negotiations concerning other issues. The values could be as simple as the president of a forest industry finding budworm to be loathsome. In an effort to have as much of his land as possible sprayed (with government financial assistance), a majority vote could be orchestrated through use of 'side-payments' on unrelated issues. Decisions were further modified by negotiations and conflicts related to territorial defense between different agencies. And during the actual spraying operations, the inevitable realities of navigational errors, unpredictable weather and misunderstandings added a further element of the random to the decision.... The structure, dynamics and constraints of the management organization are complicated, and they cannot be neglected in a proper analysis.[12]

Ordinary, everyday bureaucratic-cum-political phenomena—the ability to impose costs on others, the likelihood of divergence between plan and practice—must not be ignored.[13] If the companies involved had been required to pay the whole costs, they might have been more modest in their demands for spraying.

There are subtle ways in which the belief that it is possible to control all dangers, by creating a false sense of security, compromises coping ability. The dependence of Bay Area Rapid Transit on a computerized scheduling system that would make no errors, for example, led to a disregard for coping with all the breakdowns that were never supposed to have occurred.[14] There were no fail-safe systems. "The classic example here," Clark says, "is the ship Titanic, where the new ability to control most kinds of leaks led to the understocking of lifeboats, the abandonment of safety drills, and the disregard of reasonable caution in navigation."[15] Since theory does not ordinarily, if ever, predict all real difficulties in use, unexpected breakdowns are very likely. Hence the need for redundancy and diversity. Trials are indispensable for uncovering errors precisely because theory inevitably proves inadequate under some circumstances not known in advance.

Fear of failure inhibits learning. This cannot mean doing nothing since essential activities, such as transportation, heating, and lighting, have to take place. Rather, this dread leads to a supercaution, in which the effective criterion of choice becomes "do nothing new" or "avoid blame." While it does not excuse culpable negligence, a positive attitude toward failure can contribute to learning. No one has said this more vividly than engineer Henry Petroski:

> I believe that the concept of failure—mechanical and structural failure in the context of this discussion—is central to understanding engineering, for engineering design has as its first and foremost objective the obviation of failure. Thus the colossal disasters that do occur are ultimately failures of design, but the lessons learned from those disasters can do more to advance engineering knowledge than all the successful machines and structures in the world. Indeed, failures appear to be inevitable in the wake of prolonged success, which encourages lower margins of safety. Failures in turn lead to greater safety margins and, hence, new periods of success. To understand what engineering is and what engineers do is to understand how failures can happen and how they can contribute more than successes to advance technology.[16]

The rationale for relying on resilience as the better strategy lies in life's inherent uncertainty; for if, try as we may, we are not likely to be successful anticipators, we can always resort to resilience. Resilience is an inferior strategy only under rather strict conditions—know what, know when, know how, know how much, act as indicated. Going to extremes, of course—all resilience, no anticipation, or vice versa—would be destructive. If we have no protection against expected and controllable hazards, we would face foreseeable, avoidable emergencies that will be dealt with too late, too hastily, and too wastefully. We do, after all, take anticipatory actions all the time. We buy insurance, stash away savings against a "rainy day," tend to avoid driving on New Year's Eve or when the weather is bad, and so forth.

Analogously, economic discounting can help deal with latent risks. An appropriate example is cited by H. W. Lewis:

If we assume that we can indeed build a waste repository that will last for the necessary thousand years, but will then begin to leak dangerously, it would be prudent to invest now in a fund to deal with the problem at that time. If we therefore persuade the Bundestag to set aside one Deutschmark now to protect against this calamity in a thousand years, and invest it in a bank at an interest rate of five percent, there will be available in a thousand years the sum of over one thousand million million million Deutschmark. There are very few problems that cannot be dealt with if one has that large a fund available.[17]

Unable to put away money for the proverbial rainy day, poor countries face particularly acute dilemmas in deciding whether to undertake preventive measures. Although it was preceded by many advance warnings, and "geologists were quite certain an eruption of Nevado del Ruiz would occur," for instance, the government of Colombia hesitated to take preventive action. Specific timing of the eruption—volcanology being a young and inexact science—remained uncertain. Earthquake activity can be both a precursor of volcanic activity and an indication that pressure has been reduced. As indicators of activity grew, the government appointed three separate teams to offer predictions and advice. But, experiencing internal dissidence, a huge foreign debt, and a generally bad economy, President Beliario Bentancur did not wish to face complaints from those whose lives might be unnecessarily disrupted by evacuation.[18]

The single most important measure urged upon the government was construction of a diversionary channel to siphon off a huge buildup of water and mudflows behind a dam near the volcano. "Hesitations in construction were undoubtedly economically induced. If no eruption had occurred, the expense might have been considered wasteful to the economically depressed country."[19] So the government temporized. Damage estimates from the massive eruption of November 13, 1985 included 22,800 dead, 20,000 cattle, and much land, wheat, and equipment.[20]

Why, Michele Kenzie asks rhetorically, were residents not evacuated? Her answer is intuitive in terms of developing a theory of safety:

Scientists and government officials are trapped in a giant catch-22 in the business of handling volcanic predictions. The Colombian tragedy cries out in favor of vigorous precautionary measures. Experts are reminded, however, of a fiasco at Soufriere, a volcano on the island of Guadeloupe. About ten years ago, after extensive monitoring of the volcano, over 70,000 residents were evacuated from their homes based on geological forecasts of a violent eruption. The area was kept deserted for three and a half months at incredible political, economic, and personal expense.

The volcano never erupted.[21]

Telling people or governments to "avoid the worst" does not tell how to assess preventive measures in the context of the damage as well as the good that might result. Had Colombia been richer, the diversionary channel might have appeared to be a more worthwhile precaution. And populated areas more likely would have had a stronger infrastructure—better communications and transportation, more solid houses, controls on river flow to support industrial and recreational uses, a healthier population to begin with—that would have mitigated much of the damage. Richness is more than money; it is abundance that translates into safety. And it is abundance that makes appropriate anticipation affordable.

One country, in at least one respect, is willing to pay the cost of anticipation: under the Japanese Large-Scale Earthquake Countermeasures Act (LECA), scientists are to try to predict an earthquake loosely expected to occur in a populated corridor south of Tokyo, even if they must issue a few premature warnings. Aware that the earthquake of 1976 had cost the Chinese hundreds of thousands of lives, whereas Japan had succeeded in predicting and limiting casualities in 1975, the Japanese government made a deliberate decision to "bear the economic burden of a few false alarms" in order not to miss the "big one." Whether the Prime Minister and the scientists in charge, whose official warning will set off extensive evacuation and emergency aid programs, will be able to carry the social costs of repeated disruptions remains to be seen.[22] What matters is understanding that a strategy of anticipation should be accompanied by a recognition of its costs. Applying such a strategy in a very few areas of life is feasible. Applying anticipatory strategies in a wide range of activities would involve prohibitive costs.

Anticipatory actions do have their place in a sensible safety strategy; the difficulty is to know what mix of anticipatory and resilient measures is optimum. Given inherent uncertainties, in my opinion, a little anticipation goes a long way. Only the most likely or most overwhelming dangers should be covered, in total awareness that whatever was missed would be dealt with as and after it occurred, thereby building up resilience for handling the unknown danger that will surely come. No error (remember, mutation is an error of a sort), no learning, no new responses.

Is Prevention Better than Alleviation?

It would make sense, at least at first glance, to prevent—and thus take action to avoid—dangers rather than wait until they occur and then try to alleviate them. But talking about risks is not the same as identifying them or knowing what to do about them. Prevention by anticipation is better than alleviation through resilience only (a) when you know with a high degree of certainty what to prevent, (b) you know how to prevent it, and (c) your remedy leaves you better off than you were.

Certainty, however, is rare. Life is full of examples of misguided efforts to reduce danger to human beings or the natural environment. After deer were introduced into New Zealand and multiplied greatly, for instance, it was assumed that they were responsible for serious erosion, so massive efforts were undertaken to reduce their numbers. Decades later it was discovered that rainfall had been largely responsible for the phenomena.[23] The deleterious consequences of a sufficient number and proportion of such efforts can easily overwhelm the good that is done by other measures. But how do you know in advance which efforts are deleterious and which ones will turn out to be beneficial?

Everyone is aware of the attacks on sugar and sugar substitutes, such as saccharin and cyclamates,[24] as harmful for our health. Enter fructose, a sugar found in fruit and honey, touted as a natural and therefore wholesome sweetener. Its use has increased sevenfold in the past fifteen years or so. Now, "New research indicates that high levels of fructose exacerbate the effects of copper deficiency, a factor that has already been linked to coronary problems, including high cholesterol levels." Given that "Nature sometimes seems to have a malicious sense of humor,"[25] I do not expect anyone to have known of this indirect connection, but I do think that if matters had been allowed to run their course, it is likely that a variety of sweeteners would have a share of the market so that very large populations would not be subject to the unanticipated consequences of the few that, for the moment, are favored.

Arguing that "the full story about a preventive measure is often different from first impressions," Louise B. Russell challenges the belief that prevention is better than cure.[26] A population at risk from a disease is usually much smaller than the population to which screening methods or preventive measures would have to be applied. Consequently, the cost of treating a relatively small number of acute cases might be much less than screening or inoculating large populations. Large scale screening, repeated at regular intervals, as with suspected high blood pressure or cancer, may actually harm the recipients or lead to misdiagnosis: "But even a clearly lower risk for prevention does not mean that prevention is preferable, since more people are subject to it than to the disease and since the people who suffer from the preventive measure may not be the same ones who would have suffered from the disease."[27] There is also a moral issue. The sick person may wish to take chances in order to get better. The healthy person, rounded up in a preventive campaign, has more to lose.[28] Russell continues:

An[other] important risk is that patients will be misclassified and either fail to receive treatment when they have the disease, or undergo further testing, and possibly even treatment, when they do not. Screening for colon cancer is a case in which the risk of misclassification, specifically the risk of false-positive test results, dominates the evaluation. The initial screening test—the stool occult blood test—is very cheap. But even under the best of conditions, about 1.5 percent of people who do not have cancer will produce (false) positive test results. The expense of the additional tests required to check the initial diagnosis—about $700 in 1981 for sigmoidoscopy, barium enema, colonoscopy, and x-ray studies of the upper gastrointestinal tract—turns out to be by far the largest item in the total cost of a screening program.[29]

Prevention may still be worthwhile, she goes on, but only if an examination of its consequences suggests that society really is better off. I entirely agree that, "The sensible approach is to look at the total costs required by a preventive measure, wherever those costs occur, and to compare them with the improvement in health they produce."[30]

Perhaps a more appropriate principle is one of protecting against low-probability, highly dangerous events. The idea is to make assumptions about the worst that could happen so as to take precautionary measures. As it becomes apparent that "the worst case" is not a constant out there in nature, but a socially constructed, essentially subjective, variable, however, doubts arise as to the wisdom of this strategy. What is the worst that can happen from bottlecaps? They could be swallowed by small children, causing immense harm. Why do we allow huge planes to fly when they could crash into skyscrapers, thus setting off a chain reaction of buildings falling on one another and causing tens of thousands of deaths? We are back again, it appears, to the criterion of "no trials without prior guarantees against error," in which proof positive that a product will do no harm is required before it is allowed to come into use. Low-probability, highly dangerous scenarios, it turns out, are in abundant supply, limited only by our imagination. So they can always be made worse.

In posing alternative criteria—"(A) the average number of deaths per year that it (a given technology) will cause or (B) the potential for low-probability, high-consequence events"—Bernard Cohen shows that when we choose B over A "*we are killing extra people.*" Given the harm to health of burning coal, for example, Cohen calculates that over the thirty to forty year life span of these plants, "every time a coal plant is built instead of a nuclear plant, something like a thousand people are condemned to an early death."[31]

Assume that (I) low-probability, high-damage, and (II) high-probability, low-benefit events both occur. In order for health and safety to improve continuously over time, events meeting type II criteria must cumulatively be far more important, though less spectacular, than events covered by type I. It is the steady accumulation of these prosaic marginal improvements, I believe, that accounts for better health overall in society, as reflected in increasing longevity. The source of improvement in safety lies in the opportunity benefits of the discoveries encouraged by trial and error. The source of danger—unanticipated and drastic effects of new technology—lies, as the axiom of connectedness might suggest, in the very same process.

Suppose that something we have not figured on turns out to be dangerous. Suppose, further, that government seeks to protect people against such a possibility. Even so, prevention is not necessarily the best policy. If only a few potential disasters are in question, we might choose to prevent them, even if at high cost. But when the expectation of catastrophe becomes common, i.e., when there are a large number of speculative catastrophes, albeit of low probability, priorities among the potentially preventable have to be established or else there will be few resources left to respond to the unexpected. The difficulty is not of trying to prevent a few worst cases, such as nuclear meltdowns, but of guarding against many. A nation's entire product could be taken up in trying to reduce a given risk to zero or in trying to eliminate completely all uncertainty about a family of hazards.

Consider the costs of prediction associated with what Bertrand de Jouvenal calls "the railroad track": A pattern has always obtained in the past; therefore, although projecting it is reasonable, it can lead to absurd consequences because, somewhere along the track, a systematic reaction happens that had never occurred before (for whatever reasons that may be specific to the subject being examined). For example, suppose that the pattern that has always obtained in the past was the function of a social given (as in population dynamics). When something changes in the society, say population grows dramatically, the pattern of resource use changes too. Is it possible that the cumulative result of radical environmental changes (some of which we will not see for 50 or 100 years) amounts to a radical shift that will alter the projection? It could happen.

Knowing so little about whether a given risk will materialize (though we know that the chance is low), we are in great danger of wasting resources in the pursuit of wrong leads (the vast majority of all leads, due to the low probability involved, will be wrong leads). The inevitability and irreducibility of this uncertainty is what makes unwise the strategy of anticipatory spending to avoid such low-probability risks. Something better is needed.

A decent society, it may be said, puts a high value on life. It becomes clear, however, that when actual examples are given, spending astronomical sums per life ostensibly saved is unhealthy. As Mendeloff points out, "extending that policy from a program that prevents 200 deaths a year (at a cost of $2 billion a year) to one that prevents 2000 deaths a year (at a cost of $20 billion a year) or even 20,000 a year (at a cost of $200 billion a year) would...constitute an enormously inefficient way of improving health."[32]

When we translate the money misspent into health impaired, the loss is still greater. A brief look at a cost comparison of lives saved per dollar reveals the huge disparities involved:

TABLE 1
Cost Per Life Saved by Various Health and Safety Measures[33]

Safety Measure	Estimated Cost Per Life Saved
Nuclear Power Plant Design Features:	
Emergency Core Cooling System	$100,000
DG Sets	1 million
Containment	4 million
On-site radioactive waste treatment system	10 million
Hydrogen recombiners	3 billion
Coal Power Plant Design Features:	
Scrubbers to remove sulfur dioxide	100,000 +
Occupational Health and Safety:	
OSHA coke fume regulations	4.5 million
OSHA benzene regulations	300 million
Environmental Protection:	
EPA vinyl chloride regulations	4 million
Proposed EPA drinking water regulations	2.5 million
Fire Protection:	
Smoke protectors	50,000 +
Proposed upholstered furniture flammability	500,000
Automotive and Highway Safety:	
Highway safety programs	140,000
Auto safety improvements, 1966-70	130,000
Air bags	320,000
Seat belts	80,000
Medical and Health Programs:	
Kidney dialysis treatment units	200,000
Mobile cardiac emergency units	30,000
Cancer screening programs	10,000 +

No one can seriously contemplate spending as much as necessary, if only because national income per capita is too low. A different look at the marginal costs of preventing deaths from cancer shows how steeply costs rise as permissible limits decline.

Through this brute empiricism, we are closer to posing the right question: Under what conditions is saving a life indefensible, though perhaps

TABLE 2
The Marginal Costs Per Cancer Death Prevented Increase Sharply
as Acrylonitrile Exposures Are Reduced[34]

Permissible Exposure Limit	Total Deaths Prevented	Marginal Deaths Prevented	Total Costs	Marginal Costs	Marginal Cost Per Death Prevented
2 parts per million	7 per yr.	7	$25M a yr.	$25M	$3.5M
1 ppm	7.4	.4	36M	11M	29M
0.2 ppm	7.7	.3	86M	50M	169M

prima facie morally attractive? The obvious answer—when more lives are lost than are saved through the same action—takes us part of the way. Even if an exceedingly expensive act does not immediately cause harm, there is good reason to believe that such actions will lead to less health as well as less wealth.

Balancing positive and negative effects is considered harmful by those who, in the words of Daryl Freedman's title, seek "Reasonable Certainty of No Harm." Freedman, a lawyer who was, at the time he wrote this article, an intern with the Natural Resources Defense Council, urges greater enforcement of what he calls the "safety standard"—the absolute banning of any food additive or animal drug that shows any evidence of possible harm to humans.[35] But banishing a substance without considering the health benefits lost is a narrow and ultimately self-defeating way to promote safety. Those who want to virtually eliminate man-made risks are constructing a Maginot Line, creating a false sense of security by pouring resources into combating a few risks that will likely never materialize, all the while becoming less able to cope with whatever dangers actually do occur.

It is instructive to go back to the story of the Sabine versus the Salk vaccine. Individuals who take the live Salk vaccine are, in effect, taking a small chance in order to confer immunity on nameless others who do not have to take any vaccine to be safe. These risk takers could well say they would rather take the Sabine vaccine and leave the "free riders" with the choice of taking a safe vaccine or risking polio. I would not fault those who prefer to eliminate their own risks. From the perspective of government, however, which has to consider the overall effect on society, the better choice is the Salk vaccine because its use will greatly reduce the number of cases of polio. Despite the existence of the Sabine vaccine, government could forbid the Salk vaccine in order to eliminate the danger of polio, but in fact this could only transfer it from a much smaller number of risk takers to a considerably larger number of people who are risk averse or lazy.

Neither choice—forbidding or encouraging taking the Salk vaccine—is without physical risk or moral ambiguity.

How do I justify exposing individuals or large populations to harm? Perish the thought. Those who do in fact know with high probability how to do more good than harm by means of anticipatory measures are encouraged to bring them to our attention. Yet there is still force in the adage that it is up to the wise to undo the damage done by the merely good. For the requirements of a policy of prevention are severe. One must judge which evils are likely to manifest themselves. Predicting wrongly, when these "guesstimates" are backed up by the force of the state, wreaks havoc upon innocents: lives are disrupted, jobs lost, anxiety increased, and resources diverted from more productive and hence safer uses.

There is also the practical problem: How would government (how would anyone) know which one(s) of an infinity of hypothetical evils will ultimately become manifest? Many, which now appear dangerous, may never turn up at all, or may actually turn out to be harmless. Others may actually be a little dangerous, but the consequences of trying to prevent them may be much worse than letting them run their course. The most likely eventuality by far is that most of the low probability events will not happen, and that whatever does happen will be unexpected, i.e., it will not be among the envisioned possibilities at all. We might be better off, in fact, when faced with a large number of low-probability dangers to increase our generalized capacity to respond to realized risks than to dissipate our strength by advance preventive efforts to ward off all the hypothetical hazards that a rich imagination might generate.

For what sorts of errors (or breakdowns or dangers) should we seek to maintain a capacity for resilient response? Catastrophe comes first.

The Reverse Cassandra Rule

The main limitation of a strategy of resilience is the potential for catastrophe. No one wants to wait until dreadful events have already occurred before responding to them. Well and good. Seeking to prevent catastrophe (say, death or disability to large numbers of people or impairment of their means of livelihood), however, is not the same as doing so. There may well be catastrophes in store for us that no one knows about or, if known in advance, that no one can prevent. Resilience, for the survivors, is then all the more important.

Often there is disagreement over whether an alleged catastrophe actually will materialize. For one thing, knowledge is incomplete and uncertainty inherent, especially concerning low-probability events. That is life. Will the earth freeze or fry, the sun be blocked out, oxygen depleted, diseases spread, sunlight disappear—on and on? "Worst case" assumptions can convert otherwise quite ordinary conditions—exposure to sunlight, this or that chemical in land, air, or water—into disasters, provided only that the right juxtaposition of unlikely factors occur. The human imagination can concoct infinite modes of destruction. Yet no one can say for sure that there is a nonzero probability of catastrophe.

If the Reverse Cassandra rule were in effect—all cries of impending catastrophe must be heeded—anyone could stop anything she did not like merely by proposing a catastrophe scenario (however improbable). "The likelihood [of a major accident at Seabrook] is irrelevant," Governor Michael S. Dukakis said, upon refusing to approve the evacuation plans for this nuclear power plant. For, in his opinion, no evacuation plan was going to be possible. Dukakis suggested converting Seabrook to a fossil fuel plant.[36] The argument from catastrophe can be used to defeat all technological progress. "If government functioned only when the possibility of error didn't exist," Mayor Koch of New York City wrote recently, "government wouldn't function at all."[37]

One example of a disaster that society might try to anticipate (and defend against) would be a large meteor (of the kind hypothesized to have wiped out dinosaurs) that might well destroy a major city or worse. Shoemaker and Harris estimate the probability of an asteroid 0.5 kilometers in size hitting the earth in the next century at one in a thousand.[38] Why not install missiles explicitly designed to shoot one down if it came? The answer: a societal judgment has been made that, considering the low probability, the costs exceed the benefits.

According to C. Don Miller of the U.S. Geological Survey, huge volcanic eruptions, spewing out thousands of cubic feet of magma, occur about every half million years. He estimates that their airborne sulfates could create "volcanic winters," comparable to the projected nuclear winters, which would alter the climate and hence food production for years. He suggests keeping large supplies of food on hand.[39]

When there is widespread agreement that a catastrophe is imminent, as in regard to nuclear warfare, massive efforts at prevention are undertaken. Pure anticipation is practiced because the idea is to avoid all possibly disastrous recourse to experience. Most often, however, because we are ignorant of what the future might bring, let us ask how might we prepare ourselves for the unexpected?

Interrogating the Unknown

It is useful to distinguish between certainty—the ability to predict accurately the consequences of actions—and uncertainty—knowing the kind or class of events that will occur but not the probability of their happening. Ignorance involves knowing neither the class nor the probability of events. We know neither how likely the consequences of our actions are nor what class of consequences—hail storms, burst dams, train wrecks, economic decline—will confront us. Ignorance may be exceeded by superignorance—thinking we know but not knowing that we don't know. And superignorance itself may give way to astonishment—expecting one class of events and getting another.

Now there are at least two kinds of surprise. One might be called quantitative surprise. We know the kind of thing that can happen but are surprised by the fact that it occurs more or less frequently or in different amounts from what we would have supposed. I call this "expected" surprise because, though we know the kind of surprise, we do not know how often or how much. The other category is qualitative surprise. This is "true" (or, unexpected) surprise.[40] My thesis is that the growth of resilience depends upon learning how to deal with the unexpected, a term that Jerome Bruner identifies as striking "one with wonder and astonishment."[41]

Given that resilience is the better strategy for low-probability events, how do we develop resilience? One way is to sample the unexpected in small doses and diverse ways.

Since it is not possible to anticipate surprises, what is wanted is a method for probing the unknown. This method should seek out both potential trouble and potential advantage, sample each, and give society some experience in warding off or coping with the bad and taking advantage of the good, but without requiring huge expenditures or large-scale, premature commitment to a single approach. The more people that participate in this exploration, the more widespread the search, the more varied the probes and reactions, the more diverse the evaluating minds, positive and negative, the better. This method should be variegated—decentralized, participatory, and based on diverse, repeated probes.

This method is familiar. It belongs to the family of self-organizing systems. It represents a form of social spontaneity, not social control. It is called, though it is not just any kind of, trial and error.

Until now I have not asked a crucial question about the strategy of anticipation, namely, anticipation by whom? It is all too easy to assume that governments or other large collective entities must do the anticipating. Suppose, however, that anticipation were decentralized, with large numbers of anticipators (think of them as entrepreneurs trying out new products or users modifying old ones); each of them would pay not all, but a substantial part, of the cost of error. Should they err in predicting future events, they would bear the financial costs. If products harmed others, they could be sued. Society, instead of guessing about consequences, could hold such producers to account for the actual damage done (see Chapter 8 on the law of torts for qualifications).

The discovery procedure called trial and error, to be sure, while spurring innovation, is also creating new knowledge about actual consequences, some of which undoubtedly will be bad. But, its critics say, no one should have the right to impose unknown harm on others. Hence, they press for the rival strategy—to allow no trials without prior guarantees against error.

Alongside these undoubted costs to society, however—and unrecognized by such critics—opportunity benefits also are being created. And one of these, not previously discussed, is exploration of the unknown. For it is precisely the lack of central control and command that permits the testing of a wide variety of hypotheses that vigorously sample the unknown, and bring us into contact with events about which we would otherwise have been ignorant.

In markets, actors do not perform as if the economy operated at random. They make predictions about the future and test them through their own actions. "Entrepreneurship in individual action," Israel Kirzner tells us, "consists in the endeavor to secure greater correspondence between the individual's future as he envisages it and his future as it will in fact unfold. This endeavor consists in the individual's alertness to whatever can provide clues to the future."[42] The hypotheses tested in markets are multiple, independent, and external. There are many independent anticipators, each operating from different vantage points, trying to outguess the others. Consequently, the probability grows that someone somewhere will be alert to important future developments.

If it is experience in coping that is desired, an evident riposte goes, why not institutionalize fire drills or other exercises designed to give practice in responding to emergencies? Well, a strategy of preparing for expected surprise does have its uses, but only against expected hazards. Practice may well make perfect, though if the expected danger is long delayed, one will observe lax compliance. Emergency preparedness makes sense so long as one has the right emergency in mind. In order for trial and error to protect society against nasty surprises, however, the errors must be germane. Safety drills may well be useful in rehearsing standard responses to known dangers. Only by sampling as yet unknown dangers to get a hint of what they are like, however, is it possible to develop mechanisms for coping with surprise. It is the taking of risks, some of whose consequences are unknown, that keeps responsive ability in fine tune. For qualitative or real surprise, however, there are no ready-made drills. The underlying premise of expected surprise is that the unknown risks will be limited to the same sorts of risks that we deliberately practice to meet. Precisely because it fails to interrogate the unknown, a strategy of preparing for expected surprise—

really a form of collective anticipation—provides only the appearance, not the reality, of resilience. Deliberately planning failures to test our reactive ability does not promote resilience—which, remember, is to sample unknown hazards, so as to be always ready to cope with surprise—because the category of "expected surprises" does not include the unexpected.

The way to keep society's coping mechanisms well exercised is not through deliberately tolerating known and avoidable sorts of failure, but through economic growth and technical progress, since only new development keeps producing unpredictable risk situations. It is only by means of managing presently unknowable hazards that we can keep our coping ability in shape. Increased wealth and technical knowledge help us build up a reservoir of resilience for dealing with such problems. Even better (because such progress-related risks can be viewed as a statistical sampling from the entire universe of possible unforeseen risks), successfully coping with such risks as arise from progress does provide real information about most of the possible risks. Hence, our coping mechanisms will, most likely, be strengthened in just the sorts of ways that will be useful against the truly unexpected. This is another reason why a rapidly progressing society usually will be safer than a static one. Catastrophes can always occur. But where there is progress, we will have a much greater body of wealth, knowledge, and coping experience to draw upon; thus, growth and progress reduce the chances that "ultimate" catastrophes actually will be ultimate.

In recent years, a common prediction of catastrophe has been that the earth will within decades get much warmer or much colder. Indeed, a journal called *Environment* (on different pages of the same issue, of course) contains predictions that the earth will be getting a degree hotter and a degree colder.[43] Perhaps these trends will be unrealized, or, if they are realized, will offset each other. How might we prepare for whatever comes?

A Mental Experiment

An adage of policy analysis is that no instrument can serve every policy purpose. No single thing, so to speak, is good for everything. Conditions and context count. Were that not so, choice, and, with it, volition, would disappear because there could only be a single successful strategy under all circumstances. How dull! Rational behavior would involve following the one correct path and the study of irrational, i.e., inefficacious, behavior would become the study of pathology—willful and unreasonable disregard of the known means of fulfilling agreed desires. How uninteresting! There must be, and there are, competing strategies, better and worse under contrasting conditions. Perhaps it will help to imagine what one such set of conditions might be.

Suppose that the polar ice caps melt, thereby inundating significant areas (but by no means all) of the earth's surface; steam rises to cut off part of the sun; huge winds blow with gale force. Assuming, with good reason, that this extraordinary confluence of events cannot be anticipated, but we are aware that such unforeseen events can strike suddenly, how would we like to arrange our energy resources and facilities so that we could recover?

Flooding destroys many hydropower installations; haze cuts the output of solar power; tidal waves flood coal mines and oil fields; undreamed of, forceful gales overturn all but the largest wind machines; and nuclear fuel production is disrupted. What sort of preventive strategy makes most sense?

In the short run, as the scenario is devised to show, there is no telling which resource will remain available in what quantity for how long. Fuel supplies on hand may be used wherever transmission lines remain intact. In the medium run, coal or gas or nuclear, depending on some unknown combination of human ingenuity (i.e., a perpetually replenishable fuel; there is talk of making methane gas from algae or kelp) or the unexpected (sun and wind turn out to be undependable), may be the available fuels, quite contrary to current expectations.

The larger the number of independent sources, transformers, and transporters of energy, it would appear, the more resilient to disruption would be the supply of energy. Whatever the kinds of disruption, the more varied and dispersed the supply, the less likely any type is to be hit by the same hardship. So far so good: reliance on a sole source is bad. Or is it? Not necessarily. One rationale for a large grid is that it makes up for failures in local supply; local breakdowns are shared so the whole grid survives. What matters is how the elements within a large network are structured. Local failures can be isolated so they do not spread, while at the same time other units can be called upon for help. The structuring of the grid is such that normal failures can be contained, while "successes" can be spread through the healthy functioning of the other parts. Even so, uniformity may prove fatal if the entire grid succumbs to a particular insult.

Under certain circumstances, smaller, varied sources of energy may be less safe. Consider the conditions in the outline of disaster previously presented. The small sources which, under other circumstances, might be most resilient, suffer from serious defects. But (and it is, to be sure, a result of malice aforethought) the big stuff turns out to be in a better position to bounce back. It is easy to store sufficient nuclear fuel to last quite a while, long enough, possibly, to repair other sources of energy or to constuct new ones or to wait for sunlight to return and for windpower to become manageable. In a phrase, one way to achieve resilience is through variety. In their different ways coal, oil, gas, and nuclear power can accept different sources of supply and use different forms of processing, each being subject to failures of diverse sorts.

The conclusion to which I have come—resilience is related to variety and redundancy—appears unexceptional. A strategy of energy resilience would be concerned with retaining lots of small units but would also want to have large ones available, especially if they differed in quality from the others. Variety entails a mix of large and small. A vast dependence on large coal or nuclear plants is evidently undesirable as these might be sabotaged or destroyed in war[44] or belatedly be discovered to have terrible health effects. A balance among these various sources makes more sense than just one or the other.

Lovins Versus Lovins: Are Resilience and Efficiency Opposed?

Amory and L. Hunter Lovins have written a book advocating abandonment (I can't quite tell whether "phasing out" would be more accurate) of all large-scale sources of power (except existing hydroelectric stations) in favor of solar and wind and such smaller-scale devices exactly on the grounds that this strategy would increase resilience. And, since they rely on precisely the same work on resilience by C.S. Holling and William C. Clark from which I have derived contrary conclusions, it seems useful to sharpen the safety debate by confronting the opposed positions.

First, a few disclaimers. I am sympathetic to the decentralized market orientation of the Lovinses toward energy problems (though it might be that they would not wish this applied to social problems in which the inegalitarian outcomes of competition would be more obvious). Nor do I claim either superior understanding of energy or superior insight into the Aristotelian essence of what must be the true meaning of resilience. My aim is to explore both the similarities and the differences in our approaches so as to better understand the connection between risk and resilience.

In time-honored fashion, let us take certain truths about risk to be self-evident. As the Lovinses put it:

> Taken together, four factors—unavoidable ignorance of how some things work, unpredictable changes in the environment in which things work, the influence of unexpected events not taken into account, and changes in technology and society—make it *impossible in principle* to foresee all risks.... It is...simply beyond human ingenuity to think of all possible failure modes.... The impossibility of foreseeing and forestalling all major failures to which the modern energy system is vulnerable—that is, of preventing all surprises— requires that we take a different tack. We must learn to manage surprises and make them tolerable, to incorporate the unexpected in our expectations so that its consequences are acceptable.[45]

This quality of managing surprise might indeed be called resilience.

The Lovinses have joined resilience to anticipation. They would like to plan resilience into the energy system in advance of actual failures. One of their principles, with which I agree, is that the unexpected is bound to occur. For what kind of surprises, then, should we prepare? The concept of surprise advanced by the Lovinses is quantitative, not qualitative. If we in society are to prepare only for expected surprises, the surprise that is being referred to cannot be much of one.

Admitting that "this sought-after quality of 'resilience' is difficult to define," the Lovinses make a good try at defining it as "the ability to absorb...shocks gracefully...."[46] They distinguish between passive resilience, "the mere ability to bounce without breaking," and active resilience, "a deliberate effort to become better able to cope with surprise," or, the "adaptive quality of learning and profiting from stress by using it as a source of information to increase 'bounciness' still further."[47] This "resilient learning," this "ability to cope with stress," the Lovinses continue, is not just a passive margin of safety or substitution of a redundant element for one that broke down but, rather, it is gaining strength from stress.[48] "Stress...as a source of information" gets back to trial and error as a discovery process of sampling the unknown so as to fill in the niches that anticipation via theory must inevitably miss.

What facilitates resilience, bounciness, or whatever you call it? The Lovinses cite ecologists in support of principles with which we will become familiar in the next chapter, such as nonspecialization ("avoiding...extreme specialization"), patchiness ("temporary extinction in one place can be made up by recolonization from adjacent areas"),[49] and negative feedback. Active is preferred to static defense, learning to anticipation, a large number of small trials (and errors) to the reverse. But then, in midargument, the focus changes—from learning through experience to learning how to avoid experience; from placing minimal, to making maximal, demands on knowledge, all in the name of safety. Now we get the "other" Lovinses.

Up to this point, the reader of *Brittle Power* would not be too surprised to find a libertarian kind of argument in favor of the extreme decentralization produced by perfect (or as perfect as life will allow) competition in economic markets. Although one could not predict where help in the form of innovation would come from in time of danger, the sources would be so spread out and so numerous and diverse that in the face of catastrophe some would surely survive. These libertarians would argue that markets per se are resilient. A freely moving price system, in their estimation, rapidly shifts demand from a source of energy in short supply to other forms still in adequate supply. If market forces are allowed to prevail, however, the possibility exists that there would be a mix of large central organizations, like multinational corporations, and small ones, like garage software entrepreneurs in Silicon Valley. Apparently, for the Lovinses, this will not do.

In his earlier work on *Soft Energy Paths,* Amory Lovins defines the hard path as composed of large, centralized institutions (notably big nuclear plants) that have adverse social consequences. For, in his view, the hard path "demands strongly interventionist central control...concentrates political and economic power...encourages urbanization...increases bureaucratization and alienation...is probably inimical to greater distributional equity within and between nations...inequitably divorces costs from benefits...enhances vulnerability in the para-militarization of civilian life...nurtures—even requires—elitist technocracy whose exercise erodes legitimacy of democratic government."[50]

In *Brittle Power,* Lovins and Lovins specifically disavow, not once but several times, any intention of making a social or political argument, confining themselves, they insist, to the direct issue on grounds of cost and safety. It is not at all surprising, certainly not to a social scientist, that preferences about how people ought to live get mixed up with what is supposed, objectively speaking, to be good or bad for them. Indeed, the very same comment could be made about my own use of material from ecology. Let us try to understand, even if we cannot completely reconcile, the consequences for safety as well as for society of adopting different strategies for securing safety.

Modern, large-scale energy systems are extraordinarily reliable. They work almost all the time; breakdowns are few and rarely serious. Though the potential for disaster exists, I cannot think of any modern industrial nation that has been without electric power over an extended period outside of wartime. By any account, this must be regarded as a remarkable achievement, especially since this dependability has gone hand-in-hand with ever-cheaper energy production costs. Yet it is, as the Lovinses say, this "great reliability of supply most of the time" that "makes designers less likely to take precautions against rare, catastrophic failures which they have not experienced and hence do not consider credible."[51] Is this so? One could argue both ways: that success breeds complacency, or that such extraordinary reliability results not from complacency, but from continuous vigilance. The reliability is not passive; it is active. It is the result of constant monitoring for local failures and breakdowns. It is the active responsiveness to such breakdowns that produces the consumers' experience of reliability. Given considerable experience in trouble-shooting, failures that occur are presumed to be quickly corrected. The New York City blackout was a rare exception. Even so, the failure might well have nothing to do with having achieved reliability in the past. It might just have been an act of God, and nothing we might have done would have prevented it.

But the Lovinses believe the fact that safeguards work most of the time is precisely the problem in achieving resilience. They then quote Holling:

> But in parallel with that achievement is a high cost of failure—the very issue that now makes trial-and-error methods of dealing with the unknown so dangerous. *Far from being resilient solutions, they seem to be the opposite, when applied to large systems that are only partially known.* To be able to identify...[safe limits]...presumes sufficient knowledge.[52]

Hold on. Either these energy systems work reliably or they do not. If they do, who needs to do more? Maybe they work because resilience is already built into their systems. Or maybe, as the Lovinses fear, new stresses, such as systematic sabotage, would make them vulnerable. But then big defense, which they also dislike, might be called for. So far, energy systems have not been subject to frequent, let alone catastrophic, disruption. If they ain't broke, why are we fixing them? True, as Lovins and Lovins quote Holling, these large systems are only partially known. But they are far better known than many other kinds of systems and, as yet, there are no significant unexplained failures. Well, as the Lovinses say, maybe that is just the time to get worried.

The conclusions the Lovinses draw from their assumptions are inexorable: "If the inner workings of a system are not perfectly understood and predictable, efforts to remain within its domain of stability may fail, leading not to safety but to collapse. And if, as is inevitable, the full range of potential hazards is not foreseen, but simple precautions nonetheless give an *illusion* of security by controlling the most obvious and frequent risks, then the ability to cope with major, unexpected risks may well *decrease.*"[53] I had thought that it was precisely the "unavoidable ignorance" that the Lovinses earlier wrote about that made all systems suspect, including their preferred, small, decentralized ones. Nothing new could pass the test of needing to have a fully-known causal structure; it is precisely because the inner workings of present energy systems are very largely under control that they fail so rarely. It is external disturbances, from lightning storms to sabotage, that are less predictable.

What the Lovinses seem to be saying is that we need instances of recurring failure in order to keep our coping mechanisms in tune—i.e., to learn to keep a supply of candles on hand. Since there are enough problems in life already, I am not persuaded that we must keep punishing ourselves deliberately. Let those failures that occur be real ones, i.e., truly beyond current understanding, and we will learn from them. Why can't we just appreciate how much reliability has been achieved already, and then determine from that situation how much we need in the way of precautionary measures? After all, if the system is pretty reliable, it would be a waste for all of us to own individual emergency generators. The Lovinses' argument does not relate a necessary level of precautions to the frequency and seriousness of actual failure. It assuredly makes sense, for example, for hospitals to maintain emergency power and for high-rise buildings to do so (for elevators and ventilation). But for the rest of us? Well, perhaps a box of candles in the cupboard isn't such a bad idea.

The Lovinses claim that since it is impossible to anticipate all risks, or to come up with a design that guarantees safety in case of failure (the "safe-to-fail" method), prudence requires—if not doing nothing—at least acting small. Otherwise they assert, the ability "to *survive* unexpected stress" cannot be guaranteed.[54] Of course not. Nothing I can imagine, except preferred access to the Almighty, can do that.

For the Lovinses, it is desirable to sacrifice efficiency (read wealth) so as to win "an even richer prize—minimizing unexpected and disastrous consequences that can arise when the causal structure of a real system turns out to be qualitatively different than expected."[55] And so it would, if the premises on which this statement were based held up. The flaw in the Lovinses' thesis is that the sacrifice of efficiency, i.e., wealth, is itself a sacrifice of resilience.

How do we decide how much failure to allow ourselves in order to achieve the optimum level of fitness in our coping mechanisms? The Lovinses focus only on a single class of expected failure, namely, failures in the supply of energy. Yet unanticipated failure of entirely different sorts might occur; to cope with these we will need resilience (generalized resources, including wealth), and that wealth is exactly what we may have frittered away by tolerating frequent breakdowns in our energy system.

Note how their argument resembles homeopathic medicine: take small doses of drugs that will produce the same symptoms you already have and, somehow, this will make you better. But, I ask, having already achieved a high level of dependability, should we deliberately abandon it in order to maintain our coping ability against a hypothetical, unknowable, unpredictable failure event? One could say yes only if unknown things did occur in some predictable way so we could head them off. But they don't. Failures do happen, but not necessarily because the system fails. They also occur because we do not want to cut down every tree whose branches might break a powerline in a storm.

The Lovinses hold a deeper fallacy to which I have already alluded—the fallacy of expected surprise—namely, accepting small, deliberate failures, so as to flex our coping muscles. This presumes that big, unexpected failures will nevertheless be of types related to the small ones; otherwise, our well-exercised coping mechanisms would be useless against them. The Lovinses are trying to bound such unknown future failures by accepting some inconvenience in the present. Inconveniencing oneself is easy, but it will do no good unless the sacrifice is related to the disaster; yet there is no reason to believe it will be. An effort to ward off such surprises by accepting known types of failure is not a useful form of sacrifice.

One of the examples the Lovinses give is helpful in pointing up the limitations of sacrificing wealth to secure resilience. In recommending "local buffer storage" to cope with "fluctuations, modifications, or repairs," the Lovinses criticize the British automobile industry for keeping their stocks on hand so small that manufacturers are caught short when strikes occur. In order "to make failure-prone systems more stable," the Lovinses recommend "gradual, graceful" failures that are called "forgiving." And this "forgiveness," they point out, "is often a compromise with peak efficiency."[56] Now, in this context, forgiveness has a price too. The reader need hardly be reminded of what severe competition Britain and the United States face from the Japanese automobile industry to understand that a producer who can (as the Japanese do) keep exceedingly small stocks on hand may be in a position to outperform and undersell adversaries. Of course, keeping small stocks would indeed be incompatible with a regime of strikes, which is why it might be rational for the Japanese to minimize and the British to maximize inventory. So long as the Japanese avoid labor troubles, and the British have no compensating advantages to offer, the British will lose out economically; this will cause their car industry to shrink, if not disappear, just as sure a failure as a single catastrophic event. There is a slow as well as a fast road to extinction, a genuine dilemma with no easy answer. What the Lovinses recommend—large inventories—to reduce one hazard, the damage of strikes, lowers the strength of the industry to resist another hazard—namely, Japanese competition.

Without experience in coping with adversity, organisms and organizations can hardly become resilient. Demanding a "forgiving technology" is equivalent to requiring that it be shown to be harmless before it is allowed to proceed. By definition a technology that is "forgiving" is one that might do some good but, in any event, could do no harm. "Trial without error" has surfaced in another form.

The Distributional Question

Resilience is no respecter of persons.[57] True enough. Just as we know from experience that market processes spur innovation, but cannot say exactly which innovation will be made at what time (for otherwise we could plan to make them), the precise form that a resilient response will take must remain unknown to us. Immediately there arises the danger that innocent people who did not approve this innovation will be harmed by it, even if it could be shown that the innovation did more good for more people over the long run; hurting minorities for the benefit of majorities requires a rationale.

Just as we all sometimes benefit from actions in which we took no part, so must we expect to suffer if, inadvertently—indeed ineluctably, and at random—misfortune afflicts us. What is the alternative? Individuals, following the doctrine of trial without error, can try to ban all acts that might harm someone. Yet the loss of opportunity benefits might well leave others worse off than they would have been had the offending actions been allowed to continue. We are left with the usual balancing act, hoping to do more good than damage and wondering which sorts of strategies will best serve society.

Always there remains the distributional question: how can we choose between those who will gain and those who will suffer? Inactivity is no answer; doing nothing will also result in winners and losers. Allowing, indeed encouraging, trial and error should lead to many more winners, because of (a) increased wealth, (b) increased knowledge, and (c) increased coping mechanisms, i.e., increased resilience in general.

Before going overboard on resilience, however, I would like to make a more persuasive case. This I shall try to do by bringing in wider realms of experience not usually considered in studies of risk and safety.

SECTION II:
CONDITIONS

All the strategies I analyzed in the first section—trial and error versus trial without error, opportunity risks versus opportunity benefits, and private markets versus governmental regulation, one set emphasizing risk aversion and the other risk taking—may be subsumed under the rubric of anticipation versus resilience. Trial without error depends on anticipation while trial and error makes for resilience. The decentralized competition underlying the doctrine of getting richer and thus safer represents a form of resilience based on adaptation; the centralized regulations underlying the rival doctrine, "poorer but safer," seek to anticipate so as to ward off harm. Henceforth, in this book, anticipation and resilience will stand for a variety of rival strategies, the former seeking safety by avoiding risks and the latter by taking them.

How may we appraise the desirability of differing proportions of resilience and anticipation? One or the other set of strategies may appear promising in a particular area, but the response could well be that application to different areas of life would lead to different conclusions. While no book can cover everything, I have chosen extremely broad realms of life for study. The criterion for selection is that each realm should illustrate a different set of conditions, i.e., a different combination of anticipation and resilience. The accompanying fourfold chart displays the requisite combinations of conditions—equal proportions, mostly anticipatory, mostly resilient, and/or a little of each: (1) Nonhuman life forms operate with considerable amounts of both resilience and anticipation; (2) The inspection of nuclear power plants is largely anticipatory; (3) The human body relies more on resilience; (4) The law of torts manages to end up able to use less of each strategy. (Tort law also provides a good illustration of how to make life worse while trying to make it better.) By analyzing a broad array of conditions involving different proportions of anticipation and resilience, I seek to illustrate the relative contribution each strategy makes to safety.

I say "illustrate" advisedly. The purpose of the chapters that follow is to develop the hypothesis at the core of this book—resilience is often (though not always) superior to anticipation—by seeing how it operates under different conditions and in diverse spheres of life.

107

A Schema for Appraising Strategies of Anticipation and Resilience

Anticipation

	Less	More
More (Resilience)	(3) The human body	(1) Nonhuman life forms
Less	(4) The law of torts	(2) Inspection of nuclear power plants

To those who say that the examples used in the rest of the book are selective and anecdotal, I have two responses. The first is that these examples are the stuff of daily dispute and thus constitute a substantial sample of the instances and arguments used to justify the opposing position. The second is that arguments for risk taking versus risk aversion, summarized as resilience versus anticipation, could hardly be expected to come from the areas of life the critics of trial and error take as their own, namely, nature—the human body and plants, animals and insects. All I have to do here, using standard sources, is illustrate a negative: "nature" uses lots of resilience. Then, at least, a risk-taking strategy has a defense against the unspoken charge of being "unnatural."

Another way of making a hypothesis persuasive is to show that it leads to surprising results. No one would think that strategies employing many safety measures could be counterproductive. Nor, in my experience, are people likely to connect acts to help people who are hurt collect damages with a decline in safety. By making a plausible case that safety measures might increase danger and that punishing producers may lead to more hazardous products, I hope to break the automatic connection between *trying* to do good and *actually* doing good, between labeling acts as increasing safety and actually achieving that end. Only then can I hope to secure serious consideration for a counterintuitive theory that safety cannot be enhanced without courting danger.

As for anecdotes, there are two kinds of evidence about risk and safety. One involves stories about current controversies. In this sense, everyone in the risk debate argues from and about anecdotes. There is also systematic data on health rates that can tell us either that things have been and are steadily improving or that they are not nearly as good as they might be were certain measures taken or avoided. What is missing are theories to connect outcomes to rival strategies. My aim, under the rubric of searching for safety, is to provide one such theory. Obtaining better evidence depends on formulating the rival positions in a more coherent manner so they can be tested for predictions of opposed outcomes. Before such tests can be fruitfully conducted, it is necessary to state the conditions under which larger or smaller proportions of anticipatory versus resilient measures are expected to improve the health and safety of various forms of life. By showing in four different realms of life that safety is not just there for the taking but has to be searched for in innumerable combinations, I hope to open up doubting minds to the possibility that such a case might be made.

5

Nonhuman Life Forms Cope with Danger

Nature knows best.

—Barry Commoner[1]

I thought you'd never ask.

—Anon.

"Given the general problem of acting appropriately in a world in which the array of alternative actions and their consequences is enormous, complex, variable, and always uncertain," as Clifton Lee Gass puts it in his "Biological Foundations of Surprise," "it is a wonder that living things persist on the earth.... The fact that animal and human decision makers at both the individual and organizational level do often function effectively presents a serious challenge to our understanding of how decisions are actually made."[2] Amen!

In order to test principles for securing safety, I shall widen the domains and make an extended analogy to living organisms other than human beings. It seems appropriate to allow those denizens of the natural environment we are being urged to save to give voice to their own defense. The living organisms that ecologists study should have a number of properties corresponding in certain respects to human life. Properties of ecological systems that are conducive to systemic stability, moreover, are by definition unintended by the animal, insect, and plant participants in these systems; hence, studying them may be particularly fruitful for identifying deeper principles that are conducive to human safety. The idea of system stability, as we shall see, appears to provide a reasonable proxy for what is meant by safety, and ecologists have—along with biologists, mathematicians, organization theorists, and a variety of people from other disciplines—converged on a number of principles for maintaining stability, principles supported by a fair amount of study of insect, animal, and plant populations. Fortunately, due to such work, and especially to a seminal paper on ecological stability by Kenneth E. F. Watt and Paul Craig, these principles may be described expeditiously. First I shall describe each principle; then I shall ask whether each principle is relevant to a strategy that human beings might use in seeking safety.

A caution introduced by Watt and Craig is even more important for human than ecologic systems because people can be purposeful:

> We are specifically concerned with stability of the entire system in contradistinction to stability of each component of the system. That is, we understand that in biological, economic, or any other kind of systems, the former can be maintained at the expense of the latter. Putting this differently, if the goal adopted is to preserve stability of particular system components, the ultimate consequence can be decreased stability in the entire system. Thus, there is a tradeoff between stability in the system, or its constituents.[3]

This is a restatement of the rule of risk, i.e., no system can be kept stable (or safe) unless its parts are allowed to vary in order to protect the whole.

How broadly or narrowly the boundaries of a system are defined—the individual, the village, the nation, the universe—may decide who is saved. Thus, facts about how to achieve safety may take on their meaning from values that signify whose safety is to be sought. Which objective is chosen for a system—the safety of the whole versus the safety of the parts—is more important than the principles for enhancing its safety. Safety "for what or who" is a critical question.

A basic difference between ecological (Darwinian) and cultural (Lamarckian) evolution is that in the former, selection takes place through the genes and in the latter, "it is precisely *acquired* characteristics that are transmitted."[4] Human beings can choose who to try to protect, though, of course, they may not be successful. Precisely because we are ordinarily reluctant to achieve safety for the group at the expense of any individuals, an important constraint is put on principles of stability. There are conditions under which this constraint is violated. In "lifeboat" situations, as in war, some people may be sacrificed to protect the rest of society. But these really are exceptional circumstances; most of the time, we try to avoid placing undue costs on individuals to achieve an increase in the safety of the whole society. Do nonhuman life forms "decide" between individuals and species? Whatever the answer, whether or not "intention" may be said to be present, choices are made. I agree with Watt and Craig that "insight into mechanisms of equilibrium in human systems can be gained through examination of stability in ecological systems."[5]

Principles of Stability

Stability signifies a return to its original state after a system or a species has been subject to perturbation. A life-support system is stable when, after being perturbed, it returns, not exactly to where it was before but to an area reasonably close to its original position. The stable pattern for such a system may in fact be a cycle of changes through which it goes repeatedly without changing its trajectory. This is a stable, orbital mode of behavior. There is reason to be concerned about how long it takes for a system to return to stability. If destruction threatens, a late response may be as bad as no response at all. Also, since it is not always easy or desirable to hit the target exactly, the observed pattern may be one in which response over-shoots the target, but with each movement comes a bit closer. If safety is defined as maintenance of life at or close to its existing state, stability may be considered a proxy for safety.[6]

Of the "thirteen powerful, underlying principles of stability" that Watt and Craig derive from the ecological literature, twelve are stated with suffi-cient precision to be described here.[7] According to (1) the *omnivory princi-ple,*

> the greater the number of kinds of resources utilized by a complex system, and the greater the number of pathways by which resources can flow to dominant system components, the less likely is the system to become unsta-ble because of a supply failure of any single resource. This is the 'spreading the risk', or insurance principle, which lives in the popular wisdom as 'don't put all your eggs in one basket'.[8]

The effort of cities and nations to diversify the employment base, for instance, is premised on increasing the ability to withstand decline in any single industry. Insects that can eat more than one kind of food are more secure than those depending on a single resource. Thus Watt and Craig found that, of five types of medium sized moths, the numbers grew more stable as their ability to gain nourishment from different kinds of trees increased. There may also be a compensation mechanism at work, in that the very conditions that produce a decline in one resource may create favorable conditions for another, all providing that the organism is om-nivorous enough to make use of this new opportunity.[9]

"The higher the rate of resource flux through the system," Watt and Craig assert, naming (2) the *high-flux principle,* "the more resources are available per unit time to help deal with the perturbation."[10] Once having been disturbed, a system will take a longer time to recover if the necessary resources take a long time to reach it. Whether the resources are used efficiently may matter less than whether the right ones reach the system in time to be responsive. O'Neill's study of a variety of ecosystems, for in-stance, showed that increasing the rate of resource input per unit of life form steadily increased stability.[11] "Our version of this principle is deliber-ately worded sufficiently broadly," Watt and Craig comment, "so that it includes the effect of slow information processing on a bureaucracy. Thus, if there is a lag from the time that costs of a new supply begin to rise rapidly to the time that these costs are reflected to the consumer this can introduce instability into planning for electrical generation capacity expansion."[12] A good example would be the initial effect of price control on dampening the response to huge increases in the price of oil. When the domestic price approached the international price, demand drastically decreased and exploration showed a corresponding rise.

(3) The *homeostasis principle* can be stated positively or negatively: the positive path is that stability is enhanced by negative feedback between components; the negative path is that stability is decreased by adding components without simultaneously providing for negative feedback mechanisms. Systemic variety enhances stability by increasing adaptability. For each level of variety added, however, another must be tied to a source of feedback so the system is not overwhelmed by its own complexity.[13] Although African buffalo in Tanzania ate a lot of certain plant species, for instance, other species grew quickly to replace them. Whereas grasslands with little diversity suffered a 69 percent reduction in biomass, grasslands with more diverse plant species had their biomass reduced by only 11 percent. The increased complexity of grassland plants led to greater stability because of the presence of vast negative feedback loops. The analogy to markets stands out: "Systems of great complexity," Watt and Craig declare, "with stability maintained by a lot of fast-acting negative feedback loops are complex economies, with prices responding freely to trends in supply and demand. In such circumstances, we repeatedly see very rapid introduction of new products, or replacement of old by new products."[14]

The (4) *flatness principle* states that "the wider the base of…organizational pyramids…relative to the number of hierarchical levels, the more stable they will be." Alternatively, the larger the number of administrators relative to that of producers, the less stable the system will be. Extreme inequalities are destabilizing. Put positively, a larger number of independent actors increases stability; many responses are better than one. Placed in political perspective, democratic regimes, with widespread legitimacy (Sweden or Israel) can withstand damage to their leaders (say, assassination) better than dictatorial ones (Franco's Spain or the Shah's Iran). Events that resulted in the death of thousands of top officials would not topple democratic regimes, whereas the death of only a handful of people might well cause collapse in a dictatorship.

"System stability," (5) the *system separability principle* asserts, "increases as the mean strength of interaction between components is decreased." Stability is enhanced by separating the elements of the system from one another. The reason is straightforward: if each element of a system is closely coupled to the others through positive feedback, a break-down in one quickly reverberates throughout the entire entity. This positive feedback amplifies oscillations until the system spirals out of control. Given tight coupling and positive feedback between system elements, the larger the number of elements, the more unstable the system will become. Lawlor's research on aphid-parasitoid systems shows that their stability is compatible with either an increase in the number of species or in the connections among them, but not with both.[15] Holding the interaction between species constant, as Rejmanek and Stary did in their work on plant defoliators, the larger the number of species (the greater the variety), the more stable the system.[16]

Obviously, the speed and the coupling of interactions within a system are crucial. If each element is connected to many others, perturbation would be spread out among the elements, allowing negative feedback, provided it arrived in time, to restore stability. Dense connections would be conducive to stability only if the system were assured of feedback that was negative and speedy. Otherwise, a system whose components were more efficiently separated would be more stable. Since reliance on the principle of "trial without error" requires slow-acting bureaucratic measures, while trial and error facilitates speedy response, the "dense connections" required in a chain of command make error much more likely to reverberate throughout a system and hence make it go out of control. Tight coupling makes it especially important for bureaucratic action to be based on correct information.

The abundance of examples makes (6) *redundancy* a rich principle. Familiar illustrations come from biological organisms in which the reproduction of cells is facilitated by duplication in the hundreds or thousands or even larger numbers. Watt and Craig remind us that redundancy may also imply a high rate of loss. "If a mated pair of parents have a hundred offspring, it means that on average, 98 of these are lost to climatic extremes, predation, parasitism, disease, or starvation."[17] Failure is the seamy side of success, without which there could be no survival.

"The theory of redundancy," Martin Landau writes in his seminal paper, "is a theory of system reliability."[18] He quotes from W. S. McCulloch's "The Reliability of Biological Systems" to stipulate, "That which is redundant is, to the extent that it is redundant, stable. It is therefore reliable."[19] So long as probability applies (in that a failure of one part is independent of failure in other parts), arithmetic increases in redundancy "yield geometric increases in reliability."[20] Overlap is essential in order to permit adaptability; if there were no overlap of parts, the organism could not change, i.e., alter its behavior under certain circumstances. The overlap would permit essential functions to continue, while the extra, unneeded element could vary and evolve a new function to allow for adaptation to change. Were there no redundancy of values or of facts, Landau observes, it would be impossible for parties to agree, because there would be no common ground, and there could be no detection of error for, without any overlap among parts, none could be used to check on the other.[21] For each source of variety, therefore, to follow Ashby's famous "Law of Requisite Variety,"[22] there must be an equivalent source of redundancy in order to secure reliability. Redundancy of a part may solve a problem of malfunction in a similar part. But an error in communication can be overcome only by having diverse sources that check on one another and, if they conflict, seek something like the preponderance of the majority. How much redundancy is optimal? No one knows. In self-organizing systems, negative feedback should regulate reproduction: too little redundacy and the species dies out, too much and there is over-population.

(7) The *buffering principle* fosters stability by maintaining a surplus. Buffering is equivalent to organizational slack, i.e., a capacity in excess of immediate needs. Whether we are talking about petroleum or wheat re-serves or excess capacity to store food or water in the body, the surplus serves to buffer the system against an unexpected increase in demand.[23] Like all other principles, of course, buffering can be taken to an excess, as by those who think they can, as the folk saying has it, take their wealth with them. An unused reserve may not help the system; or it may decrease efficiency, leading to defeat by competitors or insufficient resources in an emergency. Principles must be used in conjunction with one another.

(8) The *environmental modification principle* speaks for itself. "Termites control the humidity in their environment by making a large nest; humans insure that water will be available in dry seasons by building dams and irrigation systems."[24] In the theory of organizations, similar sets of prac-tices are called negotiating the environment (by collusion on prices or by dividing market shares) so as to reduce the extent of fluctuations to which the unit in question has to respond.[25] Much depends on where the bound-aries of the system are drawn. It may be easy to save an element by building a wall around it at the expense of weakening the system. Thus, monopolies may strengthen stockholders but not necessarily the economic system on which these monoplies ultimately depend.

In systems analysis it is said that a model is robust when, without modi-fication, it still fits the phenomenon at issue under diverse circumstances. Similarly, (9) the *robustness principle* stands for the ability of a system to passively withstand environmental change. "The robustness," Watt and Craig state, "may derive from a simple physical protection, such as armor on a tank, armadillo, or tortoise. Or it may involve a complex of mecha-nisms, as in the butterfly or moth that overwinters as a chrysalis or pupa. In these cases, the robustness to very severe weather includes an external skeleton, and internal stores of calories to fuel basal metabolism during cold weather."[26] An animal accustomed to coping with large and sudden changes in temperature is robust whereas one whose mortality rate is severely affected by a drop of, say, 10 degrees is not.[27] The costs of robustness, to reinforce the obvious, may also be high, as those stalled in tanks or overburdened by heavy armor can testify if only they survive.

Referring to the internal characteristics of living systems, the previously enunciated omnivory principle increases stability through the capacity to use a variety of resources. Its external counterpart, (10) the *patchiness principle*, maintains stability by making available many different types of resources. A catastrophe afflicting one piece or patch of the environment might not afflict another nearby. Each patch is weakly coupled to the others (recall the separability principle). Therefore, if one set of resources should decline, there will be others nearby to take their place. Examples would include firebreaks, whose bare places respond differently to outbreaks in wooded areas, refuges where predators cannot find their prey, or microclimates or habitats where some species are advantaged compared to others. A smooth and uniform environment, without patches or spatial heterogeneity, might encourage flourishing life systems for a time but, when conditions changed, there would be no available alternative arrangements for some of its inhabitants. To be a bit more precise: where feedback is positive, systemic stability increases as the overlap in species or elements of a system decreases.[28] It follows that rule-bound systems, stipulating in advance the allowable and the impermissible, are likely to be less stable than those that grow up topsy-turvy.

(11) The *over-specialization principle* states that too much of a good thing may render systems unstable in the face of environmental change.[29] As Stephen Jay Gould tells it:

> All evolutionary textbooks grant a paragraph or two to a phenomenon called "overspecialization," usually dismissing it as a peculiar and peripheral phenomenon. It records the irony that many creatures, by evolving highly complex and ecologically constraining features for the immediate Darwinian advantage, virtually guarantee the short duration of their species by restricting its capacity for subsequent adaptation. Will a peacock or an Irish elk survive when the environment alters radically? Yet fancy tails and big antlers do lead to more copulations in the short run of a lifetime. Overspecialization is, I believe, a central evolutionary phenomenon that has failed to gain the attention it deserves because we have lacked a vocabulary to express what is really happening: the negative interaction of species-level disadvantage and individual-level advantage.... The general phenomenon must also regulate much of human society, with many higher-level institutions compromised or destroyed by the legitimate demands of individuals.[30]

It is through this principle of overspecialization that conflict between the parts and the whole is played out. An element (a person or group) may be advantaged by special provisions (a long neck, a tariff) that give protection within a narrow niche. When the environment changes so that struggle with different organisms or organizations becomes dominant, a protected industry or an animal with a long and vulnerable neck may not be able to change sufficiently to survive.

Agricultural subsidies provide an excellent example. When conditions change, when the international price falls, for instance, farmers have great difficulty in adjusting. And once land values have been bid up by earlier price increases, later reductions in farm income because of lower prices make it very difficult to pay off loans.

(12) The *safe environment principle* is inextricably tied in with the environmental modification principle. That is to say, the goal of the latter is, in effect, to assure the former. The idea behind the safe environment principle is to create a permanently stable environment, such as those supposed to exist at the bottom of the ocean, so that a system is immune to change. Instead of the organism adapting to the environment, the environment itself is to be so stable that no change is required to live within its welcoming embrace. Whether the belief that an environment will last forever is helpful may be doubted. Whether one speaks of the Maginot Line or the Titanic or remote villages in New Guinea, most life systems eventually do appear to experience change.[31]

What, then, proceeding from this plethora of principles, increases the safety of systems? In order to think about how they interact, it would be useful if the principles could be reduced in number without losing too much information. I will, therefore, subsume these twelve into two major principles of systemic safety—anticipation and resilience.

Anticipation Versus Resilience in Nonhuman Life Forms

There are basically two ways to seek system or species stability: adapt the organism to the environment or adapt the environment to the organism. Not surprisingly, the panoply of principles of ecological stability fall into one or the other of these strategies. Most principles (nine out of twelve, to be exact) modify the organism rather than the environment.

Since our ultimate interest is in human organisms that are capable of conscious intent and that follow diverse organizational strategies, we want to know how their usual approaches to seeking safety compare to nonhuman ecological principles. In the previous chapter, I drew out the distinction between the strategy of anticipation—deterring danger before it becomes threatening—and resilience—learning from failure so as to better cope with or bounce back from adversity as and after it occurs. Here I wish to follow the same course but in respect to principles of stability derived from observations of nonhuman life forms.

Strategies of Risk Reduction and Principles of Ecological Stability

Strategy

Anticipation	*Resilience*
1. Safe Environment	1. Homeostasis
2. Advance Environmental Modification	2. High Flux
3. Patchiness	3. Omnivory
4. Overspecialization	4. Flatness
5. System Separability	5. Buffering
6. Robustness	6. Redundancy

Under modes of anticipation, I begin with the safe environment principle. By locating an environment that will keep it stable, the organism does not have to change at all. It works a little harder by modifying the environment in advance to suit its own character. By securing spatial heterogeneity, the patchiness principle provides firebreaks and refuges so that conflagrations in one place do not spread to others. Thus, the three principles discussed so far—environment, modification, and patchiness—work by preventing environmental change so that internal adaptation is unnecessary. Fluctuations in the environment are ruled out by searching for places (or patches) that are permanently stable.

The other anticipatory measures operate on the organism, either by so attuning it to the environment that no perturbations occur, or by rendering it less vulnerable to those that do take place. The principle of specialization fits an organism to a narrow niche where the only change is in the same direction. Far less speed or information for adaptation is required when the elements of a system are separated so as to isolate disturbances if and when they occur. A sufficiently robust organism can passively withstand a wide variety of external shocks. Thus, these three principles—specialization, separability, and robustness—anticipate change by absorbing environmental perturbations.

Whether these six principles seek stability by preventing or withstanding change, they are overwhelmingly dependent on correct information. They are as slow as can be. After all, they are designed to prevent, not to respond. Other than slow evolution in a predetermined direction, as in overspecialization, the other five principles call for no movement, either because the environment is judged to be (or has been modified to be) safe, or because the organism, without altering its characteristics, can withstand the expected range and force of fluctuation just the way it is. Nor are these organisms programmed to learn. Experience cannot modify their behavior. On the contrary, from the very beginning, they are set on automatic pilot. Should the predictions or guesses of the anticipatory mode turn out to be wrong, the organisms dependent on this mode will have no way of getting out of trouble. Hence they have to be right the first time.

The cheetah is splendidly organized to travel short distances at great speed and then disable its prey. But along with this specialized advantage, unfortunately, came a disastrous disadvantage. As O'Brien, Wildt, and Bush report, "the species has somehow lost its genetic variation." Consequently, any affliction attacking a single cheetah is likely to incapacitate most of the species. A virus called feline infectious peritonitus, for example, which kills only 10 percent of infected cats, killed more than half the cheetahs in one park. Genetic uniformity, the absence of variety, threatens the cheetah's ability to adapt and, hence, its survival.[32]

The mode of resilience is based on the assumption that unexpected trouble is ubiquitous and unpredictable; and thus accurate advance information on how to get out of it is in short supply. To learn from error (as opposed to avoiding error altogether) and to implement that learning through fast negative feedback, which dampens oscillations, are at the forefront of operating resiliently. Redundancy, omnivory, and high flux are analogous to knowledge, wealth, and other generalizable resources.

The homeostatic principle means pure movement—a reaction for every action, a source of information for every component. To compensate for failure in the supply of resources, the high flux principle speeds up their provision, while the omnivory principle enables an organism to use greater variety provided along a larger number of routes. The flatness principle guards against size overwhelming intelligence by providing for several decision makers rather than a single actor. It is not hierarchy itself but extreme forms—a monopoly of power—that are guarded against. The capacity in excess of immediate needs that is the essence of the buffering principle is not a specific provision, like the armor of robustness, but rather a generalized capacity to respond to the unknown, knowing that there are bound to be unpleasant surprises, as well as opportunities, ahead. Since error is inevitable, the principle of redundancy allows for high rates of failure. Reliability is increased because overlap facilitates error detection, duplication enhances error correction, and both depend upon a diversity of independent sources of evaluation and feedback.

Whereas to pursue anticipatory strategies calls for a high degree of articulated knowledge, a strategy of resilience can get by with much less. The combination of homeostasis, high flux, and omnivorousness provide rapid provision and utilization of resources along innumerable pathways. Error is overcome by a surplus of resources (through buffering and redundancy) applied at great speed (using high flux) by independent actors (viz., the flatness principle).

Why, Coley et. al. ask, do certain plant species in resource-rich environments such as agroecosystems, oil field habitats, and many tropical regions grow so rapidly? "These species," they report, "exhibit a characteristic set of traits that include a high capacity to absorb nutrients" as well as a "biochemical and morphological plasticity that allows them to take advantage of pulses in resource availability."[33] Resource richness, which might be termed wealth, together with rapid flux and a capacity for being omnivorous (which is equivalent to speed of communication), are as helpful to plant as to human species.

Looking at the pattern of principles associated with each strategy of decision, we see that anticipation is more directly connected to the search for stability than is resilience. Do you want stability? Seek out a safe haven or armor yourself to withstand adversity. It is all up front: Seek a safe environment, modify it to suit, separate yourself from danger, specialize in a narrow niche, or build a patch of your own, or become robust. In all of this, the anticipatory organism acts by aiming directly at its target—stability. Relying on resilience is an act of indirection; it works on the organism by increasing its capacity to respond to change. Resilience depends on numerous participants interacting at great speed, sending out and receiving different signals along a variety of channels. Resilience is short on specific promises; adversity may be overcome, but exactly how remains unspecified in advance.

Conditions of Applicability

How might a person interested in the safety of human organisms choose between anticipatory and resilient principles? Anticipation seems awfully static and resilience frighteningly dynamic. Principles supporting resilience are messy. They are always indefinite, always overcoming error, and always after the fact. Anticipation is more orderly; plans may be laid and followed to find or arrange a safe haven or to adapt one's species to an existing niche. Unfortunately, if the environment changes to a greater degree than expected, some creatures following anticipatory strategies will be overspecialized, some will lack generalizable resources, some will prove insufficiently robust, and the rest will be overwhelmed because, expecting a benign environment, they took no precautions.

So far I have been proceeding on the basis of applying strategies wholesale to nonhuman life forms. In human societies, characterized by conscious intent, however unpredictable the consequences may be, there is the ever-present possibility of each part being better protected than the whole. By building moats and castles, subsidies, entitlements, or other human inventions, each part (though not every part) can hope to end up intact even if the whole has suffered. For some parts, therefore, anticipation may be the better short-term strategy. But universal reliance on resilience means that though most (or more) organisms may survive, there is no advance knowledge about which ones those will be. Since there are short-term losers, "politicking" for individual protection may make sense to those who have resources better suited to politics than to other arenas of social life.

The choice of anticipation rather than resilience depends on knowledge and the overall level of change. If the social environment is exceedingly stable or at least securely predictable, if the end to be achieved is agreed, and if adequate knowledge is available, then principles of anticipation will be more efficient than principles of resilience.

But if the facts contradict these assumptions, and if disagreement becomes the norm, anticipation would be a self-defeating strategy. Ignorance about which parts of the environment would remain stable, inability to respond to breakdowns, and disagreement about which parts should be protected, would render anticipatory methods futile, expensive, and counterproductive as general resources declined.

The environmental conditions under which anticipation or resilience are more, or less, appropriate strategies may be summarized in a fourfold table based on two dimensions: knowledge of what to do about dangers and the predictability of change.

Appropriate Strategies for Different Conditions

Amount of Knowledge About What to Do

		Small	Large
Predictability of change	**High**	More resilience, less anticipation 4	Anticipation 1
	Low	3 Resilience	2 More resilience, less anticipation

Where knowledge of what to do is considerable and the direction of change is highly predictable (box 1), anticipatory strategies should rule the day. The world most likely will stand still long enough to be predicted and controlled. Where knowledge of effective measures is lacking and change is unpredictable (box 3), resilient strategies are strongly indicated. Since, under this assumption, change cannot be anticipated, it must be dealt with if, and when, it actually occurs. The availability of preventive measures, coupled with the unpredictability of change (box 2), suggests a mixed strategy. That is, a high degree of knowledge would facilitate anticipation but because we know so little about which dangers will actually materialize, even such available measures are likely to be misdirected. To cope with the unexpected, a few anticipatory measures (to ward off the worst that can reasonably be expected) must be considerably outnumbered by resilient efforts. When we know what is coming, but do not know what to do about it to make things better (box 4), we would prefer to be anticipatory; we must, however, rely on resilience because otherwise we are likely to do far more harm than good.

Where are we in the Western world? Because there is such strong evidence of high rates of technological and social change, I think we are mostly in the second, third, and fourth boxes. Though knowledge has been growing, it appears that change occurs at an even faster rate. Thus, the conditions favoring anticipatory strategies do not apply to us. That is why I think that resilience ought to be our dominant strategy.

Why can't the safety of the whole be advanced by the sum of efforts to make the parts safer? In the next chapter, let us look at a major effort to do just this—protect every part by safety measures—through the inspection and regulation of nuclear power plants.

6

Does Adding Safety Devices Increase Safety in Nuclear Power Plants?

Elizabeth Nichols and Aaron Wildavsky, with an appendix by Robert Budnitz

> *Ironically, the origins of the Chernobyl accident lay in a decision to test safety systems.*
> —Bennet Ramberg, *Foreign Affairs*[1]

> *It is a remarkable story, providing further evidence that if something is working, an effort to test it to make sure it is really working can do more harm than good.*
> —H.W. Lewis, *Environment*[2]

Against the rather rarified wisdom of the previous chapter—nonhuman life forms do rather well by relying on resilience as well as anticipation—may be posed the urgings of common sense: if you see an opportunity to increase safety, take it. Theorists may talk all they want about roundabout strategies of resilience, but a direct strategy of anticipation, the bird in hand, is preferable. A straightforward statement of this proposition would be that to add measures designed to secure safety actually does increase safety. But is that so? Well, under the whiplash of regulation, adding multiple safety measures has been the practice of the nuclear power industry; thus, a study of the inspection of nuclear power plants provides an opportunity to explore the direct, anticipatory hypothesis: take safety measures to increase safety.

We propose to examine two aspects of the relationship between individual elements and the systems of which they are the constituent parts: (1) safety of the parts versus the safety of the whole, and (2) detailed specification about how each part is to be built and used versus measures of performance for the plant as a whole or for major segments of it. The first query asks essentially whether adding devices designed to increase safety actually works. The second query concerns process: does one enhance safety by prescribing in advance everything that should be done or, rather, by setting standards and allowing operators and constructors of nuclear plants to meet them as seems best under specific circumstances?

Do More Safety Devices Add Up to More Safety?

The Nuclear Regulatory Commission (NRC) is responsible for licensing and inspecting civilian users of nuclear materials. Although this responsibility includes several dozen research and medical facilities, the main focus of the NRC's activities is the nuclear power industry. In recent years there has been significant resistance to the continued development of nuclear power. Much of this has focused on safety—on how and whether a reasonable level can be achieved. This public concern has had an important impact on the NRC. Federal regulations, regulatory guides, inspection manuals, and other written requirements show a degree of consistency in the manner in which safety efforts are implemented. However, while regulations themselves are absolute rules, many of the implementing activities are not. Regulatory guides only indicate acceptable potential solutions to various technical issues; and certain requirements may be deferred if others come to be regarded as more pressing. General policies still leave a wide area of discretion. This allows variation and the slow evolution of regulatory strategies.

Nuclear regulators, under public pressure to show that the plants they inspect are safe, must decide how to make visible their contribution. Safe operation can only be proved, if ever, in the far distant future. Under attack, regulators must show bona fides here and now. What they can do is show that they try. The external pressures to which regulators are subject, together with the NRC's internal division of labor, tend to make it most attractive to add more safety devices or more safety reviews and procedures. The complexity of the technology involved encourages the assignment of specific inspectors and technical specialists with limited responsibility for the safety review of each plant. Since personnel most often deal with only certain parts or aspects of the plant, their chief interest is in improving their specific area. Their focus is reinforced if they can show— by pointing to safety devices—that they have done their jobs.

Whether additional safety is achieved by this approach, however, is another matter. When the nuclear regulatory apparatus was first established, no means of calculating overall safety was available. Regulatory measures tended to focus on specifiable subunits (either of hardware or procedures or plant organization). Currently available analytic techniques, while they provide a great deal of information, still cannot give complete and certain answers concerning the safety contribution of each part and the safety level achieved by the whole. Therefore, many still favor specifying both the parts the licensee will install and the procedures the regulators will follow. Such specifications at least have the advantage of being politically defensible. Yet both experience and improvements in technique have brought to light many examples of safety devices actually proving unproductive or counterproductive.

That one safety system may interfere with another has been recognized by the NRC staff. Many such conflicts seem quite mundane, e.g., when the use of thermal insulation prevents proper inspection of piping details. Yet such minor interference may prove serious if it precludes the early discovery of cracks or corrosion.[3] Conflicts in safety measures are perhaps easiest to see where the systems involved are clearly technical, but they are also visible where procedural and organizational requirements have been made the explicit subject of investigation. Nuclear security systems require careful scrutiny of personnel allowed to enter. This screening process can pose a threat to reactor safety when it delays the entry of needed expert personnel during an accident such as the one at Three Mile Island.

The Three Mile Island accident provides several other examples of conflicting efforts, each justified in the name of safety, and each, taken alone, probably productive of safety. General rules proved to be an unsatisfactory way to handle emergency situations.[4] In the wake of TMI, for instance, efforts to deal with unexpected reactor responses were hampered by the issuance of bulletins ordering operators to follow a fixed procedure in turning reactor pumps on and off. Unfortunately, such specific instructions would, under some circumstances, make an accident worse.

The concern arising from the TMI accident produced numerous new requirements that used up large amounts of inspection time. The NRC Office of Inspection and Enforcement's study of lessons learned from TMI indicated that diversion of manpower from routine inspections of equipment and facilities might contribute to decreased safety.[5] The accident at Indian Point the year following TMI, for example, may have in part resulted from this diversion.[6]

An approach that emphasizes the importance of adding devices is not, of course, always unsafe. What is required is a careful examination of the circumstances under which various strategies work well. This must include consideration of the interaction of each device with other safety measures, both mechanical and organizational. Political and institutional pressures, however, may make such advice hard to follow. There is a strong bias toward believing safety measures must improve safety.

Abstractly, there are several logical possibilities. The relationship between adding safety devices and systemic safety may be conceived as being:

(1) Linear—the more devices one includes in special regimes to ensure their reliability, the greater the safety of the system; that is, the greater the number of safety devices, the greater the safety of the nuclear plant.
(2) Nonlinear.
    (a) Curvilinear.
        (i) Positive asymptotic curve; perfect safety is never reached because there are diminishing returns as one adds more devices, but still each increment adds something to the safety of the whole.
        (ii) Inverted u-shaped curve; beyond a certain point there are actual disadvantages to adding more devices or inspecting more parts.
    (b) Conditional or contingent.
        (i) The relationship is undefined; the effect of each new addition is indefinite and no priorities can be set.
        (ii) Positive step function; contributions and interactions can be accurately measured, and the relationship will be positive, though differential impacts will not allow the function to form a smooth curve.

The assumption that linearity works—more devices equals more safety—underlies much of the past and present practice of the Nuclear Regulatory Commission and its predecessors. This notion of linearity has been most often associated with a strategy of anticipation. In regard to nuclear power, it has been generally held that we cannot afford the risks involved in trial and error learning because the consequences of error would be too great.[7] Catastrophic error must be prevented. Since, following this logic, added requirements must necessarily increase the level of safety achieved, the best way to prevent accidents is to enforce uniform requirements and to specify them as clearly and minutely as possible. That is the theory of anticipation. What are the results in practice?

Examples abound of new dangers arising from attempts to increase safety. Corrective actions themselves can do damage. Nuclear welding codes, for example, require reworking welds in which even tiny voids occur; rework itself, however, can weaken the materials used (e.g., stainless steel pipe). Given differing skill levels among those who do the reworking, it is not always clear that correction of minor defects will increase safety. Similarly, pipe restraints are often installed to prevent damage to nearby equipment from the whipping motion generated when and if a pipe rupture occurs. These restraints, however, may produce a binding of the system that decreases safety by introducing additional strain.[8]

Testing also can be counterproductive. The availability of electrical power is essential to reactor safety. Control of the plant during normal operation, and the ability to keep the plant safely shut down during emergencies, depend on maintaining a reliable system of alternate electrical sources. Because offsite power is not sufficiently reliable, installment of diesel generators is required to provide a backup, onsite source. Because these generators themselves may fail to operate on demand, there are usually two or more at a given site. If the probability of offsite power failure is relatively high, the ability to prevent any series of events that would lead to reactor core damage depends on reliable onsite diesel power. Given their importance, it might seem reasonable to require that these diesel generators be tested regularly. Testing, however, may not always be advisable, since the test itself may make the generator less dependable.

When the Florida Power and Light Company decided to build a second unit at the St. Lucie Nuclear Power Station in southern Florida, a controversy arose concerning whether emergency onsite power could be guaranteed.[9] The difficulty at St. Lucie arose from the fact that although three different transmission lines connected the St. Lucie station with Florida Power and Light's main grid, all three lines terminated at the same substation. Major grid disturbances that would disrupt power from this substation would also be likely to disrupt power from other substations to which St. Lucie might be reasonably connected. The probability of offsite power failure, given the history of the system, was estimated to be about 0.4 per year. No matter what revisions of the current configurations were made, "it would still be likely that offsite power will be lost sometime in the nuclear plant's operating life."[10]

Diesel generator reliability was therefore a key factor in maintaining safety. St. Lucie Unit 2 had two generators designed and located to be physically and electrically independent; diesel oil delivered to the site was tested and stored in separate tanks for each system; the generators were housed in a building designed to withstand hurricanes and other adverse weather conditions; a sequencer was installed to prevent simultaneous rapid loading that might cause both generators to fail.

As a means of further increasing system reliability, the company suggested at one point that, during times when its power distribution grid was on "alert status," nuclear plant personnel should "idle start the diesel engines and run them for a short period of time" to verify their availability. The NRC staff agreed that this probably was the simplest way to determine availability, but pointed out that idle starting diesel generators and running them unloaded "could unnecessarily hamper their performance in a real emergency" and might lead to equipment failure.[11] On reconsideration, the NRC concluded that such testing should not be required. The negative side effects of testing would introduce more difficulties than advantages. But the NRC is rarely on this side of such issues.

Reactor operators and other utility personnel regularly must perform dozens of required surveillance tests to determine the condition and operability of their plant. Such tests often require disengaging certain electrical circuits and/or disabling one or more safety systems. Where safety systems have been installed in redundant "trains," reactors are often switched from one to the other during tests. Valves must be properly realigned and circuits properly reconnected, or safety is degraded. Tests may also require direct intervention in everyday operations. Testing is never a simple and unmitigated good because it necessarily increases exposure to risk.

Undoubtedly, the most extreme example of the point we are making here is the accident at the Chernobyl 4 nuclear plant in the Soviet Union. This accident killed a minimum of 31 people and quite possibly hundreds will eventually die from the direct effects of exposure to large amounts of radiation. Its indirect effects, which may be very large, are still unknown. It is the only true nuclear power disaster. Yet the Chernobyl accident was the result of on-line testing. The testing was part of an effort to increase reactor safety by providing yet another source of emergency power—turbine momentum combined with existing steam.

Like U.S. reactors, Chernobyl 4 was already equipped with diesel generators, but these might fail or take too long to start. Tests were proposed to try to squeeze out an additional hour of electricity using the steam already present in the system and the momentum of the turbine. Ordinarily the turbine is shut down when the reactor is shut down. Initiating the test and keeping it going required defeating several interlocking automatic shutdown and emergency cooling systems. As a result, operators had little means of controlling the reactor once the accident began. Trying to stop the accelerating reaction in the core resulted in a devastating explosion.

Safety devices can themselves be a source of danger. Reactor coolant pumps, for example, are clearly essential safety features in any reactor. These pumps, however, are very large and require correspondingly large lubricating systems. These systems typically hold 225 gallons of oil, and are themselves an important cause of fires within reactor containments.[12]

Increasing protection in one area may create difficulties in others. Protecting against low probability events may interfere with more likely threats to system stability; seismic design standards for nuclear plant piping, for example, have been continually raised. Even in the most seismically active areas, the probability of an earthquake severe enough to damage the plant during its lifetime is relatively low. The anticipated damage from such earthquakes is, however, quite high. Extra precautions have therefore seemed justified. The difficulty is finding the right place to stop. Recently, questions have arisen concerning the consequences of adopting extra precautions to guard against such a remote "worst case."

The general principles followed in seeking seismic safety have been (1) to increase the size of the possible earthquake against which plants in a given area are designed, and, as a consequence, (2) to increase the size and number of pipe supports required. These requirements would seem quite reasonable if seismic safety alone is to be considered.

There is no completely accurate method of calculating the types of varriable stress placed on piping systems; there is, in addition, always the possibility of discrepancies between designs used to analyze stresses on the system and the actual configuration of the completed system. This gap between the ideal and the real has encouraged the conservative tendency to overdesign piping supports. Newer techniques have indicated that the supports now used are often stronger than necessary; until very recently, however, little consideration has been given to the possible negative safety consequences of such conservative engineering. The value and wisdom of a safety measure depend on the ways in which it interacts with other aspects of the same system.

The Parts Versus the Whole

Any engineering manager knows how rarely all the relevant aspects of a project can be optimized at the same time. An NRC manager, talking to one of the authors, drew an analogy to an early airplane-design session as displayed in the Smithsonian: "All these guys are sitting around a table. One is saying 'I've got to have my thirty-six cylinder engine'. Another guy says, 'I've got to have my seventeen foot propeller'. The airframe guy says, 'I've got to use steel to carry all that weight'. Then the weight reduction guy says, 'Nuts to all of this. If you guys have to have all that we have to have a hundred and fifty foot wingspan!'" In an important way, each design element is competing with the others.

Certainly, perfection of the parts may not always result in a better whole. "You can, with exquisite detail, and wonderful ingenuity in designing each system," the manager continued, "construct an aircraft totally incapable of functioning. What you have to have is compromise, though I hate to use the word when we talk about safety. In an aircraft, you reduce the weight here, so we can cut down on the wingspan, and so on." To consider only the apparent desirability of each new part of the system in isolation from other additions or modifications cannot address the question of how all these additions affect the functioning of the whole.

The organization of inspection by the Nuclear Regulatory Commission may be considered either ordinary or extraordinary, depending on one's expectations about how complex and dangerous activities might be managed. The NRC could set performance standards for operating utilities and check along the way to see that these were being met. This we call organization by performance or results. Alternatively, or in parallel, the NRC might specify in detail how each step in construction, maintenance, and operation is to be conducted, checking each part of the process for conformity to these detailed prescriptions. This method we will term "detailed specification." If we assume that a strategy of detailed specification is always a good way of improving safety performance, there is no need to inquire further. But if there is reason to believe that the two strategies can lead to quite different results, as we assert, further analysis is in order.

Although both strategies are used, the method of detailed specification dominates. Reactor owners and operators must meet a lengthy list of technical specifications and procedures that are prescriptive in character. The detail is overwhelming. For analogies, one might think of carving up the whale in Melville's *Moby Dick* or the construction of the tabernacle in the Old Testament, the exact ingredients and their usage being precisely specified. The amount and character of flux in solders or the quality and form of steel or cement are so specific that not only the composition of a screw but also the exact direction and torque and number of times it is to be turned would be determined.

The technical specifications are negotiated with Washington during design, construction, and start up, and may be further modified during operation. They are inspected and enforced largely by regulators assigned to regional offices. These "tech specs," of course, directly reflect regulations formulated by the regulatory agency. Just how each regulation is to be met, however, is based in large degree on codes, consensus documents, established by professional groups and produced by association committees. They tell users what minimal actions must be taken (in the opinion of the committee) to assure safe operation. The codes are frequently revised (some as often as every six months) and the technical specifications for each plant identify which version of any given code is considered to be valid for that particular plant.

But how safe does that leave the nuclear plant overall? No one knows what level of global safety is thereby achieved other than that each part of the apparatus has been strengthened as far as possible. The complexity of nuclear power plants makes such effects difficult to analyze. In the meantime, regulators have generally adopted the position that such additions necessarily add to the overall safety of the plant. One may dispute exactly how much they add, but all the effects must be assumed to be positive.

A prescriptive approach gives the agency a way to demonstrate its sincerity in seeking the public good (though also lending itself to the use of less well-trained and less experienced personnel). Since the type of equipment, operational procedures, and manning levels are prescribed, as well as the exact nature of the regulator's routine, safety is thought to be assured. The regulatory system has made clear exactly what materials are to be used at a site and how they are to be put together. At the same time, it also lays out exactly how agency personnel are to go about measuring the licensee's compliance. The major drawback to all this is that the regulatory workload quickly outgrows the resources of the agency. Nuclear facilities are extremely complex; the number of workers at a construction site runs into the thousands; and an inventory of parts would include tens of thousands of valves alone. Examining in detail even a small portion of a given plant soon runs into more hours than can be covered by the agency budget.

This time constraint operates even where the agency has been careful to define its task in terms of an audit function. The NRC Office of Inspection and Enforcement stands atop a large pyramid of inspections and reviews. At the bottom, each element is subject to inspection through the quality control program maintained by the architect–engineering firm, subcontractor, or utility subdivision responsible for building or operating the plant. The adequacy of such programs is monitored by the quality assurance component of the licensee's organization, which in turn is assessed through NRC inspection. Just as the licensee's quality assurance unit samples the quality control work of others, so the NRC samples (or, to use its term, audits) the work of quality assurance. Only if errors begin to slip through the quality control system does the NRC undertake full-scale inspection.

Despite this screening system, regulatory personnel are often swamped with prescriptive tasks. A section chief remarked that previously he had been assigned to inspect two large construction sites several hundred miles apart. He was to go out to each site once a month for a week. "There were 7500 workers on those two sites. The head of Inspection and Enforcement said some place that we inspect one percent of all construction. No way could I have looked at one percent of everything done! People can write requirements forever. But it's a case of the alligator mouth and the hummingbird stomach. Even in an operating reactor you have 250 people; you can't do a comprehensive check of everything they do."[13] Adding more inspection personnel might boost the number of parts inspected into the 1 percent range, but the discrepancy between tasks prescribed and tasks performed would still be very large.

The conscientious effort of regulators to follow a prescriptive safety regime conflicts with their need to be responsive to current safety concerns. Looking after the parts becomes increasingly burdensome because there are more and more parts to oversee, and inevitably becomes inadequate since it does not take into account their interaction relative to the regulated whole. Indeed, actual operating incidents—from which lessons about safety might be drawn—often do not fit into the neat categories that inspectors use in their day-to-day work. Yet the way in which nuclear regulation is now organized makes it hard to break away from a strategy of detailed prescription.

The Nuclear Island

Why has nuclear regulation taken on these characteristics? How did this enormous growth in detailed prescriptive regulation take place? What was its chief dynamic? Over the past thirty years there have been some important shifts in the way the "whole" to be regulated has been defined. These shifts have taken place along two dimensions. The scope of what is to be included has steadily increased. The relevant whole was once conceived as a "nuclear island" located in the middle of an otherwise rather unremarkable power plant. But today the relevant whole has grown to include not only a major portion of the nonnuclear hardware surrounding the nuclear island, but many of the human and organizational aspects as well.

At the start it was assumed that the nuclear aspects of the plant could be separated from the rest. The nuclear steam supply system was distinguished from the turbine generators and other systems that directly produced electric power. "The utility people had an image that their previous experience with coal and oil would be sufficient for dealing with nuclear power. They thought they were adding just one element of new technology." Nuclear regulators were to be responsible only for the nuclear parts of the plant. That was, as one interviewee put it, "the bill of goods that was sold to the utility industry. The Atomic Energy Commission, the predecessor of the NRC said, 'You really ought to get into this business!' When industry expressed concern about regulation, they said, 'No, no, we'll regulate only the special nuclear stuff. There's this nuclear unit, and all that's needed is you to hook it into your plant and you're all set to make power.'" But things turned out to be not quite so simple. The exact limits of the "nuclear system" were indeed often hard to define.

This concern of each individual and group with the parts meant that the whole necessarily grew increasingly complex. New protection devices continually were added and upgraded. The number of subsystems and components mushroomed. And, in turn, the increasing complexity of the nuclear plant itself further encouraged the tendency to look only at the parts. The division of labor became finer and finer as the number of things that had to be reviewed or inspected increased.

"Reviews," a safety official told us, "used to be largely a matter of getting the right people into the room at the same time. But that time is past. It is no longer possible for you as an engineering manager to look around the room and count on your fingers the people you need, core physics, structural people, and so forth." The size of the plant and the complexity of both the plant and the requirements have made such informal procedures difficult. Detailed reviews are now carried out through correspondence and fieldwork by many different groups.

As the division between the nuclear and nonnuclear aspects of the plant turned out to be hard to maintain, the notion of the nuclear island was modified. A new distinction arose between systems that were "safety-related" and those that were not, which did help to reinforce the line between what was to be regulated and what was the sole concern of the licensee. But this distinction, too, met with significant difficulties.

Well before the accident at Three Mile Island, there was disagreement over which systems could be defined as "safety-related" and what components were included in each system. After the accident, the Kemeny Commission's report tended to discredit the whole notion that adequate safety could be assured by oversight of only certain parts or systems. The accident did not result from the kind of large pipe break or other catastrophic failure that had been anticipated and guarded against by the NRC policy of strengthening the parts. Instead, it was due to a number of lesser failure conditions combined with the operators' misunderstanding of the situation confronting them, an error easier to make as the plant grew more complex. Following the accident, an NRC official said, "[t]he concept of a 'nuclear island' and a limited regulatory purview was dead. You have to look at the whole plant. There was still some debate about it until TMI, but there was no debate afterwards." But while there was no debate about the importance of systemic failure, there was still disagreement over the implications of this for nuclear regulation.

Today, as an NRC manager explained, "we regulate to the extent a system or function has an important part in operation or shut down albeit totally nonnuclear."[14] The definition of the relevant "whole" has expanded from the nuclear steam-supply system itself to include all systems needed for safe shutdown. But what these systems and functions are and how they interact with one another remain problematic. Should regulatory purview, for example, include oversight of management and personnel systems as well as hardware? Should only offsite releases be monitored, or also the safety of the physical plant itself? And how, exactly, can we estimate the importance of each part for the whole?

System Interaction

Before TMI there had been a general belief that if each subsystem was built to withstand a major accident, then one need not worry about lesser accidents. The safety of the whole could be assured simply by strengthening the parts. It was assumed, for example, that any system that could safely overcome a large (l)oss (o)f (c)oolant (a)ccident, or "LOCA," could also withstand any sort of small LOCA. Plants were to be built to withstand a "design basis" accident. Though nuclear regulators and their critics disagreed chiefly over just how large the design basis accident should be, there was no real disagreement in principle.

The "maximum credible" accident against which the plant was to be secured was the main focus of attention. Estimates of what was credible were continually revised upward, and safety devices and requirements were piled one on top of the other to cope with the revisions. Some of the revised estimates resulted from actual operating experience, but not others, especially those dealing with potential seismic events. Instead, estimates were based on reinterpretation of already available data or on new research. The experts disagreed among themselves. But public concern with the possibility that an earthquake could produce a major nuclear accident was increasingly taken into account in regulatory rulings.

Certain sites (e.g., Bodega Head on the northern California coast) were declared clearly unsuitable. For others, where it was still believed possible to engineer one's way around such difficulties, utilities were told to double or triple their efforts. Pipe supports to protect piping systems from earthquake damage increased in number and size. Mechanical snubbers to damp pipe vibration were added in ever larger numbers. Designs changed significantly. "Four snubbers have become 4000 or 5000 snubbers"; as one inspector pointed out "even to list them all is perhaps one-third of the technical specifications for some plants."[15] This reinforcement of the piping system against earthquakes has important negative consequences for the viability of the system as a whole.

Negative consequences arising from interaction between safety systems and the rest of the plant have received little attention until recently. Much more familiar are negative consequences of interaction between failed safety systems and other parts of the plant. NRC design review groups are very much aware of this type of system interaction: "Water is, of course, required for fire fighting systems," an official observed. "This water is distributed by pipes running in places where there is electrical equipment important to safety. We would be very concerned if there was a possibility that a given failure might be worsened through the design of the fire fighting system. This is why we require that it be seismically designed and properly supported. The Code of Federal Regulations (10 CFR 50) tells the licensees that they must take action 'to assure against failure due to inadvertent operation' of the fire protection system."[16] That is, the licensee must make sure an earthquake does not rupture the fire safety system and thereby create further danger by damaging other safety devices. But this attention to safety devices fails to address the question of whether even properly operating supports and snubbers may themselves contribute to negative results.

Snubbers are attached to piping and anchored to the reactor building. They are intended to absorb ground motion and therefore make it less likely that piping will be disturbed. Great reliance on snubbers can, however, create difficulties, especially where pipe whip restraints and other safety measures have already made the system less flexible, since: (1) Snubbers are hydraulic or mechanical devices with failure rates of their own; they further complicate the system and decrease reliability. (2) Rigid systems require more careful alignment so that reinstallment of snubbers, which must be removed for inspection, increases the likelihood of poor alignment. In sum, the strategy that tells us to add more supports and safety devices leaves us with several other safety related problems.

Many older nuclear power plants have been subject to retrofitting requirements to bring them up to newly imposed seismic standards. Since these plants have relatively small containment structures, the ability to maintain and inspect piping and equipment is compromised. Workers who must perform these services are more likely to be exposed to higher radiation doses, since they must spend more time to do the same job. Even in newer construction, to alter requirements may present serious difficulties when major structural features are already in place. Spencer Bush, a senior staff consultant with Battelle Northwest Laboratories, cites testimony from the maintenance manager at the McGuire nuclear station in North Carolina, which indicated that "they would have to cut through two walls to obtain access to components in the piping system." The order in which requirements are added, then, must also be considered when we ask what is the relationship of the parts to the safety of the whole.

The degree to which it turns out that increasing safety in one area may lead to decreased safety in another area will be a major determinant of what level of safety finally has been achieved. Bush, for example, has pointed out that thermal stress on piping from rapid heating and cooling is far more common than is dynamic stress from earthquakes. "My concern for several years," he writes, "is that the unforgiving nature of stiff systems may lead to the failure we are trying to prevent with the heatup and cooldown probability much higher than the seismic."[17]

In other areas as well, it is clear that there are conflicts between how to increase safety in one area while maintaining or increasing safety in others. The still-controversial issue of how to control hydrogen produced within containment during an accident sequence is an excellent example. Following the accident at Three Mile Island, the NRC ruled that new plants such as the Tennessee Valley Authority's Sequoyah 1 would have to be able to withstand a hydrogen burn at least as large as that at TMI. After careful calculation, TVA reported that the containment for their new plant would withstand three times the previously required pressure, but would survive a TMI-sized burn with very little margin. Several alternative control methods were available. One could install glow plug igniters to deliberately burn off any hydrogen as it was generated. (This was the method chosen by TVA.) Or one could use carbon dioxide or other burn suppressants, or replace the air in the containment with inert nitrogen gas. All these methods, however, have undesirable side effects.

The "inerting" of containment has a particularly instructive history. Under Criterion 50 of 10 CFR 50 Appendix A governing containment design, the pressure and temperature conditions resulting from any loss-of-coolant accident must be sustained without exceeding the design leakage rate. The criterion recognizes explicitly that experience and experimental data (and therefore knowledge) are limited. In calculating the ability of the containment structure to withstand possible operating pressure and temperature conditions, a margin must be included to protect against conditions not explictly treated in the initial analysis. High pressures resulting from metal-water interactions and other chemical reactions following degradation of the core cooling function are to be taken into account. The design requirements for emergency core cooling systems (ECCS) assume that it will function well enough to prevent more than 1 percent of the metal in the core from reacting with water present in the containment. Only if the function were impaired to an extent that allowed more than 1 percent of the metal to react with water would there be enough hydrogen generated to cause concern. Filling the containment with an inert gas would be one solution. But hold on.

In regard to the Vermont Yankee Nuclear Power Station, the Nuclear Regulatory Commission staff's evaluation of the proposed containment structure assumed there had been a 5 percent metal-water reaction and that a correspondingly large amount of hydrogen had been produced. Since the evaluation based on these assumptions indicated some difficulty in sustaining a satisfactory margin of safety, the NRC staff insisted that the utility "inert" the atmosphere of their containment building whenever they were operating at 80 percent power or above.

Vermont Yankee Nuclear Power Corporation, the utility involved, objected on the grounds that filling the containment with an inert gas (e.g., nitrogen) would have a number of disadvantages in terms of safety. Entry into an inert containment would have to be made with self-contained breathing apparatus. Working in close quarters with high temperatures and humidity, surrounded by projecting equipment that could easily snag air lines, and burdened with the weight and bulk of the breathing apparatus itself, plant personnel would face a significant risk. Entering a "de-inerted" containment for routine inspections during scheduled outages would also be more hazardous, due to possible gas pockets remaining. The dangers involved in entry into inert containments would greatly reduce inspection capability and therefore increase the risk of a serious accident. In testimony before the Atomic Safety and Licensing Appeals Board, the utility's witnesses identified two instances in which safety problems within containment were discovered and corrected during inspections that would no longer be possible with an inert atmosphere. In one of these instances, had the defect gone undetected and unrepaired, there might have been a very serious (Class 8) loss-of-coolant accident as a result. Ironically, it is this very type of accident that inerting is intended to ameliorate.[18] The Atomic Safety and Licensing Appeals Board eventually ruled in favor of the utility and against inerting the Vermont Yankee containment, but the question of how best to control hydrogen generation remains.

Adding new safety devices and procedures is no guarantee of increased safety. Operational safety is not merely additive or linear, but highly conditional and contingent. Unforeseen interactions may foil the purpose of the new addition. New dangers can arise from the added safety effort itself. Even when interactions are already known or can be anticipated, it may be difficult to identify an optimal choice. Recognition that added safety precautions may produce diminishing returns, or that time and resource constraints can make additional requirements counterproductive, are partial correctives to the linear view underlying much current regulatory practice. But to clearly define the relationship between additional requirements and achieving safety, one must be able to attain an adequate overview. This means being able to understand the significance of each part for the whole, the ways in which various safety measures may reinforce or counteract each other, and the time dependencies of these interactions. Without this understanding, the real consequences of regulatory actions cannot be known.

In the meantime, regulators must continue to regulate one part at a time. The task is an onerous one if only because the specificity of the prescriptions complicates effective regulation. As an NRC engineer explained, once the difficulties he has observed in the field are translated into regulatory language, the official complaint against the licensee is reduced to a series of minor deviations. The real issue, the result of the combination of these deviations, is not addressed. Because translation of the technical problem into narrow legal categories often trivializes it, "The licensee winds up thinking we're just picking on him."[19] More concern with the consequences of system interaction would help redirect attention away from detailed specifications and toward how the plant is actually operating.

How could we achieve a more resilient nuclear power industry? In line with our analysis of counterproductive safety measures, we would like to have far less detailed specification and a far higher proportion of performance standards. Not being nuclear engineers, though we relied on interviews with them, we asked physicist Robert Budnitz, formerly head of research at the NRC, to devise an approach to performance standards emphasizing its limitations (where it should not be employed) as well as its strengths.

Toward Performance Standards

Robert Budnitz

The effectiveness of nuclear reactor safety regulation would be substantially enhanced by a shift away from prescriptive regulations and standards governing specific activities affecting safety, and toward more general regulations prescribing levels of performance that safety systems and operations must attain. There are two overlapping objectives: first, to move toward regulation by performance standards; second, to move toward operational approaches that can take maximum credit for learning from experience. These objectives are mostly congruent but not entirely so, because some regulatory initiatives can satisfy one of the two with little if any impact on the other.

If it were possible, the best approach would be to ask the operating utilities to design, build, and operate reactors so as to preclude large accidents. Such a performance objective at the highest level of aggregation would be the ideal approach in principle, since all the regulatory authority need do is to establish the level of safety *sought*. The Nuclear Regulatory Commission has been wrestling with just this issue and has proposed some tentative "safety goals" that, if ultimately adopted, would set an overall performance objective for the safety levels that reactors would need to achieve. Framed in terms of the (calculated) likelihood either of large untoward consequences to the public or of highly damaging core-melt accidents, these goals would set an overall safety standard for the reactors. Unfortunately, there is a broad consensus in the technical community that there is not now an adequate technical means to calculate accurately enough whether the safety goals, in the form in which they have been proposed by the commissioners, would be met.

It is apparent that any system of performance regulations, therefore, must settle for some lower level of aggregation. One might, for example, regulate the performance of specific reactor systems or of specific reactor functions. One might alternatively have performance measured through tests on actual operation. Another approach would be to require an analysis showing that the reactor could successfully cope with a specified accident, with only the end-point outcome state specified by NRC. The difference between this approach and the present method of regulation is that the level of specificity of requirements could be greatly reduced. The operating utility would be free to find the best way to meet the performance standards. This would allow utilities room to innovate; it would also limit the number of mandated changes.

In practice, the regulatory approach suggested should leave as much freedom to the reactor designer and operator as possible, consistent with meeting the regulatory objective. A good example of this would be the method for regulating against what are known as "design-basis accident initiators" such as a large pipe break, an external flood, or an earthquake. For such accidents, the performance standards would specify the design-basis initiator in some detail (say, the size and timing characteristics of the external flood or earthquake). Also specified would be the desired end state for the reactor system, which would usually be some safe shutdown situation like hot-standby shutdown or cold shutdown. The standard would in principle then leave it entirely up to the applicant/licensee to demonstrate, by whatever means he chooses, that his plant's systems and operating procedures could cope with the selected design-basis initiator.

This suggested approach, unfortunately, is not satisfactory for some of the important initiators—the analytical techniques now available are in many cases not advanced enough to reliably demonstrate safe plant performance. In these situations the applicant/licensee would be forced to introduce conservative assumptions into his analysis, to simplify the analytical problem and to bound certain technical difficulties on the "safe side." However, the applicant/licensee could choose his conservatisms as he saw fit, rather than have them imposed by regulatory fiat. True, the burden of proof would shift to the applicant/licensee to demonstrate the validity of his approach and assumptions, but this seems a small price to pay for the benefits of operational flexibility. Compliance with the performance specifications would remain as an engineering judgment made by NRC staff— just as at present, of course, but with judgments made about a different set of technical issues. In the end, there cannot be any avoidance of engineering judgment by the regulatory staff.

It is a little too extreme to expect that no specific pieces of equipment need be shown to be "earthquake-proof" or "flood-proof." For reasons based on sound engineering practice, and also because we are probably ignorant of at least some important engineering issues, it would remain highly desirable for regulators to continue with prescriptive standards requiring certain critical items to meet certain design standards. However, the demonstration that the plant as a whole could safely survive the postulated accident initiator would shift significantly away from the stylized calculational methods now used to more realistic, performance-oriented analysis. One steep cost of such a shift would be to complicate the problem of regulatory review, since regulators would need to delve quite deeply into the specific analyses presented by the applicants/licensees to fully understand them (and, in principle, the analyses presented by the many applicants could all be different). The benefits would be a more realistically based design process, a review process closer to actual plant performance than to some stylized conservative calculation, and ultimately a collection of more innovative design and operational approaches to the safety problems that, after all, everyone wants to overcome.

Another regulatory arena where performance specifications might profitably be introduced is the area of test and maintenance procedures and intervals. At present, detailed regulations and requirements specify these maintenance activities for many (perhaps most) safety-related items—the diesels to be tested at specified intervals, the circuit-breakers to be maintained on certain schedules, and so on. A performance approach might establish certain desired performance requirements for these items, while leaving it up to the utility operator to devise appropriate maintenance schedules, tests, checks, and documentation. The utility operator would have to demonstrate, through whatever combination of tests and calculations he chose, that his equipment met performance specifications. Here again, flexibility as a benefit is traded off against specificity (also a benefit); while either approach can attain the safety objective, the one places the initiative and the burden of proof with the operator, while the other deprives him of initiative, makes compliance "easier" if not more effective, and is less well linked to the actual, desired end point of safety. Again, the regulatory review is more difficult in the performance-specification case, but in many situations the safety benefit would be worth the extra effort.

No regulatory standard can be effective unless a satisfactory scheme can be developed to monitor it. Indeed, one of the main virtues of the present system of prescriptive standards is that it is easy to determine compliance or noncompliance. For performance standards, this is much more difficult, in part because the data base of actual experience is inevitably inadequate; for the issues of interest, we know a priori that failures will be rarely observed. Here the approach must be to rely on a well-conceived system that combines some analysis with a thorough effort to gather the relevant experiential data. The analysis must be designed to pose and answer the important question—"What if?"—in a way that satisfactorily assures the adequacy of system performance. Today's regulatory approach, for example, includes specific dicta about avoiding electrical interference between various redundant (or even diverse) sensors performing similar functions. The dicta involve specific prohibitions in electrical wiring and the like. Nevertheless, there is an occasional discovery, through experience, of situations that violate long-established dicta. If the dicta were to be supplemented by performance standards (ultimately one might imagine the dicta being *supplanted* by them), the necessary approach would have to be a thorough analysis of all such past events, and all events occurring in the future, to ascertain the extent to which violations could compromise performance. This analysis would require the standard setter to think through and write down what performance he was intending to attain at a level of specificity that is seldom accomplished today, since the standard setter now is not usually called on to evaluate either the consequences for system performance or his decision. Analysis of experience would be keyed to that level or quality of performance sought by the standard setter. Ultimately, it would be desirable for designers to work toward the performance criteria rather than within the dicta.

For purposes of regulatory compliance in this highly stylized example, the monitoring process would take the form of a continuing evaluation by both the operating utility and the regulator of relevant events as they occur; for each such event, an analysis would reveal whether the event itself or implications derived analytically from it were serious enough to compromise the performance standard. If not, fine; if so, corrective action would be called for. Again, in the spirit of our proposed philosophy, it would fall first to the operating utility to propose and defend a modification to achieve the desired performance. The regulator would review and affirm the proposal, or modify it interactively. The motto of performance standards is: Tell the operator *to* fix it, *not how* to fix it.

A shift to performance standards might profitably occur in a large number of areas. It does *not*, however, encompass *all* areas of safety regulation: there are some areas where a continuing need for detailed regulation exists. These are safety areas where either no valid test (either operational or calculational) can be devised even in principle, or where none has yet been developed in practice. Assuring that the primary pressure vessel integrity remains adequate against the likelihood of a large mid-line rupture is an example. Here, the full-scale experiential base is almost nonexistent, and calculational methods are inadequate. Furthermore, despite much analytical and experimental progress, there seems little hope that a performance specification could be developed soon in this area. Hence the anticipatory approach, relying on conservative engineering practice, seems likely to remain as the best regulatory strategy.

On the other hand, there are important areas where movement toward using performance standards would now be feasible. An excellent example is the regulation of ECCS (emergency core cooling system) performance. ECCS requirements were first established in NRC regulations in 1973 through adoption of Appendix K to 10 CFR 50. At the time, there was insufficient understanding of the basic physical and engineering phenomena involved in ECCS performance during a large-break, loss-of-coolant accident. No one could reliably calculate ECCS performance, and experiments had not been performed (indeed, had not yet been planned). When the regulatory authority perceived the urgent need to establish a position on ECCS, there was no other choice but to regulate through prescriptive measures concerning what an applicant needed to do to demonstrate compliance. A decade later, however, this particular situation has shifted significantly: advanced calculational methods, and extensive experiments along with information from operating experience, have given engineers an ability to understand the important phenomena adequately. Today, if Appendix K were to be rewritten, one could easily imagine a regulatory approach that went quite far toward embodying performance specifications to replace the prescriptive approach still in force. The performance standards would need to contain significantly more detail than merely the demand for the licensee to "demonstrate that ECCS works to keep the core cool." Yet it could afford the licensee much more flexibility in meeting the requirement and in demonstrating conformance through a mix of calculation and supporting experimental data.

Still another example is NRC's set of regulations in the area of containment system behavior during an accident. NRC now is working actively to modify the regulatory approach as part of the larger question of the size of the "severe accident source term." Within the next few years, it is anticipated that a large body of regulation will be brought into being to provide stronger assurance to NRC that accidents progressing through core melting will have a diminished likelihood of producing large offsite releases. In this regard, recent important insights gained from probabilistic studies have told the safety community that large offsite releases can be mitigated (and perhaps avoided) in many core-melt scenarios by effective performance of containment and its active systems, such as sprays, suppression devices, and the like. The regulatory issue will be how to devise regulations and standards to optimize the risk-mitigative properties of containment systems. Here there is almost a "golden opportunity" to think through a regulatory approach that seeks performance rather than prescriptive analysis of prescriptive properties of these systems. Subtopics where this approach might be very useful include hydrogen control, steam-spike control, plateout or adsorption, and operability of engineered systems such as fans and sprays.

Given the opportunity to institute performance standards, it is important not to overlook the possible trap lurking in this approach. The trap lies in considering a system or an operation out of the context of the accident sequence(s) in which it is involved (i.e., falling back and once more looking at only the parts, not the whole). It is absolutely vital to consider carefully those important accident sequences in which the regulated item or activity is involved. Failing to concentrate on plant operation as a whole might produce many different kinds of suboptimizations (or even counter-to-safety designs or procedures). In this regard, the discipline of probabilistic risk assessment (PRA) can play an important role, since it can illuminate not only which sequences are involved with a particular system, but also the relative priority or importance of the several sequences.

It is probably too much to expect a fundamental reevaluation of the full range of safety regulations. The likely place to begin is with regulations in those areas that are already of active interest today, such as the "source-term-containment" area (or where and in what amount radioactive material would go after a major accident) or the human-factors area. Even though these areas represent only a part of the whole fabric of safety regulation, adoption of the performance-specification approach for them could shift the emphasis away from regulation by prescription and set the stage for a gradual reexamination of many other regulations and standards.

Pressure to Be Perfect

Because in today's regulatory climate the whole is not allowed to be perturbed, pressure to be perfect is put on the multitudinous parts of nuclear plants. Showing tangible evidence of stronger parts becomes a substitute for actually improving safety. Therefore, the flexibility needed to relate one part to other parts is subordinated to the rigidity of the whole. And while it may be less likely that any damage will occur, because rigidity brings a certain amount of resistance, the likelihood that grave danger will occur goes way up as the system is in greater danger of snapping.

The rule of risk is violated twice over: neither whole nor part is allowed to vary. Parts become heavy and immobile; they don't bend; they are difficult to get through or around or to move out of the way. Worse still, each part is directed against an external challenge, without being connected to the other parts that interact with it. At one and the same time, the whole becomes rigid—so that defects in parts rapidly reverberate—and unpredictable—the movements cannot be specified in advance because the parts have not been put together in consideration of one another. Accordingly, there is less safety for the whole than we are capable of creating.

In the nuclear power industry, anticipation does not seem to work well as a dominant strategy. Let us shift to the subject of maintaining the human body and ask whether resilence as a dominant strategy does better.

7

The Battle Within:
How the Human Body Defends Itself

Dennis J. Coyle and Aaron Wildavsky

*All substances are poisons; there is none which is not
a poison. The right dose differentiates a poison and
a remedy.*

—Paracelsus[1]

*The resiliency of the cell is remarkable. No single
process is so precious that the cell will not survive a
temporary dislocation of it. While we should not
presume to impose intentionally or chronically on
the cell's reserves, we find it reassuring to discover
they exist.*

—Brabec and Bernstein[2]

*The immune system is clearly essential to survival;
without it death from infection is all but inevitable.
Even apart from its vital function the immune system is a fascinating example of biological ingenuity.
The cells and molecules of this defensive network
maintain constant surveillance for infecting organisms. They recognize an almost limitless variety of
foreign cells and substances, distinguishing them
from those native to the body itself. When a pathogen enters the body, they detect it and mobilize to
eliminate it. They "remember" each infection, so
that a second exposure to the same organism is dealt
with more efficiently. Furthermore, they do all this
on a quite small defense budget, demanding only a
moderate share of the genome and of the body's resources.*

—Susumu Tonegawa[3]

149

The human body is under constant attack. Partial failure of the body is not rare, as we know from the incidence of disease and accidents; ultimately, of course, failure is fatal—and inevitable. Given the precarious and fleeting nature of life, it may seem remarkable that *Homo sapiens* has been rather successful, at least to the extent that the species has managed to persist, expand in numbers, and exercise considerable control over its environment.

How is this possible? How does the body defend itself against varied but ever present danger? We will review the nature of risks the body must confront and the defenses it employs and analyze the basic principles that characterize human defense systems.

The body does indeed have recognized defenses. Yet the parts are not protected to the detriment of the whole. Safety mechanisms are treated on a priority basis, not piled on top of one another as if more necessarily were better. Richer (if by richer is meant a higher level of resources, permitting greater diversity, redundancy, speed, and energy) is safer. The axiom of connectedness, by which safety mechanisms such as the immune system can become killers, receives resonance from repeated observation in this very different context. The human body is a successful example of combining a modicum of anticipation with a mass of resilience so as to secure a reasonable degree of safety on, as Tonegawa says in the headnote, "a quite small defense budget."

The Risks

The human body faces risks that are multiple, varied, and unpredictable: multiple in that there are many sources of potential injury, varied in that the body is vulnerable to many types of damage, and unpredictable in that the body cannot know which disturbances it will encounter and when. No system or organ of the body is immune from damage: the skin may be punctured, burned, or damaged by disease; the air passages of the lung can become clogged or collapse; hearts can stop and blood vessels can be blocked; bones can break or become malformed; nerve cells can be destroyed. The agents of attack can come from outside the body, such as invading viruses or foreign chemicals, or from inside, from the reactive products of normal metabolism or the destructive actions of immune cells. The line between enemy and friend becomes blurred; many substances or organisms may be beneficial at low concentrations and damaging at higher concentrations, or may even be both essential and damaging at any level. Oxygen, for example, is basic to human life yet produces potentially harmful products when metabolized. Certain substances may increase tumors at one site while decreasing them at others.[4]

Organisms and compounds may damage the human body by disturbing its structures or functions. Tissue can be damaged by traumatic injury or by biochemical alteration of cellular structure. Many substances may also trigger DNA mutations, leading to cancer, birth defects, and other abnormalities. Foreign substances may interfere with normal processes by binding with, and thereby locking up, key compounds, or by causing harmful reactions. The body temperature and the levels of oxygen, carbon dioxide, nutrients, wastes, and organic ions in the blood and intracellular fluid must be kept within close tolerances by homeostatic mechanisms. Any agent that disturbs this balance can cause considerable damage.[5]

The human body can limit risks but never eliminate them entirely. Damage limitation is the preferred strategy, partly because no defense system is perfect; rather than rely on one, supposedly fail-safe strategy for defense, the body uses many different mechanisms and strategies. No single one is perfect, but together they provide adequate protection most, though not all, of the time. In fact, if a defense mechanism were entirely adequate to suppress the hazard at which it was aimed, the mechanism itself might cause considerable harm. Just as people often discover that their ostensible protectors are as dangerous as their foes, so may such defensive devices as the immune system do the body in. The impossibility of creating perfect defense systems is largely due to the ambiguous nature of risk. It is hard to launch an attack if the body's defenses cannot be sure what the enemy is.

Safety might be simpler if everything inside the body was good and everything outside potentially bad. Then the body could concentrate on careful external screening of incoming substances and not worry about internal processes. But sources of danger always exist. Always present in the gastrointestinal tract, bacteria actually aid digestion by breaking down substances; some may even be manufactured by the body. Cholesterol, for example, blocks arteries and contributes to heart attacks, yet 80 percent of the body's cholesterol is made by the liver.[6] Enzymes and antibodies produced in the body to detoxify harmful substances and destroy invading organisms actually may make matters worse by increasing the potency of some compounds or by attacking internal tissue. Particular genes, called oncogenes, may make cells particularly vulnerable to transformation into cancer cells; and compounds that trigger mutations may come not only from the dangerous world outside the skin, but may also be produced by normal metabolism. Danger is always present: "Mutations are not rare events. All of us," M. Alice Ottoboni observes, "normally carry within us a certain number of mutated cells."[7] Seeking a simple division between purity within the body and evil outside obfuscates the dangers faced, for the axiom of connectedness—that good and bad are intertwined—applies with full force to the human body.

The degree of danger, whether from internal or external sources, depends on the context. Mechanisms that allow the body to relax muscles and lose consciousness may be very helpful during surgery, but may be hazardous to a body engaged in activity.[8] Most people are not allergic to most chemicals, but any chemical may cause a reaction in someone. Organs within the human body also vary in susceptibility to substances: carbon tetrachloride is most toxic to the liver; DDT attains its highest concentrations in fat deposits, where it does the least harm.[9] The degree of danger depends on the specific location. Where a substance ends up, not where it comes from, is most relevant to assessing risk.

Substances may be both beneficial and dangerous. The same cholesterol that blocks arteries can be used to manufacture hormones, vitamin D, and nerve-fiber sheaths. The most striking example of a double-edged sword is oxygen, which may be deadly if it forms compounds known as "oxygen radicals." Fridovich notes that "molecular oxygen is both benign and malign. On the one hand, it provides enormous advantages; on the other, it imposes a universal toxicity.... Any organism that avails itself of the benefits of oxygen does so at the cost of maintaining an elaborate system of defenses."[10]

The chief principle of toxicity is that it depends on the dose. Substances may be deadly at high doses but harmless or even beneficial at low doses. Toxicity depends not only on the total amount of a substance that enters the body or is manufactured internally, but also on the route and length of exposure. Substances that permeate the skin, for example, may reach a vulnerable organ only slowly and partially. Ingested toxicants may be caught in the liver before they have a chance to reach other organs. Materials that may pass harmlessly through the digestive tract might block air passages in the lungs if inhaled. The critical exposure level is not how much enters the body but, rather, how much reaches a vulnerable organ.

Acute toxicity can result from a single exposure to a substance, while chronic toxicity is produced by moderate exposures over long periods of time. A compound may be dangerous in one case and quite harmless in another, and may affect quite different organs or biochemical systems, depending on the dose. Gradual exposure may allow the body's defense systems to temper the effects of a hazardous compound by converting it into something useful or by eliminating it. "Every one of us," Ottoboni writes, "ingests many lethal doses of many chemicals, both natural and synthetic, during the course of a lifetime. A shocking thought!"[11] Vitamin D, for example, can be acutely toxic, though beneficial in small, regular doses; long-term deficiency can produce rickets. Other substances, such as mercury, may not be harmful in acute doses but can be chronically toxic, due to slow absorption by the body.

Pharmacologists have formalized the principle of dose dependence in the "therapeutic index"; this is the ratio of the toxic dose to the curative dose for a given substance. Vitamins may greatly benefit the body, for example, but too much of a good thing can kill: fat-soluble vitamins such as A and D may exceed the body's capacity for elimination; water-soluble vitamin B6 can cause nerve damage at high doses.[12] (Indeed, even water itself can be fatal if the rate of intake exceeds the body's capacity to process it.) Hormones such as estrogen can cause cancer; oxygen is directly toxic at a pressure of 2.5 atmospheres.[13] The dose, the time period involved, and the susceptibility of target organs help determine whether the results will be harmful or healthful.

Substances may be dangerous at high doses, though essential in some moderate amount. Enzymes can cause all kinds of havoc if they are either excessive or deficient.[14] Many vitamins and minerals must be closely regulated by the body to ensure an optimum supply: zinc is used to maintain cell membranes and produce protein and energy; either too much or too little can lead to reduced growth;[15] iron and molybdenum also must be kept at moderate levels.[16]

H. N. Smyth, Jr. and other scientists suspect that small amounts of otherwise useless or harmful substances may actually do good by forcing the body to react. They note that animals exposed to low levels of toxic substances in experiments often show more growth than animals in the control group. "There are data in the toxicology literature," according to Ottoboni, "which indicate that our bodies are not just indifferent to trace quantities of synthetic foreign chemicals, but that such exposures may actually be beneficial.... Homeostatic mechanisms must be kept active if health is to be maintained."[17] Regular testing of the body's responses improves its resiliency.

If any substance can be both harmful and helpful, and if dangers can arise within the body as well as come from the environment, then safety can never be certain. Risk is unavoidable and largely unpredictable, since the nature of future exposures cannot be fully controlled. In this mine field of uncertainty, how can the body possibly maintain sufficient safety? We will next look at how the body fights uncertain risk with flexible defense.

Goals and Strategies

If all these risks are unavoidable and unpredictable, it might seem prudent for the body to devote virtually all its resources to defense, to protect fully against every conceivable risk; damage would then be minimized. But if active risk avoidance is carried to an extreme, the body might use up all its energy in a vain effort to defend against unknown dangers or those that fail to materialize. Though the resources available for defense of the body can be increased over time, they are limited at any one time and are never infinitely expandable. Therefore, they must be used judiciously. Defense alone does not ensure survival; organisms must develop effective growth mechanisms if there is to be anything left to defend. Life must go on after the battle is won.

Strictly speaking, biological mechanisms lack intention; they cannot follow strategies. But defense mechanisms do have certain characteristics in common that would be considered strategies in organizations capable of intentional action. The concept of strategy helps categorize the biological mechanisms of defense; it is not intended to imply that we have discovered some biochemical miracle of cellular thinking.

In its defense network, the body uses what might be called "combatants" and "noncombatants." Combatants are mechanisms that combat threats directly, either by fending them off or by rendering them harmless; if they are successful, damage from disturbance is minimized. Limiting damage might seem to be all that is required of defense systems, but restricting our discussion to these mechanisms would give a distorted view of how the body achieves safety. Because growth is as crucial as defense for survival, growth mechanisms ought to be considered part of the protective network. We have grouped together as noncombatants those mechanisms that do not directly fight enemies. Rather, they provide the growth needed for the body to avoid danger or to recover quickly if damage is sustained. Mechanisms for growth and repair do not destroy enemies, but they are vital to the defense effort.

Some defense mechanisms seek to prevent disturbances while others deal with the consequences of disturbances that have occurred. Strategies for preventing disturbances may include the use of both combatants, such as barriers that directly block harmful substances from entering vulnerable systems, and noncombatants, such as growth systems that keep the body strong and agile, able to escape contact with dangers. Forces that deal with the consequences of disturbances also include combatants and noncombatants. Some enzymes and immune cells, for example, react to invasions by directly attacking the enemies. But an attack triggers other, noncombatant enzymes to repair or replace damaged cells and their parts.

The distribution of defense mechanisms into the four categories created by these two criteria represents the variety of basic strategic "choices" made through mutation and selection (see Model 1). The body's defense system utilizes each strategic option—insulating vulnerable organs from harmful substances through barriers and excretion, attacking invaders by trapping, detoxication, and immune processes, compensating for damage through repair and replacement, and avoiding damage through growth and prudent behavior.

Model 1
Defense Mechanisms in the Human Body

	Combatants	Noncombatants
Prevention	Barriers Excretion	Growth Behavior
Mitigation	Trapping Detoxication Immunity	Repair Replacement

Defense Mechanisms: Taking the Offensive

The body apparently values growth over defense. Many defensive measures fail to reach levels that might, if viewed in isolation, be considered optimal. Since bones may break, it might seem logical to make them as strong as possible so as to survive intact any stress or accident. When Alexander tested bones, he concluded that the strengths of many limb bones were surprisingly low.[18] Perhaps this is only an odd fluke of evolution, but more likely maximal strength in each bone did not prove advantageous. Why not? Well, if bones were sufficiently massive, the human body might be too much like a tank: hard to destroy with a direct hit, but clumsy and slow. When survival may depend on outrunning predators—or dodging falling limbs, surging floodwaters, or drunk drivers—it might be well worth trading some strength for greater agility.

Or take skin, which, although it functions as a protective barrier, is really rather thin. Perhaps the greater sensitivity and transferral of materials thus made possible makes up for the added vulnerability. Internally, the liver and kidneys are important centers for detoxication and elimination of harmful substances, yet they take up only a modest portion of the body's space and resources. The energy and materials devoted to the immune system are also modest; only when challenged by a specific toxicant does the system begin to deplete general reserves and produce antibodies in large quantities. The benefits of these defenses are balanced through selection with the need for growth and maintenance systems, such as the lungs and circulatory system. Health requires energy, endurance, strength, and skill as well as preventive defenses.

Behavioral learning is a critical element for defense. The human species shares with many others the physiological capacity to take certain actions to avoid danger. But humans are exceptional in their ability to process information from the environment, store it away, communicate it to others, and modify future behavior accordingly. The elaborate structure of the brain that makes this possible is itself an indirect, but essential, mechanism for defense.

Mechanisms of growth and behavior that help the body avoid damage are the "diplomats" of the body's defense system. They provide the potential to detect threats and make appropriate adjustments to avoid confrontations. If this global growth strategy works, the body need not do battle. But when diplomacy fails, the body must turn to its combat forces.

Pulling Up the Drawbridge

Many safety measures, such as detoxication by enzymes and immune cell activity, are triggered by the presence of foreign or harmful matter. These are resilient defenses, because they are activated only when a specific danger threatens. But there are other defenses, which are always present or function regularly. Though their effectiveness does not depend on the stimulation of harmful substances, they nonetheless play major roles in the body's defenses. These techniques—such as barriers and mechanisms for elimination—help prevent damage by keeping sources of disturbance away from critical internal systems. They are operational before any specific hazard presents itself, and thus are anticipatory.

Sensitive organs and vessels are best kept isolated from the experience of dangers that lie outside the body. Such barriers as the skin keep many harmful substances from entering the body or reaching critical systems. The skin also keeps the body from drying out. This is a chronic, not an episodic, hazard, and so an anticipatory mechanism is appropriate. The relative impermeability of skin prevents compounds from filtering through the surface; the skin's keratin layer provides moderate protection against abrasion and the effects of sun and wind. Through induction and selection, concentrations of melanin in the skin have been increased to provide further protection in populations most exposed to the harsh sun.

Mucous membranes in the mouth and throat, the cornea of the eye, and membranes in the ear, which capture many harmful substances before they can enter the body, are also protective barriers. Deeper within, the lining of the digestive tract restricts the passage of materials into blood vessels and organs. The extensive surface of the lungs also plays a prominent role in blocking the entrance of material from the air. This surface is extremely thin—as little as a single cell in places, which hardly seems like a formidable barrier. This vulnerability is partially compensated for by the elaborate structure of the lungs, which hides some of the most fragile surface deep in a labyrinth of passages. Only the tiniest particles can stay suspended in the air long enough to reach the inner passages; larger particles are deposited on the throat and nasopharynx.[19]

Perhaps the most significant internal barrier is the blood-brain barrier that separates the central nervous system from everything else. Made up of glial cells, brain capillaries, and extracellular space and fluid, it defends by restricting the passage of materials. This is not an absolute barrier; it does not cover the entire surface of nerves and the brain. But the blood-brain barrier is supplemented by a related technique of cushioning the most vulnerable parts. Thus, the sensitive and irreplaceable neurons (nerve cells) are protected by layers of replaceable glial cells, which also act somewhat like immune cells. They can multiply to provide additional protection when nerves are under attack; some microglia may serve the same function as phagocytes (cell-eating immune cells) by devouring invaders.[20] Within the neurons, the vulnerable nucleus is more isolated than the myelin, axons, and dendrites.[21]

Mechanisms of elimination dispose of materials accumulated on the body's barriers. Elimination includes evaporation, exhalation, and excretion. The cilia of the lungs move particles outward by their waving motion. Coughing and sneezing are ways to increase the expulsion of substances into the air. Toxic substances can be excreted in sweat, tears, and milk, although the major vehicles are urine and feces. Excreted substances may have passed through the digestive tract without ever entering the bloodstream, or may have been processed by the liver or kidneys in what Ottoboni calls the "sewage treatment plants of the body." Cells that are in regular contact with harmful materials, such as the lining of the digestive tract, are regularly shed and excreted to prevent contamination from reaching internal systems.

The Battle Within

None of the body's barriers is perfect. That is not a design defect; letting in nothing would soon cause death. A totally impermeable barrier would hurt the body, which needs also to receive many beneficial substances from the environment. Of course, once materials do pass into the body, it becomes extremely difficult to allow in only the good things. Choosing between good and bad is particularly difficult for substances that are beneficial at one concentration but harmful at another, or that are essential but dangerous at the same dose. Relying merely on isolation from a hostile environment is not a sufficient defense strategy. Thus, mechanisms to deal with harmful materials that have entered the body are vital. These are the reactive, defense mechanisms of trapping, detoxication, and immunity.

One way to handle dangerous materials is to put them where they will not do harm. The body traps many toxicants by binding them to other substances. Proteins in the blood, such as albumin, attach to foreign compounds to prevent them from entering organs where they might do damage.[22] Thionen in the liver traps cadmium and sequesters it away.[23] A good example of an inducible, or reactive, response, the synthesis of thionen rises significantly following exposure to cadmium; the more danger, the more defense. This threat has not been anticipated; this is a resilient response that depends on knowing the exact degree and type of exposure, so the remedy may be adjusted in proportion.

When the concentration of a harmful substance exceeds the ability of the body to process and eliminate it, the substance may be stored where it is least likely to do harm. Lead, for example, may be stored in bone, and DDT in fat. Storage keeps such material out of the bloodstream and away from sensitive nerves,[24] thereby providing a buffering mechanism, like a reservoir that keeps water supplies constant. Substances can then be selectively eliminated as intake drops.

Not all harmful materials can be bound and stored. Some toxic materials must be eliminated or turned into useful (or at least harmless) materials; this is the job of the enzymes of detoxication. The body contains a wide assortment of enzymes needed for normal metabolism, which help to transform nutrients into energy and structure. And the detoxication enzymes of the liver can be induced in response to specific toxicants. The diversity of enzymes provides a built-in defense. When a previously unencountered, harmful substance enters the body, there will likely be an enzyme already present that can break it down.[25] Although enzymes are specific in that they are most effective against a single substance, most will react with (albeit less efficiently) a broad range of substances. This versatility allows the body to concentrate its resources on actual dangers as they occur. Commonly encountered substances will be treated by specific enzymes, while rare materials can be handled by the general nature of detoxication enzymes.

Enzymes are entirely reactive; no substrate (that is, a substance to be acted upon), no reaction. The greater the presence of a substrate, the greater the need for large quantities of a specific enzyme. Substrates trigger, or induce, the synthesis of enzymes. Such feedback allows the body to tailor its repertoire of enzymes to its past and current exposures. The inducible nature of enzymes means that high doses of harmful materials may be tolerated if the body is given adequate time to build up reserves of the specific enzymes. The capacity to build up tolerance explains why the long-time drinker finds that a couple of drinks do not give him the buzz they once did. The Styrian arsenic-eaters of Central Europe provide a curious example; they ingest doses that would spell the end for most mortals, yet live long lives.[26]

Most specialized of the body's defenses is the immune system. Its major function is to destroy foreign or dead material within the body. Therefore, the body's capacity to distinguish between itself and foreign matter is essential. Should its information detection fail, the body would make war on itself. Immune cells circulate continually throughout the bloodstream, reacting only when they recognize foreign matter. As enzymes modify foreign compounds, immune cells destroy foreign organisms, such as bacteria, viruses, and fungi. The immune system has two main lines of defense: humoral immunity, in which "B cells" release chemicals that destroy pathogens (or agents of disease); and cellular immunity, in which organisms are directly attacked by "T cells." The first technique is a sort of chemical warfare; the second can be compared to a carnivore devouring its prey.

Like enzymes, immune cells can be both broad and specific in their selection of victims. Broad, or general, immunity allows the body to respond quickly to an invasion. Macrophages (literally "big eaters") and natural killer cells roam the bloodstream, ready to consume any cells detected as foreign. They are complemented by chemical antibodies that can recognize and attack a variety of antigens (the configurations that identify foreign substances). These broad defenses provide rapid reactions, but cannot recognize and destroy particular invaders as efficiently as more specific measures. Each type of antibody, for example, has a unique shape that will lock with a specific antigen. An antibody may also hook up with a roughly similar antigen, thus making broad immunity possible, but the connection will not be as tight and effective. An encounter with a new pathogen induces the production of T cells and antibodies specifically targeted for that pathogen. Just as one cannot maximize contradictory objectives, the body also compromises between specificity and versatility.

As the battle against an invader is won, the immune system gradually shuts down. Suppresser cells send chemical signals to stop the production of new specific T cells and antibodies. If the body reduces its defenses too soon, monitor T cells may trigger the resumption of production. After an attack subsides, the quantities of T cells and antibodies targeted for the invaders decline. But a residuum of "memory" cells will remain in the body for its lifetime, providing a modest "peacetime army" in case of reinvasion. According to Mizel and Jaret, "Before the first infection, there may have been one helper T cell in one million programmed to recognize the antigen of the hepatitis B virus; after the infection there will be thousands more of these antigen-specific cells."[27] These memory cells provide the immune system with a resilient, learning capacity; future preparations are determined by past experience. As in trial and error, the most effective techniques are retained.

Recovery Through Growth

Defensive strategies that only limit damage are not sufficient to achieve health and safety. The body must get on with its business, which is to grow so as to survive. Crucial functions must not be interrupted for long. After attack and defense, the body is rather like a victorious, but devastated, postwar nation that must rebuild its economy.

The body meets the need for recovery by sending in the "medics": mechanisms that are triggered by a disturbance but do not directly attack the invaders. Rather, they repair and replace damaged parts so that normal maintenance and growth is disrupted as little as possible. In contrast to the general growth processes discussed earlier that protect safety by promoting the avoidance of damage, these types of growth mechanisms are targeted to compensate for specific damages. For example, there are several different enzymes that detect and correct lesions in cell DNA. Repair restores cells that otherwise could become mutagenic and carcinogenic to their normal state.[28] Where repair is not possible or practical, functions may be transferred from damaged cells to sister cells. The presence of large numbers of identical cells makes this interchangeability possible. When the needed material is not at hand, it may be quickly obtained. Small metabolites damaged by foreign compounds may easily be replaced by similar parts that circulate in the normal metabolic flux. A deficiency of a substance that has been destroyed by a toxicant may induce the synthesis of a replacement supply.[29] In order for repair and replacement to work, however, the general level of the body's resources must be high enough to contain and sensitive enough to control the necessary parts.

Holes in the Armor

Not one of the body's defenses is invulnerable. Invading organisms and foreign compounds may slip through gaps in the defense or overwhelm them. Defense mechanisms may make errors that create new dangers. Risk is ever present. The defense systems can only increase the body's chances of survival; they cannot ensure immortality.

Barriers alone could not adequately defend the human body because, once breached, they are ineffective. The body cannot anticipate, and insulate itself from, all dangers. Harmful substances do find their way through the skin, eyes, ears, lungs, and digestive tract. After invaders penetrate the body, external barriers (with their limitations) are reminders of the dangers of overreliance on anticipation, but of no help in the immediate fight. The blood-brain barrier also is not absolute. Lipid-soluble, nonbound compounds can penetrate; bacteria can pass through and cause meningitis. Indeed, some vulnerability must exist if the central nervous system is to get the necessary nutrients. Moreover, partial openness allows harmful substances that did get in to be passed back out. Nerve cell axons are exposed at the nodes, making it possible for the ion fluxes of nerve signal conduction to take place, but also increasing the risk of damage.[30] Toxins that get through the barriers can do considerable damage; they can strip the myelin off neurons and interfere with nerve conduction. The nervous system pays a higher price for damage than most other systems because nerve cells are irreplaceable; unlike other cells, nerve cells do not divide once they are mature. If too many cells are destroyed, functions are lost forever.[31]

The immune system has potent weapons to seek out and destroy invaders, but this benefit is not without cost. Immune cells must distinguish between self and nonself and turn on and off as needed but, like every other component of the body, they are not perfect. The immune system may turn on the body. The need to quickly identify and overwhelm foreign invaders makes the immune apparatus so sensitive that it can indeed get out of control. Arthritis, and perhaps even cancer, may involve bodily self-destruction by immune cells and other body chemicals. Organ transplants, blood transfusions, and even fetuses may be rejected by the immune system. If nerve proteins are chemically modified, they may provoke an immune cell attack.[32] Even when cell-eating phagocytes are consuming the right enemy, they generate oxygen radicals that may cause mutations.[33]

Growth makes rapid recoveries possible, but it too has its risks. Ames and Saul speculate that a relatively low basal metabolic rate may aid human survival by creating fewer mutagens.[34] Species that live fast and die young—like those denizens of the laboratory, rats and bacteria—have much more rapid dissemination of possibly beneficial genetic mutations through the population. Life may be just a flash in the petri dish for each individual, but for the species as a whole rapid adaptation to environmental changes becomes possible.

If risk is unavoidable and no defense is perfect, it would make sense at least to maximize safety by exploiting more than one strategy at once. And that is exactly what the body does: barriers, excretion, detoxication, immunity, and growth function simultaneously, providing overlapping layers of protection. If one thing doesn't work, perhaps something else will. The nervous system, for example, relies heavily on barriers, but also on glial cells to attack invaders and mechanisms to repair DNA damage. Duplication and overlap in the human body is so prevalent that it can be considered a basic principle of safety.[35]

Diversity of Form and Redundancy of Function

The human body is an extremely complex organism; trying to make sense of the body's defenses requires dealing with a wide range of systems and organs, strategies and tactics. Why can't the body make up its mind? Why can't it conserve its resources by selecting, and sticking with, the most effective defense technique? In part, of course, the body doesn't have a mind to make up; except for gaining or losing a few pounds or staying in or out of the sun, there is little we can consciously do to affect the design of our bodies. But we can rephrase the question to ask why selection pressure has not forced the emergence of a single, superior safety strategy. Given what we know about evolutionary theory and the risks and benefits of defense systems, a reasonable answer could be that reliance on single strategies or systems doesn't work very well.

Diversity means surrendering the dream of invulnerability to the practical advantage of survivability. When a harmful organism or substance invades the human body, structural diversity lessens the threat of catastrophic harm and increases the chance of a quick and effective defense. Many invaders attack only certain types of cells or react only with certain enzymes. Having a diversity of cell types means any invader will likely find something to attack, but only a limited number of cells will be attacked at one time.

Sexual reproduction provides an important defense for the species by increasing genetic diversity. Though the species may not be perfect, it will be resilient:

> One advantage of sexual reproduction is that it produces variety.... Without knowing what environmental changes are apt to occur, it is impossible to predict which are the best possible traits.... Nevertheless, for any environmental change that is not dramatic, there is a good chance that at least some members of the species would have just the right traits to enable them, and the species, to survive.[36]

Variety ensures that human beings will differ greatly in their susceptibility to different substances. Any environmental change will likely hurt some people, but diversity helps limit the size of any vulnerable group. Diversity can aid entire populations as well as individuals.

Enzymes provide protection to cells and their parts by trapping and detoxifying harmful compounds. A wide variety of enzymes is needed to meet the diverse needs of normal metabolism. This diversity enables the body to handle new, possibly harmful compounds, because enzymes designed for similar but more common substrates will already be present.[37] Similarly, the great diversity of antibodies makes it more likely that some will be able to handle any invading bacteria.

Redundancy is essential to defense based on diversity. That is, safety would not be promoted if each structure were specialized and separate, because that would merely increase the number of irreplaceable parts. For diversity to be advantageous there must be duplication and overlap of function, so that some parts may be sacrificed without jeopardizing the whole. Barriers, excretion, enzyme actions, immunity, and growth all promote safety. If one mechanism temporarily fails, others may provide sufficient protection. And redundancy also abounds within each technique. Functions may be transferred when cells are destroyed because there are so many duplicate cells to take over the burden. A substance that can damage cells may be overwhelmed by the depth of the body's reserves. "The mass and redundancy of carbohydrate molecules in the cell," Brabec and Bernstein inform us, "simply render the target too diffuse and inert to suffer attack directly by an exogenous chemical."[38]

The defense systems of the body are highly redundant. A few examples: Several antibodies are capable of binding to a single antigen, increasing the probability of a rapid match; there are more than a trillion lymphocytes, so considerable losses can be absorbed.[39] There are several different repair mechanisms for DNA. Cell-eating macrophages can be variously attracted by neuropeptides produced by immune cells or the nervous system, or by the blood-clot peptides, or by bacterial products.[40] There are two kidneys, critical organs for trapping and eliminating harmful substances. Blood pressure can be regulated by either heart rate or blood vessel size; oxygen in cells can be controlled by varying blood flow or the oxygen content in the blood. Body temperature can be regulated by dilation of blood vessels that brings skin temperature closer to the core temperature, thereby increasing conduction, by sweating to increase evaporation, or by increasing heat production through activity, such as shivering. The body has a wealth of reactive, redundant mechanisms. But how can it afford to maintain such elaborate defenses, and how does it know when to employ what?

Plasticity, Flux, and Feedback

Redundancy and diversity allow the body to absorb some damage and continue to function. If resources were unlimited, the best defensive strategy for the body might be to have as much duplication and overlap of every form and function as possible, so the body could absorb major simultaneous losses in many systems and still carry on. If unlimited redundancy were possible, the body would be like a very complex organization with an infinite degree of slack. An abundance of excess capacity would ensure survivability.

But the supply of energy and materials is not infinite. The body's limited resource base means choices must be made, priorities set. As Jakoby observes, there cannot be a specific enzyme ready to deal with every compound that might someday be encountered, because there is a "continual supply of unfamiliar products" into the body that would monopolize its resources. Instead, the body relies in part on the ability of enzymes to catalyze a broad class of substrates. This versatility does not provide the rapid removal and delicate regulation possible with specific enzymes, but is more economical and effective when the broader needs of the body are considered. By limiting the supply of specific enzymes, the body is "saving expensive capacity in the machinery for information storage and protein synthesis."[41]

Since choices must be made, however, the body runs the risk that its choices may be wrong. With its limited selection of specific enzymes and antibodies, for example, what will happen when the body encounters an entirely new type of invader? Must defense depend solely on broad, inefficient measures? Although the general versatility of antibodies and enzymes contributes to the initial defense, the body also has the capacity to respond to an attack by producing specialized defenders. This ability to aim accurately is possible only because resources can be transferred from other forms and functions to fight the new danger. Thus, materials must be plastic (that is, convertible or generalizable), able to be reformed or redirected as needs change.

The essence of the body's defense system is this rapid transformation of energy and matter in response to an attack. Enzymes, phagocytic T cells, and antibodies specially designed to attack invaders can be produced in a matter of hours and days. Defenders already present in substantial quantities, such as macrophages and nervous system glial cells, can reproduce quickly to provide even more firepower. When the immune system swings into action, it can divert energy as needed from other sources, such as the muscles. The body puts up with a short-term hindrance, muscle weakness, in order to speed up victory. In the same way—although cells depend on fats, protein, and carbohydrates to meet their metabolic and structural needs—when the exogenous supply of any one of these is limited, cells can transform other materials to make up for the shortage.[42] Plasticity gives the body the potential to meet urgent needs while still serving its normal needs efficiently.

How does the body decide when and how to transfer its resources? A system of chemical communication provides organs and cells with the information they need to produce certain substances or adjust settings so as to maintain their equilibrium. The high flux of materials through the blood promotes rapid communication; chemicals such as interleukins and lymphokines send messages between cells. Helper T cells travel between the lymph nodes and sites of infection, stimulating the production of specialized immune cells.

The high flux of materials through human systems and rapid feedback make possible highly sensitive homeostatic mechanisms. The body can quickly detect what adjustments are needed, find the necessary resources, and convey them to a particular site. Plasticity and homeostasis are essential to a highly reactive, or inducible, defense. Replacements will be synthesized for compounds destroyed by toxicants, specific enzymes produced when new substrates are encountered, and ongoing processes modified to meet changing needs. Lymphocytes enlarge, divide, and secrete if stimulated; also, when nerve cells are threatened, glial cells multiply. The body will increase its internal temperature, bringing on a fever, to increase the effectiveness of immune cells.[43] Synthesis of thionen, which traps cadmium in the liver, will increase after exposure to cadmium.[44] Melanin will be induced in the skin in response to harsh sun; eye pupils will be shut down to limit damage from light. Through rapid feedback of information, the body is able to quickly disturb the status quo when it must to fight an attack, then rapidly return to homeostasis.

All this—diversity, redundancy, plasticity, homeostasis—depends on the overall resource capacity of the body. Just as body weight is proving to be a crucial indicator of an infant's future health, so the body's global capacity, the extent of its general resource base, limits what it can do in the way of self-protection.

Anticipation and Resilience in the Human Body

Diversity and redundancy in a system means the ability to absorb disturbance and survive. Plasticity and feedback provide the potential and mechanism for change. Increases in global resources raise the level of safety. By inculcating these principles, the body has created a set of defense mechanisms that allow it to survive constant attack.

The body cannot afford to devote all its resources to a buildup of combat forces to prevent any possible disturbance. Just as defense spending alone does not a healthy economy make, the body also must concentrate on the growth that makes for survival. And while the variety of dangers faced is infinite, the body's resources are not. To identify enemies often involves ambivalence, as some of the many invaders bring benefits as well as dangers to the body. A fully anticipatory defense would seek to protect the body by preventing every possible danger before it could do damage; yet clearly this is impossible.

The lack of total anticipation does not leave the body defenseless, however, because the human organism has developed a sophisticated set of resilient defenses to supplement its anticipatory mechanisms. When danger occurs, the body will respond. A flexible defense admits both the fallibility of the defenses and the ambiguous nature of the enemy.

Plasticity and feedback epitomize resilience by allowing forms and functions to change rapidly in response to emerging needs. Mechanisms, such as inducible repair enzymes, that most fully exploit these principles are the most resilient, as are patterns of diversity and redundancy. Although they may exist before trouble strikes, the specific disturbances that the body encounters determine the future characteristics of its redundant defenses. Small amounts of specific enzymes, for example, will remain in the body once a new substrate is detected. There will be several enzymes designed to handle known (or previously experienced) and common dangers, such as oxygen radicals—enzymes concentrated in the organs or cell parts where encounters are most likely. Specialized immune cells and antibodies also will remain in the body after an invasion; this is why giving someone a small dose of a disease may confer immunity. Persons who as children survived influenza in the 1890s, for example, in their nineties still had specialized antibodies floating in their bloodstream.[45] Each individual's defense systems thus become unique, modified in response to different experiences. The redundancy of large numbers of different cells and chemicals uses the resilient responses of the past to prepare for highly individualized future needs.

The body places only a limited emphasis on anticipatory mechanisms. In a strict sense, none of the body's defenses are anticipatory, because the body cannot consciously anticipate future needs and intentionally modify its structure. Rather, defense systems presumably arise from a long process of selection, resulting from mutation and the survival of those forms sufficiently suited to the environment. Evolution is a resilient, not an anticipatory, process, allowing stability through change.

But some of the body's defenses are more anticipatory than others. If we return to grouping defenses by strategic choices of form and function, we can see that these criteria, modified slightly, describe anticipatory and resilient defenses (see Model 2). The most anticipatory defenses are preoccupied with the elimination of risk; they seek to maintain the purity of the body and avoid all errors. Elaborate safety measures are taken to keep out anticipated dangers. Barriers and excretion mechanisms best fit this category. Conversely, these are the mechanisms that least follow the more resilient principles of feedback and plasticity.

Model 2
Anticipatory and Resilient Defenses
Investment in defensive forces:

Goal:	Heavy	Light
Avoid disturbance	Barriers Excretion	Growth Behavior
Cope with disturbance	Trapping Detoxication	Repair Replacement

ANTICIPATION

RESILIENCE

Barriers are the most anticipatory of the body's defenses, since the level of danger does not greatly affect their form or function. But even this is not entirely correct; barriers change (consider the concentration of melanin in the skin) in response to environmental conditions. Nor are barriers the ideal defense; the central nervous system depends heavily on the blood-brain barrier to keep out of trouble, since its nerve cells are not replaceable. Yet the AIDS virus has breached that barrier, leaving the nervous system vulnerable to attack from related diseases.

Resilient defenses assume that enemies cannot be known until they attack. There is less investment in specific defensive measures and a greater acceptance of risk. The mechanisms for repair and replacement are the most resilient of the body's defenders. They most fully pursue the principles of homeostasis and plasticity, relying on quick feedback and resource transfers when enemies strike. General growth is not exclusively devoted to creating safety measures to avoid anticipated risks. Growth also limits the robustness of body parts in order to increase agility. In this way, growth increases future resilience.

The trapping forces of enzymes and the immune system blend anticipation with resilience—anticipatory in that they are designed to combat specific risks and may be present before a disturbance occurs, but primarily resilient, since they may increase rapidly and go into action only when danger strikes. Enzymes trap and detoxify harmful materials and induce manufacture of replacements only when stimulated by substrates. Immune cells multiply, eat cells, and secrete antibodies only when there is (or is perceived to be) an enemy present. And the distribution of forces is influenced greatly by previous experiences of danger. Like behavioral learning, inducible enzymes and memory cells use past resilience to anticipate the future.

Resilience (to borrow an analogy from Samuel Florman) is tragedy. Resilient defenses admit the failings of the human body: prediction is never perfect; recognition of enemies is flawed. The great irony facing the body's defenses is that they must ultimately fail; risk is constant and death inevitable. The body's defenses can only fight off as many enemies as possible for as long as possible, while at the same time getting on with life. If resilient defenses are successful, the species may succeed, though each individual will eventually die. The body's defenses are remarkable not because they are ultimately victorious, but because, through a complex network of anticipatory and resilient mechanisms—more the latter than the former—they make possible, however briefly, vigorous life amidst inevitable danger.

As we shall see in the next chapter, it is possible to do worse. The law of man does not always heed the lessons of nature.

8

From Resilience to Anticipation: Why the Tort Law is Unsafe

Daniel Polisar and Aaron Wildavsky

Separate sections of the *Oakland Tribune* on August 15, 1985, featured three stories whose full import could be understood only by considering them all together. The front page, under the headline "Pollution insurance drying up," carried a feature article explaining how companies seeking to clean up hazardous wastes were forced to curtail their work because they could not obtain liability insurance for a reasonable fee. On page one of the Lifestyle section, interested readers could learn that midwives and obstetricians were in dire straits because they were unable to get medical malpractice coverage, a specific type of liability insurance. Many were abandoning their profession or starting underground practices. The reader who continued perusing the paper could find out on the third page of the Sports section that a jury had awarded $180,000 to a woman who had been struck by a ball while watching a baseball game at the Astrodome; because she had not been warned that spectators faced the danger of being hit by foul balls, the owner of the Houston Astros was liable and had to pay her damages.

In each of these situations, the behavior of large groups of people was affected, and in each instance judges and juries, rather than government regulators, were behind the changes. The waste disposers and midwives faced across-the-board higher insurance costs because of court cases in which their insurance agents had been forced to pay compensation to people allegedly injured by their practices. Owners of ball clubs throughout the United States had to face the prospect of redesigning stadiums or issuing warnings to their fans. The courts' rulings concerned particular instances, but entire classes of people, uninvolved in those legal proceedings, were pressured to alter their behavior. Actions remained voluntary but incentives changed. What is going on here? Why is everyone acting as if they are being regulated?

Legal scholars take great pains to draw distinctions between government regulation and adjudication in the courts. In theory, there is little difficulty in doing so. Government regulation is the more direct way to mandate safe behavior. A regulatory commission determines what it considers safe, leaving individuals, corporations, and governments the choice of complying or facing punishment. Regulators measure behavior against standards which are quantifiable or otherwise capable of being measured. The rules they establish determine, say, how thick a retaining wall must be, how many parts per billion of a substance will be tolerated, or how far a car window may roll down. Failure to meet a safety standard is a violation, whether or not an accident results. Regulators and courts can force compliance with standards and procedures even if no harm has occurred.

In addition to its own role in enforcing regulations, the judicial system also possesses a distinct mechanism for promoting safety. Judgments in tort cases, unlike enforcement of regulations, are made only after an accident occurs. An injured person brings suit in court, trying to convince a judge, and usually a jury as well, that another party was responsible for his injury and should be forced to pay compensation. No injury, no case; a plaintiff who could prove the existence of the world's most egregious safety hazard still would have to find some mechanism other than tort law unless he could demonstrate that harm had been caused. Regulation is preventive, setting up standards before the fact; the law of personal injury (tort law) is reactive, providing redress after the fact. In form, the tort law is a classic instance of resilient response.

Tort law has undergone tremendous changes during the past century. For the most part, these changes have made it easier for injured parties to collect compensation. A central justification has been that by making unsafe behavior costly, tort law makes society safer. But has it? Certainly, tort law and liability insurance have become ubiquitous. It isn't possible to be born, work, drive a car, or go to a doctor without being profoundly affected by some aspect of the law of personal injury. Almost as certainly, behavior is being altered. Decisions made about the products we buy, the services governments provide, and the environment we live in are shaped by people who are deeply aware of the implications for behavior of legal changes. That this myriad of changes also has reduced risk is much more problematic.

How do stories about foul balls and midwives fit in? They are bench marks of the changes that have transformed tort law in practice from being largely resilient to mostly anticipatory. By making tort law resemble regulation—where penalties are prescribed in advance in order to prevent practices known or believed to be harmful—tort law has lost the quality of resilience, the flexibility to fit the remedy to the harm in individual cases.

A Brief History of American Tort Law

Before the middle of the nineteenth century, American legal scholars did not think of tort law as a unified body of knowledge. There were laws about personal injuries, descended from the English system of writs, but these were discrete actions, legal remedies tailored to particular harms.[1] In the 1850s and 1860s, the trend towards classification in scientific thought affected the legal profession also, resulting in a search for principles that would unite law under a comprehensive and logical set of doctrines.[2]

After sifting through thousands of cases decided by English and American courts, legal theorists settled upon a few principles whose application seemed most consistent with the outcomes reached. For unintentionally inflicted injuries, the standard of conduct was generally considered to be negligence.[3] If one actor had acted negligently, causing injury to another, then he was held to be liable for damages suffered. To establish that behavior was negligent, the injured plaintiff needed to show three things: the defendant's action had caused the injury; the defendant owed a duty of care; and the defendant had violated that duty. Central to this was a proof of fault; causing injury was not enough. Unless the defendant had done something wrong, he was not liable for damages. In a famous 1873 case, *Brown v. Collins*, a pair of horses had shied off a road after being startled by the noise from a passing train. In doing so, they damaged a lamppost on property belonging to Brown, who then sued for compensation. But the court ruled that Collins, who was driving the horses, "was in the use of ordinary care and skill." Since there was no showing of "actual fault," Collins did not have to compensate Brown for the broken lamp.[4]

Competing with negligence as a principle for determining who should pay whom was another: strict liability, or liability regardless of fault. If you do harm, negligently or not, you pay. The classic statement of strict liability was in the case of *Rylands v. Fletcher*, decided by the House of Lords in 1868. Fletcher's mill had caused water damage to Rylands's mine. The Lords ruled that Fletcher had to pay, despite the fact that he had run the mill properly and had used ordinary care in preventing accidents. They based their decision on the fact that Fletcher's activity was extremely hazardous and the very act of doing business made him responsible for the hazards he created. American courts generally did not follow the precedent of this case and, instead, used negligence as a standard of conduct.[5]

By the 1870s, negligence—the defendant had to do wrong to be liable— was firmly entrenched as the principle guiding decisions in tort cases. In

1881, Oliver Wendell Holmes wrote in *The Common Law* that "No case or principle can be found...subjecting an individual to liability for an accident done without fault on his part."[6]

Negligence was actually a cluster of related doctrines delineating the responsibilities of all parties to an accident. The actions of the injured party were considered as well as those of the alleged injurer. Only a fault-free victim was legally entitled to compensation. A plaintiff whose own negligence was causally related to his accident was barred from receiving compensation.[7] If the plaintiff knew about the danger and chose not to avoid it, a related doctrine stated, he was said to have assumed the risk; no one else could be expected to pay for the consequences of his own action. If a danger was obvious, then a person who failed to heed it had no one to blame—or to compensate him—but himself.

In the 1916 case of *MacPherson v. Buick*, the behavior to which tort law could apply was vastly expanded. MacPherson was injured when the wheel of his Buick broke, causing him to lose control of the car. He sued Buick, which defended itself by pointing out that its only obligation was to the dealer, to whom it sold the car, and with whom it had a contract. Writing for the majority, Justice Benjamin Cardozo rejected that argument on the grounds that duty could exist without a contract; impersonal markets required that duty be extended to strangers with whom one had no direct contact. Other courts accepted the precedent during the next two decades.[8]

From Negligence to Strict Liability

By long established precedent, a higher standard of care was required of manufacturers involved in making "dangerous" substances, such as dynamite or poison. Conduct which would be judged acceptable if engaged in by a toy manufacturer might be judged negligent if an explosives factory had used no more than the same level of care. The greater the danger, the greater the duty to exercise care; if extraordinary damage could result, then "ordinary care" had better include the taking of all possible precautions.

During the 1930s and early 1940s, changes in tort law made it easier for plaintiffs to prove negligence. A 1937 case, *Pearlman v. Garrod Shoe Company*,[9] expanded the category of dangerous goods. A boy developed a blister as a result of a defective shoe lining, starting an infection that eventually killed him. In ruling that the company owed damages, the Appeals Court held that shoes constituted an imminently dangerous instrumentality. Hence, the burden of proof on the boy's family to show negligence was reduced. Only a negligent company could allow something as dangerous as a shoe to leave its factory without making sure that it was free of defects.

The presence of the defect strongly implied that there must have been negligence—even if it could not be proven concretely.

Even more striking was the case of *Noore v. Perlberg, Inc.*, decided in 1944.[10] The first time that Noore wore a gown made by Perlberg, it burst into flames immediately upon contact with a cigarette. Purchasing agents of the manufacturer, which bought thousands of yards of cloth from a variety of sources, were unaware that this particular material had been treated with a highly flammable substance. By the commonly accepted definition of negligence, Perlberg was not negligent, since the company had used ordinary care in making dresses. The court found for the plaintiff, however, ruling that a woman's dress is a "dangerous instrumentality," and that Perlberg had not exercised sufficient caution in its dangerous enterprise.[11]

Summing up the trend reflected in these and several other negligence cases, a legal scholar concluded that, "The jury is allowed to find liability on extremely slight evidence of negligence, or the burden of proof is placed on the defendant to show the use of all possible precautions."[12] A second scholar concluded that the case of the gown maker showed that negligence was beginning to resemble strict liability (liability without fault).[13] That is, as judges began to create the presumption that accidents implied fault, it became easier for injured plaintiffs to receive compensation with only a slight showing that there had been wrong action. Accidents or bad luck were going out of style as explanations; if there was injury, the producer or seller must have been at fault. Harm and fault were becoming equivalent.

In 1944, in *Escola v. Coca-Cola*, the growing disenchantment with the requirement of showing fault was treated explicitly. Gladys Escola, a waitress in a Merced, California restaurant, was severely injured when a Coke bottle exploded in her hand. She sued Coca-Cola for having negligently made the bottle. Her lawyer argued that although it was impossible to prove negligence, since the explosion had destroyed the evidence, the lack of any other plausible explanation created the presumption of negligence. If the bottle had been made properly, he argued, it would not have exploded. It was up to the defendant, Coca-Cola, to prove that some other explanation could account for the explosion.

According to a long established doctrine of negligence law, if every cause for an accident is ruled out except negligence of some party, then the presumption is that that party indeed was negligent. This doctrine is called "Res Ipsa Loquitur," meaning, "the thing speaks for itself." Typically, it was applied to the sort of case in which a person walking near a building was struck by a brick. Without witnesses to explain where the brick had been placed and how it had fallen, it was extremely difficult to prove that someone had acted negligently. Absent negligence, however, bricks don't fall from the tops of buildings. Therefore, negligence could be assumed unless the defendant could provide a more plausible explanation for what might have happened.

After a trial judge ruled that the facts in the Escola case supported the use of "res ipsa," and after a jury found Coca-Cola's arguments of other causes unpersuasive, the case was appealed. Eventually it reached the California Supreme Court, and all seven justices upheld the decision. This not only made it far easier to prove fault in negligence cases but, through the con-curring opinion written by Justice Roger Traynor, it also opened the door to decisions of liability without fault. Traynor argued that accepting simple negligence as the basis for Coca-Cola's liability required a tenuous stretch-ing of the definition of negligence. He therefore rejected a ruling based on fault, but decided for Escola on the basis of strict liability. Coca-Cola should be held liable even though fault could not be demonstrated or even inferred. The rationales Traynor used in reaching his decision are similar to arguments for strict liability still used today:

> Even if there is no negligence, however, public policy demands that respon-sibility be fixed wherever it will most effectively reduce the hazards to life and health inherent in defective products that reach the market. It is evident that the manufacturer can anticipate some hazards and guard against the recur-rence of others as the public cannot. Those who suffer injury from defective products are unprepared to meet its consequences. The cost of an injury and the loss of time or health may be an overwhelming misfortune to the person injured, and a needless one, for the risk of injury can be insured by the manufacturer and distributed among the public....[14]

Judges had been subverting negligence doctrine by allowing juries to award damages in cases where negligence, in Traynor's view, had not been shown. Traynor agreed with their sentiment, but wanted a more honest approach: "It is needlessly circuitous to make negligence the basis of recov-ery and impose what is in reality liability without negligence. If public policy demands that a manufacturer of goods be responsible for their quality regardless of negligence there is no reason not to fix that respon-sibility openly." Here we have it: Traynor explicitly views the law as a tool of social policy, not of justice for individuals. His intent—"public policy de-mands" that responsibility be fixed on manufacturers regardless of negli-gence—is explicitly regulatory.

Other judges might have been less anxious thus to dabble in public policy, believing that to be a task for the legislature, but Traynor was known for his espousal of judicial activism. If public-policy considerations are to play an explicit role, then tort law no longer consists of discrete responses to particular situations. It becomes another means of regulation by at-tempting to balance a variety of social costs and benefits.

In establishing negligence, one favored rationale among judges was that market relations are marred by inequality between buyer and seller. Judges' decisions since the 1940s have been replete with references to the helplessness of consumers in the face of new technologies.[15] Increasing complexity, judges argued, had rendered the individual consumer incapable of understanding the vast panoply of potentially dangerous products. Only manufacturers could understand what they had wrought, so consumers could not be asked to assume the risk for a product they had purchased. By the same token, manufacturers had to assume more care in exorcising hazards from their products, including all possible uses to which innocent consumers might put them. Justice Jackson's comments in a 1953 case were typical: "Where experiment or research is necessary to determine the presence or the degree of danger, the product must not be tried out on the public, nor must the public be expected to possess the facilities, or the technical knowledge to learn for itself of inherent but latent dangers. The claim that a hazard was not foreseen is not available to one who did not use foresight appropriate to his enterprise."[16]

Courts in other states quickly adopted standards of strict liability for products whose defects were not the result of fault on the part of the manufacturer. No matter how it was used, if a product that was supposed to function safely caused an injury, then it was defective, and its maker was liable to anyone who suffered damages as a result. Within two years, this extension of strict liability to products (called products liability) was an established part of tort law.[17]

In 1972, the California Supreme Court ruled that manufacturers were responsible for making products safe for any "reasonably foreseeable use," replacing the 1965 standard of "intended use."[18] In other words, if a chair was made with the intention that someone would sit in it, but instead a particular customer decided to stand on it, causing it to break, the chair manufacturer could be held liable for any injuries suffered, on the grounds that the company should have anticipated the possibility of the chair being treated in such a fashion. Once individuals are assumed to be powerless to learn about the products they buy, the range of uses which can be called reasonably forseeable, particularly in retrospect, is immense. A product that is safe for a wide range of uses might still be ruled "defective" if it fails to perform safely even when used in doing things for which it had not been designed.

In one instance, a manufacturer was held liable for damages because of a failure to warn purchasers of special "baseball sunglasses" that if a baseball struck them going at full force, they could crack.[19] In 1980, a court ruled that a pajama manufacturer should pay damages for not having done more to make pajamas flame-resistant. The court cited the small percentage of research and development funds devoted to flammability as evidence that the company was at fault for "not reducing (the) danger to a fairly acceptable level."[20]

However, since tort law, unlike regulation, has no quantitative standards, how can a company make decisions about an acceptable level of danger? Would three times as much money spent on R&D have been sufficient? When the definition of "fairly acceptable" is up to a court to decide, especially after the fact, a manufacturer is hard pressed to prove how much research on flammability is enough (and at what cost to other research).

Moreover, foreseeability is also problematic. In retrospect, everything is foreseeable. The most improbable occurrences look inevitable from the future. What historians can do for past events, good plaintiffs' lawyers can replicate for accidents. And any company too callous or careless to foresee the inevitable certainly deserves to compensate the victims of the accidents it has caused!

Planning to Fail: The Crashworthiness Doctrine

Auto manufacturers are liable if a defect in the car they made causes an accident that otherwise could not have occurred.[21] Under the doctrine of simple negligence, only defects attributed to manufacturer fault implied liability. With the advent of strict liability, however, the presence of any defect, even if the manufacturer used proper care, entails liability. In 1968, a new burden was added, and now cars must provide maximum protection for their occupants during and after an accident. Damage that could have been avoided with a different design is called "enhanced injury," and triggers liability for the manufacturer.[22] The seminal case for "crashworthiness" suits was *Larsen v. General Motors Corporation*.[23] Larsen was injured in a head-on collision. He sued GM on the grounds that his steering wheel mechanism was pushed rearward at impact, causing greater damage than would normally occur. Though the Court of Appeals noted that, "Automobiles are not made for the purpose of colliding with each other," it stated also that since collisions are "a frequent and inevitable contingency of normal automobile use," injuries are "readily foreseeable as an incident to the normal and expected use of an automobile." The manufacturer is therefore under duty "to use reasonable care in the design of its vehicle to avoid subjecting the user to an unreasonable risk of injury in the event of a collision."[24] The Court therefore ruled that GM owed Larsen compensation for the injuries he suffered due to the "defective" steering wheel.

In 1980, the standard of crashworthiness was applied in the case of *Dawson v. Chrysler Corporation*.[25] Dawson was driving his police car when it went out of control, struck a steel pole at a 45° angle, and literally wrapped itself around the pole. Dawson, who became a quadriplegic as a result of the accident, sued Chrysler on the grounds that a stronger frame would have prevented the pole from piercing the car. Expert witnesses for the plaintiff argued that a continuous side frame and a cross member would have been sufficient to protect the driver during the accident. Experts for the defendant countered that in most accidents deformation of the vehicle body is desirable because it absorbs the impact of the crash, allowing slower deceleration for occupants. If Chrysler were to adopt the reforms suggested by the plaintiff's witnesses, then in another accident case it could be liable for precisely the opposite reason—that the frame had not been flexible enough. Nonetheless, the jury demanded that Chrysler pay Dawson $2 million in damages. An Appeals Court upheld the jury's decision, despite noting that a different jury could plausibly have concluded that the design used was the safest possible.[26]

A problem with crashworthiness cases is that juries focus on only one part of the automobile, and under only one set of circumstances. Since cars can strike or be struck from any angle, at varying speeds, it is extremely difficult to design a car that affords optimal protection in all types of accidents. In one case, expert witnesses testified that injury was enhanced because a seat was anchored and failed to give way. In a different case, experts argued that failure to anchor a seat had led to greater injuries.[27] Perhaps both were right in the specific instance, but the impossibility of predicting what kind of accident a particular car will be involved in makes a manufacturer wrong no matter what choice he makes. Using hindsight, and focusing on the performance of one part of a car that crashed a certain way, juries can find liability for almost any injury. Despite the insistence of judges that they are not expecting manufacturers to build an accident-proof car, the separate decisions of juries cumulate to exactly that effect.

A study was conducted to determine what the implications would be of a car designed to prevent serious injury in a variety of accidents, including straight-on collisions of up to 50 mph.[28] The Experimental Safety Vehicles (ESVs) would have to weigh 4,900 pounds, compared to 3,000 pounds for the heaviest cars now on the road. They would wreak so much damage in collisions with smaller cars that the national death toll would actually climb for several years, until all small cars had been replaced.[29] As Samuel Peltzman has demonstrated from a study of accident records in Sweden, people driving these cars also might well be more reckless since they would feel safer. This could be disastrous for pedestrians, cyclists, and people driving smaller cars. Peltzman's data shows fewer and less serious injuries to those in heavier cars but more frequent and more serious damage to pedestrians. Hazard has, in effect, been displaced from drivers (and passengers) to pedestrians. Since the ESVs would undoubtedly be more expensive, moreover, consumers would be loath to replace existing cars.[30]

One rationale for products liability is that producers of unsafe goods should be forced to internalize the cost of the hazards they inflict on society. Companies will compensate people hurt by their products, and the costs will in turn be spread to all customers. Fewer dangerous products will be purchased, and people will be safer. This analysis ignores the fact that society does not compensate companies for every life their products have saved. Penalizing them for every life that is lost thus creates a disincentive to accept small risks that reduce larger risks. If the company should pay, say, $1 million for every life lost, then they should be paid the same per life saved; but they are not. This asymmetry is clear in the vaccine industry. If companies must limit themselves to designing products that are not only risk-reducing for most people but also risk-free for all, then the incentive to reduce already existing risks through trial and error will diminish sharply.

Of course, we do not claim that companies ought to be compensated for the lives their products save. Our argument is that a standard of negligence is preferable to one of strict liability; for when it is necessary to prove negligence, this imbalance between penalties for lives lost without rewards for lives saved would not exist.

From Contributory Negligence to Deep Pockets

At the end of the 1960s and the beginning of the 1970s, most states modified negligence law to make it still easier for injured parties to win compensation. Two types of new laws emerged. In states where the "Wisconsin rule" is in effect, plaintiffs whose share of fault is determined by a jury to be less than 50 percent may collect damages. The judge or jury divides up fault among the various parties to an injury, and also rules on how much compensation the plaintiff should receive. That award is reduced by the percentage of the fault which lies with the plaintiff. If a cyclist is held to share 20 percent of the fault for an accident and the motorist who injured him 80 percent, and if the award is $1 million, then the driver, or more likely his insurance company, must pay $800,000.

Under a "pure" comparative-negligence standard, anyone who contributed in any way to the occurrence of an accident can be sued and, if found liable, must pay based on contributory percentage of the fault. A landowner who fails to follow an ordinance requiring shrubs to be cut back and is ruled 1 percent at fault for an accident that might have been avoided were it not for diminished visibility must pay 1 percent of the damages—which, in a $1 million case, amounts to $10,000. Pure comparative negligence was given a substantial boost when the California Supreme Court adopted it in

1975, at the same time eliminating the use of contributory negligence as a defense (*Li vs. Yellow Cab Company*). Defendants in personal-injury cases could no longer point out the plaintiff's fault so as to avoid paying damages. Relative fault mattered only in determining how much the defendant would have to pay. The consequences of weakening if not abandoning the principle of contributory negligence have been profound, opening up an entirely new class of suits by people whose accidents are largely their own fault.

With the advent of comparative negligence, it became necessary to inquire into the percentage of fault of each party to an injury. Formerly, juries had to assume that each defendant was equally liable, since no means existed to distinguish degrees of fault. Whereas formerly an actor minimally involved in an accident might be left out of the suit, on the grounds that his responsibility could not fairly be held equal to the others, now everyone could be sued in accordance to his share of fault. More important, the new law allowed an accident victim to sue for damages even from an injury caused largely by his own negligence. Hence, plaintiffs have a special incentive to sue "deep pockets" (corporations or municipalities that are capable of paying large sums of money), for if they are found at fault to any degree, such organizations can be held responsible for the entire costs.

Through the first half of the twentieth century, governments had immunity from civil suits, even if they were guilty of negligence. State courts whittled away at that doctrine starting in the 1950s,[31] and a major Supreme Court ruling in 1961 led to the end of governmental immunity.[32] Now municipalities are the hardest hit by "deep pocket" suits, since almost every accident that takes place is at least partially attributable to some condition over which some city had jurisdiction. Municipally-maintained roads could have been wider, or flatter, or banked, or better lit, or straighter. Since no road is accident-proof, no municipality is suit-proof. The duty of a city to abate public nuisances even further extends the city's liability. The right to cut down bushes or trees on private property if required by the public interest can become the obligation to do so in order to improve safety. In short, any condition can be said to be the fault of the city and, even if the fault is small, the potential liability is for the entire payment.

The League of California Cities cites several examples of applications of the "deep pocket" principle. An eleven-year-old boy riding his bicycle was struck by a car, after brake failure caused the cyclist to lose control and to cross into a lane of oncoming traffic. The city of Los Angeles was named as a defendant because a bush on private property was alleged to have prevented the boy and the driver from seeing each other. Since the city had an easement on the land allowing it to widen the street, the jury ruled that it was at fault for not requiring the property owner to cut the bush. Los

Angeles had to pay $1.7 million of a $2.5 million verdict.[33] An injured motorcyclist sued the City of Signal Hill after being caught between two colliding cars. The jury's determination was that the road was not wide enough, and the city was forced to pay $1.5 million.[34]

These cases are unusual in that they were decided in court. Most municipalities prefer to make generous settlements outside of court in order to avoid higher legal fees and the possibility that the jury will award greater compensation out of sympathy for the victim. A case in the City of Escondido illustrates the pressure on cities to negotiate: A motorcyclist proceeded incautiously into an intersection, where he was struck by a car that had the right of way. The motorcyclist's lawyer sued Escondido for $3 million, contending that although his client was partly at fault for not yielding at a stop sign, the other driver had been speeding, and also that the city had negligently built a retaining wall that obstructed the cyclist's vision. The driver, whose insurance was limited to $50,000, quickly settled his claim rather than risking a trial. The city was then faced with the remaining claim. In effect, with the driver no longer a party to the dispute, if the city went to court it would assume his degree of fault (minus $50,000) in addition to its own. Under the "good faith" settlement law, the cyclist could no longer sue the driver, since their agreement had ended any claims between them. The city had no way to force the driver to be a codefendant. If Escondido wanted to make the driver pay his fair share, the city would have to assume the entire payment to the cyclist, and then sue the driver in a separate case. Very likely, Escondido would have lost the case, on the grounds that it was in a better position to pay; even if the city won, collection would be problematic because the driver had little means of paying beyond his exhausted insurance policy. Facing the $3 million lawsuit alone (actually $2.95 million, since the driver's settlement accounted for $.05 million), the city chose to settle out of court by paying $1.1 million.[35]

Large cities like New York or Los Angeles can self-insure, setting aside a certain portion of their budget to be used for paying compensation. Small and medium-sized cities are less fortunate. They need liability insurance, since losing a single suit can mean shelling out a sum substantially greater than their revenue. Insurance companies, watching their bills outstrip their income from premiums, have begun raising rates and canceling policies. Actuarial tables can predict roughly how many accidents will occur, but divining how judges and juries will behave is an undiscovered art form. Fearing the worst, insurers raise rates according to a best guess of what the year will bring. Or, unwilling to assess risk without information, they refuse entirely to sell insurance. As a consequence, many municipalities have found their rates soaring in the last year; some, unable to afford policies, must gamble on self-insurance or even consider disincorporation. Lodi,

California saw its rates go up 405 percent, from $48,900 to $247,000 in a single year. San Rafael fared better, as its premium climbed only 238 percent. The 14 cities in Contra Costa County, which insure jointly, were hit by a price increase of 372 percent.[36] Tehama, California's smallest municipality, found that its insurance costs, formerly one-fifth of annual expenditures, have now risen to the point where they might consume the entire town budget, forcing the town council to decide whether it should cut vital services, raise taxes drastically, or disincorporate.[37]

Insurance, Anticipation, and Safety

Plaintiffs' lawyers, whose contingency fees are generally one-third of the settlement figure, defend deep pocket suits on the grounds of compensation—injured people need and deserve financial help—as well as on the grounds of forcing municipalities to improve safety. For deterrence to work, however, there must be a way to avoid punishment that is within the city's means. If purifying the water, maintaining a road system relatively free of potholes, and fielding a fire department capable of responding to most emergencies is sufficient to keep municipalities free from massive liability payments, a city is usually able to fulfill these obligations. But when any far-fetched kind of fault is enough to make a city liable—the narrowness of roads and the height of bushes on private property being considered evidence of such wrongdoing—who can eliminate every condition leading to liability? A wise city councilman might vote against all spending to improve safety, knowing that the joint and several liability doctrine—a party that is deemed even minimally at fault must pay the entire settlement if the party mostly at fault lacks the resources to do so—makes any degree of fault the equivalent of the whole thing.

Particularly perverse in this respect is the rising cost of liability insurance, which takes money out of town budgets whether or not their safety records are poor. Insurance companies set rates on the assumption that towns, unlike motorists, cannot take a few simple steps that will drastically reduce their liability. Any town can be struck with a major suit, regardless of its past "clean" record. It is a good bet that most towns whose rates are being driven up have never paid a penny in a liability case. Enough cities have been struck, however, to make insurance companies raise rates for all. Higher insurance premiums, of course, reduce the amount of money available to vital town functions: police, fire, water, sewage disposal. Hence, the need to pay a premium to cover accidents for which the city is not genuinely at fault might paradoxically result in decreased safety, as municipalities cut budgets for accident-preventing measures. Insurance is anticipatory, with a pessimistic twist. Instead of using resources to combat known or suspected dangers, you use them to prepare for the new known quantity—the failure to avoid liability. Total safety is reduced in the name of deterring unsafe behavior. When large sums are paid for small degrees of fault, the connection between future action and safety consequences becomes attenuated. In Oakland, California, for instance, a motorist was paralyzed after being hit by an uninsured driver on a poorly lit street. The city settled out of court for $2 million, even though it considered itself at most only 10 percent at fault. Why did Oakland not go to court? The city attorney cited the expense of litigation—involving such exotic specialists as an engineering photographer, a cartographer, a physicist, and an economist—as well as the fear of a huge jury award. But would the city, then, in the interests of safety, change the lighting at the intersection where the accident occurred? No, the city attorney explained, "We'd be spending money to kingdom come to remove such a small degree of liability from every intersection."[38]

Empirical evidence of trends in tort law is hard to come by. Legal scholars are interested in doctrines that emerge from cases, not in the data grubbing necessary to establish rates, frequencies, dimensions, and other attributes of quantitative analysis. Fortunately, Mark A. Peterson and Audrey Chin of the Rand Corporation have come up with the first rigorous test of awards under contemporary tort law. Their study of winners and losers and compensation for injury in more than 9,000 jury trials took place in Cook County, Chicago, Illinois, between 1975 and 1979.[39] As the *Rand Research Review* sums up the two studies,

> A typical serious injury suit might be that of a 35-year-old white man who falls down a stairway and fractures his leg in several places. He has substantial medical expenses, misses work for six months and winds up with a permanently fused knee. Depending upon whom he sues, he gets a markedly different result. If he sues an individual and wins, a Cook County jury is likely to award him $37,000, but if he sues the government and wins, he is likely to get $98,000. If he sues a corporation and wins, the jury is likely to award him $161,000.[40]

No doubt the availability of resources ("deep pockets") makes a difference.

Regulation

Before discussing the impact on safety that many of the changes in tort law have had, it is useful to consider what advantages it is supposed to have over regulation, the rival means of assuring safety. Tort law is deemed superior to regulation because it punishes only conduct that actually leads to injury. Individuals and corporations are free to innovate so long as their behavior does not harm others. Being more knowledgeable about the specific circumstances of their actions, individuals and particular corporations supposedly can distinguish safe and unsafe better than could a regulatory commission. Fear of liability, goes the argument, causes them to avoid being negligent about safety, while allowing them to continue trying to provide consumers with cheaper, safer, and more useful products and services. Regulation, because it deals with the general rather than with the particular, necessarily results in forbidding some actions that might be beneficial. Regulators cannot devise specifications sufficiently broad to serve as guidelines for every contingency without also limiting some actions that might increase safety. Because regulation is anticipatory, regulators frequently guess wrong about which things are dangerous; therefore, they compensate by blanket prohibitions. Hence, they run afoul of the axiom of connectedness by throwing out the baby of benefits with the bathwater of hazard.

Juries in civil trials can consider all of the facts of a particular case, since they make their rulings after an accident has occurred. Regulators must try to make rulings in advance, ignorant of what the specific circumstances will be. Thus, actors subject to civil law can act flexibly, knowing that if they vary from the commonly accepted practice, they need fear punishment only if an accident occurs. Even then they will have the opportunity to convince a judge and jury that there was good reason for their behavior. Subjects of regulation must act within constraints which might not be well-tailored to their situation.

When a negligence standard was the dominant rule, tort law did encourage strategies of resilience. Decision making was decentralized, and actors were not required to anticipate every possible danger. Liability resulted only from failure to anticipate and prevent dangers that could have been reasonably foreseen. Resources were saved that could be used to reduce damage from accidents that did occur.

Safety Consequences

Four trends have produced disincentives to risk reduction, causing anticipation to replace resilience, and tort law to acquire some of the worst features of regulation.

(1) Strict liability standards, particularly for design defects, have caused juries to avoid balancing smaller risks against larger risks. Actions or decisions that mean accepting a minor risk to avoid a major one can nonetheless lead to liability. Court decisions that find against vaccine manufacturers exhibit this unbalancing act; these decisions work to increase net risk by providing disincentives to innovation, going so far as to threaten con-

tinuance of current risk-reducing immunization programs. Under a negligence standard, a court considering this situation would not impose liability because vaccine manufacturers are using a high level of care and are saving far more lives than they lose.

(2) Acting under uncertainty, regulators tend to make requirements too restrictive for fear of making a mistake that would implicate them directly in an accident. Their prime obligation is rarely to reduce already existing risks. Regulators are not to blame for those. Because accountability for them means preventing future risks, an incentive pattern arises that favors the status quo. For example, the law of personal injury may look very different if the people being sued are not "fat cats" with "deep pockets," but social workers assigned to deal with cases of child abuse. As always, a few instances of gross neglect or abuse of authority do crop up. For the largest part, however, social workers are caught up in balancing suspected abuse against family solidarity. As suits have begun to proliferate, then, social workers feel compelled to take defensive action: under "great pressure to take no chances"—meaning that they "take children from their parents whenever they might be criticized for not doing so"—caught between the devil and the deep blue sea, social workers now are being countersued by parents. Although the intent of the tort law undoubtedly was not to bias government toward breaking up families, that is exactly what has come about by the burden of proof being put on defendants. Now some social workers have organized a campaign to convince judges that a decision made in good faith to leave children with their families ought not be penalized.[41]

(3) Changes in tort law have forced needless anticipation, even under conditions of high certainty. When doctors or inventors consider how they can defend themselves in court, they will tend to prescribe too many tests, or add on too many safety features. Their decisions must be made with reference to what a jury can be made to believe, rather than what is actually safest. Where everyone is held to the highest standard in the industry, the innovator has to make sure that no expert witness could point to some available safety feature that he missed. Where the range of common practice is wide, a jury intent on compensation might easily be persuaded that the optimal practice was the very one that such an innovator had failed to undertake. Over-ordering medical tests reduces safety by sapping and diverting resources. And for products, safety devices raise costs, thus making many products unaffordable to lower income people who do without or continue to use older, less safe substitutes.

(4) The movement toward strict liability has tended to keep new products or services off the market. When a defendant who has acted on as much information as possible can still be held liable because of new de-

velopments revealed only years later (through trial and error), then the incentive to innovate is reduced. Companies are forced to act as regulators, avoiding any product that might cause direct harm and ignoring or discounting tangible safety benefits that might accompany the innovation. Under the old negligence standard, some additional risk might result from innovations that do turn out to do more harm than good. The majority, however, would be products that, while not risk-free (what is?), might increase risk for a limited group while decreasing it overall. The axiom of connectedness tells us that good and bad, safe and unsafe, cannot be wholly segregated from each other.

A byproduct of large liability awards is that people who want a product that is considerably better for them than existing alternatives may not be able to get it. When the Dalkon Shield, an intrauterine birth-control device, turned out to have adverse effects, manufacturers of related products found they could no longer get insurance. An immediate result is that research suffers. "If there are no insured investigators," Henry Garelnick (a biomedical engineer affiliated with the National Institute of Health and Child Development, which does research on contraception) told Frank James, "we just can't do the studies." Another consequence is that IUDs have largely gone off the market, thus penalizing women who need and want something other than the pill, sponge, and condom, and who are willing to accept the small danger of their opportunity.[42]

Economics as applied to liability law needs major revision. The current wisdom regarding accidents is that liability should be assigned to the party who is able to avoid the accident at least cost. Such liability assignments are believed to enhance efficiency because the cost to society of attaining a given level of safety is minimized. From this perspective, it may be appropriate to find a ballpark owner liable for injuries sustained by a patron, to find a city liable for not lighting an intersection where an accident occurred, and in general to support all of the judicial decisions that this chapter calls into question. The least-cost approach, like all economics, however, depends on often unacknowledged social understandings. One of these is that torts have been concerned with finding who is at fault, not with redistribution of income. Once that social understanding changes, the economic principle becomes perverse converting a mechanism of resilience into one of anticipation. When everyone is trying to minimize costs, it makes sense to let those who know how to do something best tackle the job. When the desire shifts to making "deep pockets" pay, however, principles of economizing end up by supporting uneconomic purposes.

Let us put the point another way: when the original emphasis on resilience was replaced by insistence on anticipation, tort law ceased to promote safety. Instead of searching for safety by finding actual cases of harm reasonably related to negligence, tort law tried to become smart ahead of time by defining damage as negligence. Once blame was assumed, all that remained was to find someone nearby who could pay. Unfortunately, changing the standard presumption from innocence to guilt did not provide instruction on what could be done, other than impoverishing oneself, to improve safety. By locating the richer rather than the responsible party, the connection between prevention and safety was lost.

In this roundabout way, we have come to see that the tort law was never just a mechanism for resilient response. It enhanced safety not only because it reacted to realized harms, but also because it produced preventive measures proportioned to real responsibility. The secret of the tort law was that in proportioning the punishment to the crime, it created a viable balance between a good deal of resilience and a lot less anticipation. Yet these anticipatory-cum-preventive measures did yeoman's duty because the costs were so strategically placed as to yield a large stream of future benefits. By making the tort law mostly anticipatory, huge expenditures have reaped minimal safety benefits, advantages so small they are undoubtedly overwhelmed by decreases due to declines in the standard of living.

Limiting ourselves thus far to four studies in widely varying contexts—nonhuman life forms, regulation of nuclear power plants, the law of personal injuries, and the human body—has enabled us to explore in some depth the viability of various strategies for securing safety. Balancing anticipation with resilience appears to work well; relying on anticipation alone has severe defects. In the next chapter, I go on to review a much broader array of efforts to improve safety that have instead increased harm. By categorizing these defects, I hope to come closer to proposing a more promising set of principles.

SECTION III:
PRINCIPLES

9

Why Less is More:
A Taxonomy of Error

William R. Havender and Aaron Wildavsky

No Paradox, No Progress[1]

*A standup comic on a Mississippi River boat:
"When my father heard that three-quarters of all
accidents occur within 25 miles of home, he moved."*

The United States was startled in 1985 by a spy case involving Navy personnel that was widely described as "the most serious since the Rosenbergs," possibly compromising the security of what hitherto had been regarded as the most secure of the three legs of strategic deterrence, the U.S. nuclear submarine fleet. The spy ring had been in operation for nearly two decades and was finally cracked not by the superior sleuthing of U.S. intelligence, but only when the embittered former wife of the ringleader spilled the beans to the FBI.

Given the elaborate efforts by the military to shield its most sensitive secrets against release to the enemy through its document classification and security clearance system, how could such a serious breach of security have gone undetected for such a long time? According to an account in *Newsweek*,[2] it was precisely *because* of the elaborateness of these efforts. The deliberate effort to sequester every piece of potentially sensitive information had caused so many documents to be classified unnecessarily—the Pentagon creates 16 million new classified items each year, and estimates of the total number of classified documents in government, defense, and related industries reach into the trillions—that huge numbers of people (more than 2.5 million in the Department of Defense alone) had to be given security clearances to handle them. This desire to reduce risk to the

189

vanishing point overloaded the capacity of U.S. security agencies to monitor the loyalty of those involved. According to Federal Bureau of Investigation Director William H. Webster, "If you have too much that is classified and too many people (who) have clearance to see that information...there is a tendency to lower your threshold of sensitivity." In this way, the assiduous effort to reduce as much as possible the chance of important information leaking to an enemy brought about exactly the opposite result: It became impossible to detect such leakage when it was taking place.[3]

Another example of the Gresham's Law of risk—false alarms drive out true ones—comes from experience with the implementation of laws on child abuse. Douglas Besharov reports that:

> Back in 1975, about 35 percent of all reports turned out to be "unfounded," that is to say, they were dismissed after investigation. Now, ten years later, about 65 percent of all reports nationwide prove to be unfounded. This flood of unfounded reports is overloading the system and endangering the children who really are being abused. And the rules and regulations prompted by federal solicitude are a major part of the problem.... [T]hese unfounded reports have created a flood that threatens to inundate the limited resources of child protective agencies. Forced to allocate a substantial portion of their limited resources to unfounded reports, these agencies are increasingly unable to respond promptly and effectively when children are in serious danger. As a result, children in real danger are getting lost in the press of inappropriate cases.[4]

The last two decades have seen an explosive growth in concern about risks to health and physical safety. There has been a metastatic increase in the efforts by government agencies to reduce such risks as much as possible. New bureaucracies have been created or expanded to deal with the risks of foods and drugs (FDA), the environment (EPA), the workplace (OSHA, NIOSH), and consumer products (CPSC). Major new legislation has been passed (TOSCA, RCRA, CERCLA, the Clean Air Act, the Clean Water Act, etc.). Personal injury lawsuits representing billions of dollars in claims have been brought against corporations and governments, a large fraction of them either being won outright by, or else yielding substantial settlements to, defendants. Cities face huge increases in insurance costs. And new scientific doctrines, such as the "one molecule" hypothesis of cancer causation, have been advanced to rationalize a preoccupation with what are often very small risks indeed.

By and large, however, there has been little debate about the desirability and wisdom of this concern with safety. The general consensus has been that everything should be made ever safer, either through direct government regulation or else by means of the deterrent effect of large legal awards in tort actions. The nearly universal assumption, as in nuclear regulation, has been that any number of safety measures do in fact increase safety. Hence, virtually no attention has been paid to the many ways in which the direct effort to reduce identified risks can, perversely, bring about a net increase in those same or other risks. Numerous examples of this paradox—less risk is more—can be cited, and the beginnings of a "taxonomy of risk errors" can now be suggested. We propose six categories of such errors:

(1) Ignoring opportunity benefits, i.e., overlooking those existing risks that will continue unabated by the choice to delay the introduction of new technology that could reduce them.
(2) Ignoring the "safety" risks associated with a proposed remedy.
(3) Ignoring large existing benefits while concentrating on small existing risks.
(4) Ignoring the effects of economic costs on safety.
(5) Ignoring the inevitable tradeoff between errors of commission (Type I) and errors of omission (Type II).
(6) Ignoring the displacement of risks onto other people as a consequence of reducing risks for some.

These categories are not mutually exclusive, and indeed all of them might be viewed as special examples of the same basic error, focusing only on one dimension instead of the multiple interactive dimensions of safety and risk.

Ignoring Opportunity Benefits

Decisions to delay introducing new technologies may be motivated by a fear of new dangers associated with the innovation. But, all too frequently, opportunities to reduce existing risks through innovation are merely ignored, and thus are never properly brought into the balancing of risks and benefits.

A classic instance of opportunity benefits foregone is "drug lag." Here, in the wake of the thalidomide tragedy, FDA required that new drugs be proved "safe" before they could be marketed, a step that has added several years to the approval process of a new drug. While delay does reduce the chance of another thalidomide kind of episode—an unforeseen, serious health hazard resulting from the hasty introduction of a new drug—at the same time it raises risks of another sort, namely, the prolonged illnesses and unnecessary deaths that result from the delayed introduction of new and improved drugs, especially those that after prolonged testing in fact turn out to be safe and efficacious. Drug lag has been extensively documented by Sam Peltzman, William Wardell, and Louis Lasagna, and the conclusion of these researchers is that far more lives are lost from delayed introduction of beneficial new drugs than would be lost even by another tragedy as devastating as thalidomide.[5]

Food irradiation is another instance of foregoing the opportunity to reduce existing health risks because of fears of new technology. This process can be used in place of pesticides for many purposes, such as killing insects in stored grain and certain fruits. Though since the mid-1970s FDA has had radiation for those uses under consideration, it has not yet approved this process. Thus, once again, delay in approving a new technology has led to the continued use of pesticides, some of which (like EDB, methyl bromide, and carbon tetrachloride) show up as carcinogens in animal tests; hence, a potential reduction in carcinogenic risk is not being realized.[6]

Another instance of the error of ignoring opportunity benefits concerns human growth hormone, which has been found to be effective in treating the deficiency known as hypopituitary dwarfism, which affects about 2500 people in the U.S. The sole natural source of this hormone is the human pituitary gland, which must be extracted from cadavers, usually accident victims. In the spring of 1985, however, it was found that three people who had been treated with this natural hormone several years back had died of Creuzfeldt-Jakob disease, a virus infection that leads slowly but irreversibly to mental deterioration and death. It was thought that this virus somehow might have been contaminating the growth hormone preparation given to these patients, and for this reason distribution of the natural hormone was stopped in April 1985.

Now genetic engineering has produced an equivalent hormone. The human gene responsible for this hormone has been introduced into bacteria, and the isolated hormone (since it no longer must be purified from human tissue) lacks the viral contaminant. This artificially produced hormone has been undergoing clinical testing for more than three years, but still has not been approved by FDA, nor has it, as of this writing, received a "compassionate" exemption. The treatment of pituitary dwarves is thus being indefinitely delayed pending approval, even though a virus-free, clinically effective treatment is immediately available.[7]

Similar considerations arise in connection with artificial hearts. FDA approval is needed before a mechanical heart can be implanted in a human. So far, only the Jarvik-7 heart has received this approval, although four other artificial hearts are also being developed. At their present stage of design, these four hearts are intended to keep dying patients alive until a transplantable natural heart becomes available. Even for this limited use, only one of these hearts has received a limited approval for emergencies.

And this despite the fact that patients are dying because they have no means to stay alive while the process of FDA approval grinds on.

Of even greater importance is the delay that slow approval procedures mean for development of these hearts. The technology is far too new for anyone to say yet which of the several hearts being developed will turn out to be the most reliable and cause the fewest side effects. Indeed, the question of possible side effects is of extreme importance; results already obtained with the Jarvik-7 suggest that one unresolved and grave problem is the formation of microscopic blood clots by the mechanical action of the heart. If these clots accumulate in the brain, lungs, or kidneys, the result can be strokes, lung failure, or kidney failure, any of which could be fatal. Clearly, improvement in the details of design of these hearts—the materials, the nature of the pumping action, the nature of the heart/blood vessel junctions—will be needed to overcome this flaw. The only way to evaluate the relative success of these various mechanical hearts will be by means of further implants in people for whom the only alternative is rapid death. But with FDA approval currently going to a mere handful of implantations, using only one design of heart, it will be a long and slow process to analyze and solve problems caused by clots as well as other, currently undiscerned difficulties. Tens of thousands of patients die of heart disease every month (heart disease is the chief cause of death in the U.S.), so that each month's delay in the ultimate development of a truly practical, implantable heart means that patients will die unnecessarily who might have been saved had a heart been available sooner.[8]

It is not merely regulatory agencies, however, that generate delay in adopting new technology and thus retard the reduction of existing risks. Jeremy Rifkin, a private citizen, has successfully brought suit against the National Institutes of Health to overturn their approval of the first experimental test in the open environment of a genetically-engineered organism. The organism in question is a bacterium that grows on the surface of leaves and, in its normal form, carries a protein on its cell surface that seems to serve as a nucleation initiator for ice particles in sudden freezes. That is, the protein promotes the growth of ice crystals, and in this way greatly aggravates frost damage. The genetically-engineered bacteria lack this surface protein; it was hoped that deliberate inoculation of the altered organism would displace the wild ones on a test crop and so protect it from frost damage. Lawsuits by Rifkin and others, only recently rejected, held up the field test pending an environmental impact study—not merely on this particular test, but on all possible future tests involving the release of genetically-engineered organisms.

It is particularly ironic that the only reliable method for determining the impact of the organism on the environment—field testing—has itself been banned until all answers are known in advance—a Catch-22 situation. This, in effect, mandates the ends (complete knowledge of impact) but bans the means (field testing) of discovery. Any resulting impact statement can be only speculative and controversial, and quite rightly labeled "inadequate."

During this time the Florida orange crop has been wiped out by frosts for the last two years running; had this field test not been delayed, we would at least know by now whether this altered bacterium could prevent such losses in the future. So far, public debate had centered exclusively on the possibly harmful effects of releasing inadequately tested, genetically-engineered organisms, and has entirely ignored the substantial damage to society (think of the owners and workers in the orange groves and plant nurseries) that can result when a significant reduction in existing risks is foregone because of the delayed introduction of such advances. As the Florida freezes show, the financial costs alone can easily run in the tens of millions of dollars each winter for this one item alone.[9] These losses translate into lost jobs, reduced income, and failed businesses—factors that themselves, as argued in Chapter 3, reduce health. Crop losses translate into higher prices and shorter supplies for consumers who, particularly if they are poor, will have less fruit in their diets.

Among the experiments held up by the moratorium on genetic engineering is an interesting effort to make crop plants selectively resistant to certain herbicides. Some of the newer herbicides, such as sulfonylureas and imidazolinones, are effective in very small doses—only a few grams per acre are needed, rather than the kilograms per acre required for older herbicides—or else are much less toxic. But, being nonselective (in contrast to such herbicides as 2,4-D or 2,4,5-T), they will kill the desired crop as well as the pests. Both Calgene (a small genetic engineering company in Davis, California) and DuPont have developed genetic engineering methods for making crops selectively resistant to such herbicides, which would allow existing herbicides to be displaced with these environmentally safer ones. Again, no consideration is given to lost opportunity benefits (health benefits delayed or denied) that result from the moratorium.[10]

These examples show that readily realizable opportunity benefits have often been foregone. But, as discussed in Chapter 2, significant benefits of products or processes often do not reveal themselves until they are used. Thus, we have no way of knowing how many important but unanticipated benefits are being thrown away through the fear of new technology and the delay of its introduction.

Ignoring the Risks Associated With a Proposed Remedy

The pesticide DBCP was widely used as a soil fumigant to kill nematodes (a microscopic soil worm that can drastically reduce crop yield), and the successful control of nematodes is vital to the economic viability of growing many kinds of crops in certain areas of the country. DBCP is unique in that it can be used around and between plants without harm to the crop. This selective property is of primary importance in citrus groves and vineyards, since such trees and vines are expected to remain productive for decades. That DBCP could be used around them without harm meant that it could be applied in relatively small doses, repeated as needed. However, when it was discovered that DBCP could cause sterility in unprotected factory workers chronically exposed to high doses, the EPA banned its use. It was replaced by ethylene dibromide (EDB), a substance that could not be used in the vicinity of living plants. EDB, therefore, could be applied only before the crop was planted. To make this preplanting soil treatment effective for long-lived crops, huge amounts had to be used to reduce the nematode population so that it could not recover for at least a decade. This massive application of EDB contaminated the groundwater, showing up in drinking water wells in Florida, Texas, Arizona, and elsewhere. Since EDB is a carcinogen of substantial potency in animal tests, after its water-contaminating properties became known, it, too, was banned by EPA in the fall of 1983 for the purpose of soil fumigation. EDB in turn was replaced by Telone II, which also cannot be used around living plants. Last year, this substance was reported to be a carcinogen, so it, too, faces a likely ban in the near future.

EDB was also the central actor in another recent episode involving fear of cancer: the contamination of grain-derived food products in supermarkets that so exercised the nation at the beginning of 1984. This contamination resulted from a different pesticidal use of EDB, namely, fumigation of stored grain and of milling machinery. EDB was banned in these uses, too, because of the unacceptably large cancer risk it was alleged to pose to the public. Yet some method of insect control in stored grain is essential, because grain-eating insects are ravenous and, if uncontrolled, multiply explosively. EDB has been replaced by methyl bromide, phosphine gas, and a 4:1 mix of carbon tetrachloride and carbon disulfide, the only substances currently registered by EPA for this use. As it happens, none of these has yet passed with a clean bill of health a long-term, high-dose animal cancer test (of the type that it took to reveal EDB's cancer hazard). Methyl bromide and carbon tetrachloride are both carcinogens, carbon disulfide is still under test, and phosphine has never been so tested at all. Consequently, there is no way to know that the public isn't being exposed to a cancer risk from these replacements that is as great or greater than that from EDB.[11]

In the early 1970s, the Consumer Product Safety Commission (CPSC) required children's pajamas to be treated with TRIS, a fire-retardant chemical. A few years later it was discovered that TRIS was highly mutagenic in bacterial tests and hence might be carcinogenic as well. Later animal tests confirmed this suspicion; children who absorbed TRIS through the skin could face an increased risk of cancer. Entirely overlooked when CPSC had made its original decision, the cancer risk was ultimately deemed to outweigh the lives that might be saved from fewer fires, so TRIS was banned from children's sleepwear.

In December 1984, the City of Los Angeles substituted a substance called chloramine for chlorine in the treatment of drinking water. The change was made because chlorine reacted with organic matter in the water to produce a class of compounds called trihalomethanes, some of which (such as chloroform) proved carcinogenic in animal tests. EPA ordered this switch to reduce the theoretical cancer risk, even though not a single case of human cancer in the U.S. has ever been shown to be due to trihalomethanes in drinking water. Then, only seven weeks later, the use of chloramine had to be suspended, because it was found to be causing illness among dialysis patients. Without special treatment, it turned out, the water could not safely be used for this purpose. Nearly twenty patients developed anemia and required blood transfusions.[12]

The decaffeination of coffee was once accomplished by treating whole beans with chemicals such as benzene or chloroform. Both of these, now known to be carcinogens, were replaced by trichloroethylene (TCE), which also turned out to be a carcinogen; TCE has been replaced with methylene chloride. Just this spring, methylene chloride was reported to be a carcinogen. Some coffee manufacturers are now turning to ethyl acetate.

Storage tanks for solvents used in the semiconductor industry in Silicon Valley were required by local municipalities to be placed underground as a fire safety measure when these plants were built in the 1960s. This made it difficult to detect leaks; now solvent residues are showing up in local drinking water supplies.

When a substance is in use, we learn a lot (though, needless to say, not everything) about it. We certainly, for example, get a pragmatic sense of how great (or small) its risks are. Even if it has adverse effects, there is no point in abandoning it unless we are prepared to do without, or know of something better. The lesson we learn is not that chemicals should never be used unless we know about all their future effects but, rather, that continuity is likely to be safer than change because the likelihood is that we know more about the existing substance (since it has been tried) than we do about its replacement (which, in general, has yet to be used for this purpose).

Ignoring Large Existing Benefits While Concentrating on Small Existing Risks

Many times the remedy is worse than the disease. Safety precautions may lower small risks while increasing more major risks.

PCBs were originally used in electrical equipment, such as transformers, because, in addition to excellent electrical properties and low toxicity, they had the advantage of being fire-retardant—a highly useful property where electrical fires are an endemic hazard. PCBs replaced mineral oil, a petroleum derivative that is very flammable indeed. Many municipalities made it a requirement that transformers containing PCBs be installed. Then it was discovered that PCBs could cause cancer in animal tests; PCB-containing electrical equipment is now being banned in city after city. What about the fire hazard problem? Well, mineral oil is making a comeback. Thus, the immediate and real risk from fires is being increased in order to reduce the hypothetical, and in any case long-delayed, risk of cancer (cancer typically has a latency of some two or three decades between exposure to carcinogen and onset of the disease).[13]

For the same reason—fire retardancy—asbestos had long found wide use in building construction. Now that it is known to be a human lung carcinogen, it is being removed from school buildings. Ironically, asbestos is virtually harmless as long as it remains on the walls and is not flaking off and being dispersed as a fine dust that can be inhaled. The very act of stripping asbestos from building walls makes asbestos dust airborne, thereby creating more hazardous conditions than if it were left alone. Moreover, one thereby loses the fire-retardancy of asbestos, so that this risk rises as well.[14]

Whooping cough vaccine causes minor side effects and, in rare cases, severe reactions that can lead to death. The incidence of such deaths is about one or two in 100,000 treated individuals. This chance of severe side effects has led parents to resist having their children vaccinated. One such episode occurred in the United Kingdom in the late 1970s. Parents refused to bring children in for inoculation after publicity about the hazards of the vaccine. The result was a major outbreak of the disease, which has an associated mortality rate in children of about 60 per 100,000 cases. The same thing happened in Sweden, where the government stopped producing the vaccine in 1979 because of safety fears. Then, in 1982 and 1983, Sweden experienced the worst whooping cough epidemic in decades. In

Japan, use of the vaccine dropped because of safety fears, only to be followed by an outbreak that killed at least 40 children.[15]

Ignoring the Effects of Economic Costs on Safety

If wealthier is healthier, then it is important for global resources to be large, growing, and flexible. The Clean Air Act required that all new sources of air pollution (primarily utility plants) had to install the best available technology for reducing sulfur oxide emissions—that is, scrubbers—regardless of whether or not the standard could be met by using low-sulfur fuel. As a result, there was no financial incentive for the utilities to use low-sulfur coal, which was costlier than high-sulfur coal. The use of high-sulfur coal with scrubbers had a perverse consequence, however, for it turns out that scrubbers are unreliable and break down often. During breakdowns, the utility continues to operate and spews out enormous quantities of sulfur oxides into the atmosphere so that, on average, the amount emitted is substantially greater than if standards were being met by means of low-sulfur fuel. The decision to lower the risks of emissions by requiring scrubbers, regardless of the type of fuel used, actually raises those same risks. (To be sure, another motive also was at work in the decision to require scrubbers, namely, the attempt to protect Eastern producers of high-sulfur coal from competition with Western producers of low-sulfur coal).[16] Scrubbers not only are less effective at reducing emissions than is the use of low-sulfur coal, they are also more expensive. Hence, resources that might be put to more efficient use elsewhere are tied up in inefficient pollution controls, effectively lowering the level of global resources that is critical for safety.

Two forms of smoke detectors are currently available in the U.S. One uses a tiny amount of a radioactive element to detect smoke and is called an "ionizing unit." The other uses a photoelectric cell. Ionizing units cost as little as one-fourth as much as photoelectric units, and so are much more commonly used. Yet, because they emit radiation, there is a move afoot to eliminate them as an unnecessary and unacceptable source of cancer risk. Entirely ignored in this thinking is the demand curve for smoke detectors. Quadrupling the cost of having any smoke detector (which would be the result if only the more expensive photoelectric units were available) inevitably will lead substantial numbers of people at the margin to decide to forgo purchasing smoke detectors entirely, or else to buy fewer of them. Since current estimates are that 7,500 lives are lost each year that might have been saved by smoke detectors, the risks associated with having no smoke detectors at all are neither insubstantial nor hypothetical. Opponents of the cheaper ionization unit are trading an immeasurably small cancer risk for a quite significantly larger, and also much more immediate, risk of death and injury from fire.[17] Raising the cost of smoke detectors lowers the buying power of consumers; hence, less wealth means less health. Low-income consumers must either do without smoke detectors or forgo other expenditures that might also increase their safety.

FDA's requirement for testing to establish the efficacy and safety of new drugs does not result only in delaying introduction of new drugs; it also increases substantially the costs of getting new drugs registered. Higher costs mean that it has become increasingly uneconomical to develop drugs for which the potential market is small. Such drugs have been termed "orphan drugs," since no company is willing to sponsor, register, and produce them. One result of the effort to ensure the safety of new drugs, then, was that many drugs for rare conditions were in danger of not being developed at all. In an effort to deal with this problem, in 1983 Congress passed the Orphan Drug Act; this provides federal aid for developing and marketing drugs that otherwise would not be commercially feasible. So far, sixty-one products have been designated orphan drugs under the Act. As with FDA's "compassionate" exemptions for new drugs for AIDS patients, it remains to be seen whether this legislative remedy will prove equal to the problem. To qualify for orphan drug classification, a disease must affect fewer than 200,000 people.[18] Even when the costs of lengthy testing and registration procedures do not prevent drugs from being produced, they still add significantly to the price. This price increase may cause low- and moderate-income consumers to do without beneficial drugs. Higher cost can be a particular problem for the elderly, whose prescription costs are not covered by Medicare.

Ignoring the Inevitable Tradeoff Between Type I (Errors of Commission) and Type II (Errors of Omission)

There is a kind of irreducible statistical uncertainty that limits how safe we can become, namely, the complementary relationship between Type I and Type II errors. An error of commission (Type I) is one that falsely raises an alarm when no hazard exists, and an error of omission (Type II) is one that falsely ignores a hazard that is in fact real. Both kinds of error are well exemplified in the tale of the boy who cried "wolf." His first alarms, being false, were errors of commission, while the failure of the villagers to heed his final alarm—which was valid, since the wolf was indeed there—was an error of omission. The interesting thing about this tale is that it raises in a graphic way the profound question of what sort of decision criteria the boy should have used in order to reduce his Type I errors of commission. His constant cries of "wolf" might well have been born of conscientiousness rather than mischievousness; or, possibly, they could have arisen from his having only limited and uncertain information as a basis for deciding whether a wolf was present—possibly only a tuft of hair on a bush, or a footprint, or a dropping, any of which could have come from a coyote or dog as well as from a wolf. Given this uncertainty, he might well have opted to be "prudent," reasoning that no one would be seriously hurt if his alarm turned out to be false, but that the village would be grievously injured if he failed to raise the alarm when a wolf truly was there. In this situation the boy might have decided to "err on the side of safety," by calling out a warning every time an ambiguous bit of evidence came to his attention. As the tale illustrates, there was an unforeseen catch to this decision strategy: the villagers' inability to distinguish true from false alarms became so great that *all* alarms came to be ignored, with the perverse outcome that a decision strategy chosen purposefully so as to reduce to a minimum the chance of missing a true hazard led instead to an increase in that very risk.

The same problem occurs with the current government regulatory posture toward identifying carcinogens. Enormous scientific uncertainties surround the use of animal tests as surrogates for humans in identifying cancer-causing chemicals. What species and strains best resemble humans in their physiological response to a given carcinogen? What doses should be used? What shape should be assumed for the dose response curve in trying to extrapolate risk down from the experimental doses to human exposure levels? Should an increase in benign tumors or in nonlethal, microscopic tumors be regarded as a carcinogenic response? How should conflicting findings on the same substance in different species (as frequently occurs) be resolved? Scientists have formed no consensus about the answers to any of these questions; and regulators, faced with so many uncertainties, have responded by "prudently" deciding that, if error is inevitable because of unresolvable uncertainties, then it is necessary to "err on the side of safety." In order to avoid missing any true carcinogens, in short, researchers have intentionally biased the decision criteria so as to raise substantially the chance that a suspect substance will be judged to be a carcinogen.

But, like the boy who cried wolf, this kind of conservatism had an unforeseen result. Regulatory agencies were inundated by a flood of "carcinogenic" chemicals in need of regulation, and so identified by means of the biased decision criteria. Such a supercautious attitude has been the genesis of virtually all cancer scares over the past fifteen years.

Roughly half of all chemicals tested in animals under the conservative rules of conducting and interpreting animal tests have turned out positive, i.e., have been judged to be "wolves." Hence, regulatory agencies are

swamped by a huge backlog of chemicals awaiting regulatory consideration. The core problem is that no one can know which of these, if any, are
the chemicals that pose a truly significant risk of cancer and therefore
deserve to be regulated first. Once again, as with the boy crying "wolf,"
valid cancer signals are getting lost among the swarm of signals from trivial
or falsely identified risks, so there is a tremendous loss of *discriminatory
power* inevitably associated with erring "on the side of safety." The result is
that substantial regulatory resources are being expended to reduce risks
that are already trivial, while the public's exposure to carcinogens that
matter is being prolonged.

Noise that screens out valid signals also occurs in laboratory tests given
to preoperative hospital patients. A series of blood tests is routinely admin-
istered to surgical patients whether or not there is a clinical indication of a
need for the tests. A recent study of 2,000 patients by researchers at the
University of California in San Francisco found only four cases where
abnormalities were indicated by the preoperative blood tests, and these
were in fact simply overlooked in the operating room. "One of the consequences of routinely ordering tests," says Dr. Cohen, one of the researchers, "is physicians don't think to read the results. If you order too
much, you might miss things you would really care about."[19]

This same principle can be seen in the case involving naval security with
which this chapter opened. Deciding to "err on the side of safety," that is,
on the side of overclassifying documents, made it necessary to give so
many people security clearances that it became impossible to investigate
them adequately, and especially to do follow-up checks on their loyalty. In
this way, a breach of security now admitted to be of enormous impact went
undetected for some 20 years.

Ignoring Risk Displacement

The Clean Air Act mandated uniform maximal pollution standards
across the country, specifically ruling out exemptions from the national
standards for the localities immediately adjacent to power plants. These
"hot spots" were, of course, the prime source of such pollutants. The solution? Disperse pollutants over a wide area by means of smokestacks a
thousand or more feet in height. Dispersal did succeed in bringing local
pollution levels into compliance with the mandate—but only by causing
the offending substances too be wafted away by the prevailing winds to
come down elsewhere, perhaps in the form of acid rain.[20]

Under the "Superfund" legislation, EPA is supposed to clean up toxic
waste sites. If other measures fail, EPA is obligated to truck the wastes to
secure disposal sites where escape of toxicants into the environment is

supposed to be impossible. Unfortunately, no one knows how to construct a site that is truly secure. "Of the [EPA disposal] sites looked at carefully, all are leaking," said William Myers, an EPA hydrologist, in the spring of 1985. Thus, in "an elaborate shell game" (as Rob Wyden, an Oregon congressman, calls it), we are spending millions of dollars to truck hazardous wastes from one insecure site to another.[21]

It takes labor to produce equipment or undertake the measures needed to make things safe for the public, and workers themselves run risks in carrying out such tasks. In this way there is a redistribution of risk from the general public to the workers—imposed risks that may be substantial. The EDB episode supplies a particular instance. Only methyl bromide, phosphine gas, and the 4:1 mixture of carbon disulfide and carbon tetrachloride are currently approved by EPA for use as substitutes for EDB in fumigating grain. Both phosphine and methyl bromide are more poisonous than EDB; in fact, all uses of phosphine are classified by the EPA as "restricted" (meaning that only certified applicators may work with it), as are most uses of methyl bromide. In contrast, none of EDB's uses in grain and fruit fumigation were restricted. Worker accident records with methyl bromide and phosphine are substantially worse than those for EDB. Methyl bromide is particularly insidious because, while lacking an odor at normal work concentrations that could warn a worker when a leak inadvertently occurs, it can cause lasting, central-nervous-system damage. In contrast, EDB smells. Phosphine, for its part, is highly flammable (both methyl bromide and EDB are flame-retardant), and so care must be taken when it is used in situations where grain dust, itself highly explosive, is commonly present.

EDB also has the right mixture of gaseousness and toxicity to make possible a unique mode of fumigating milling machinery called "spot," i.e., local, fumigation. A few gallons could be injected through special ports directly into the machines, and concentrations toxic to insects would be reached before the gas dissipated. Both methyl bromide and phosphine are much more volatile than EDB, and, if used in the spot mode, would dissipate before the insects had been killed. These substances can be effective, according to the EPA, only when the whole mill building is closed off and fumigated, a procedure requiring hundreds of gallons of fumigant. Obviously, the risks of exposure to workers are substantially larger.[22]

The patterns of unanticipated consequences covered in this chapter, from loss of opportunity benefits to displacement of dangers, suggest a madness in the method. Our categories of errors have in common placing inordinate emphasis upon anticipatory measures to the neglect of resilience. Ignoring the trade-offs between errors of omission and errors of commission, prevention is preferred to learning from experience. The error, in both categories, is to focus inordinately on the dangers of new things and not enough on the risks of doing without them. Demanding that costs be compensated, but that benefits not be weighed in the balance, goes contrary to the axiom of connectedness, i.e., that desirable and undesirable safety effects come from the same substance or activity. Companies discover that the inadvertent harm they do is valued more negatively than the good they provide is valued positively. This disparity is seen in the vaccine problem: for every life saved, a company should accept, say, a dollar in profit, while for every life lost, it should pay $1 million. Inability to get credit for improving safety, as we have seen in the law of torts, makes insurance far more expensive than it would otherwise be.

Now we know what not to do: increase anticipatory measures. What, acting positively, can we do to increase resilience so as to improve safety?

10

The Secret of Safety Lies in Danger

Hotspur was right. It is out of the nettle, danger, that we pluck the flower, safety.

—Peter Huber[1]

No available evidence about safety and danger is likely to resolve current disputes about the consequences for life of new technology. Aside from the lack of sufficient knowledge, the main reason is that these conflicts are largely social, not scientific. Supporting one's vision of the good life is bound to matter more than evidence that can hardly be compelling. Indeed, as philosophers of science tell us, it is people who must consent to validate facts, a social-cum-political process in which the rules scientists have evolved for what counts as evidence do play a part, but not necessarily (when social differences run deep) a conclusive part. Since perceptions of what is safe and what is dangerous also imply judgments about the societal institutions that produce these goods and bads, perception is partly a political act.

As a political scientist, I am always aware that questions about the distribution of dangers to different groups, and not only the sum total of damage, are at stake. If there are changes in perception of who gains and loses, there are also likely to be changes in willingness to assume risks. As Douglas Easterling recently wrote me in commenting on a draft manuscript:

> This is one area where my thinking is beginning to change. I think most of the public is under the impression that innovations benefit society in a disproportionate manner: those who implement the activity stand to gain the most, whereas those with the least political power and knowledge will undoubtedly bear the brunt of the costs. In other words, the reader may buy your argument that some individuals will suffer if society as a whole is to prosper (obviously, some individuals suffer regardless of whether a program is tried or not); however, technological "advance" poses the appearance of a *non-random* allocation of risk and benefit. Some members of society (those already with a

disproportionate share of the resources) are seen as able to target specific subgroups who will be exposed to risks (we site dumps where we expect the least resistance).

On the other hand, I have a feeling that those who stand to gain the most are also in a position to suffer the most. The innovators expose themselves to lawsuits (at least under current legal interpretation, as you point out). In addition, they may also expose themselves to health risks as great as those assumed by the unsuspecting. Comments we received in our survey of muta-genesis researchers indicate that *management* working in high-risk factories suffer just as much damage to themselves and their families as do laborers. Management may have more knowledge about the risks than does labor, but it does not have all the knowledge it needs; such are the inherent equities of trial and error—we *all* learn as we go.

"The poor" have apparently replaced liberty as an excuse for excess regulation. It is said that the poor, being less well protected, suffer more from risk. No doubt; richer, to be sure, is safer. One reason for wishing to raise standards of living is that people of low income generally have worse health. But by the same token, poor people have more to gain from prog-ress. Stopping wherever we are now, pulling up the ladder, while some of us are ahead, does not seem to me a doctrine in aid of social mobility. Of course, systematic harm imposed upon the most defenseless people in society should be a cause for concern. The question is whether help or harm results from a risk-averse or risk-taking posture. I am not aware that the health and safety of the poor is notably better in less technological societies.

In our book on *Risk and Culture,* Mary Douglas and I related varying ways of life (or cultures—shared values justifying social practices—as we call them) to differing perceptions of risk as part of the processes by which people seek to hold each other accountable for what goes wrong. Thus we had no difficulty in accommodating those who see disputes about what is deemed risky as struggles for power, or who view the acceptability of risks as a social, that is, a profoundly human, not merely technical, subject.

We do not berate ordinary people for failing to adopt the same sense of rationality as do the scientists who accuse laymen of ignorance or bias. A limitation of the study of risk perception, however, is that it may appear (wrongly) to dispose of the subject by reducing differing views to their social context, as if the facts did not matter at all. Facts do matter, even if they are not all that matters; but more important is the theoretical frame that makes the available facts more or less persuasive. The questions we ask, our attention-directing and information-rejecting frameworks, help determine the answer we seek.

Should we look upon safety as something we already know how to achieve, aiming directly at it by central command? Or should we view safety as something largely unknown, aiming at its achievement indirectly through a decentralized process of discovery? Should we weigh the safe against the dangerous, seeking more of the good and less of the bad, or should we focus only on avoiding or reducing harm? In one way, my message has been absurdly simple: because risks are inherently mixed with benefits in life, they should be balanced by the safety they can provide. Merely considering the potential health-giving effects of things that also may do harm would make a big difference in risk assessment. To say it another way, I have proposed a more complex (because indirect) understanding of safety as a search process. Here I would like to summarize these views and spell out their implications for the way—if a safer society is our common objective—we ought to think and act about risk and safety.

Safety is a Balancing Act

Nature does not take a Hippocratic Oath: Do no harm. Looking to the world of nature—the human body, animals, insects, plants—we find strategies not based on choosing the wholly benign but, rather, on balancing the safe and the dangerous. Trial and error, not the prevention of trials if they seem to contain the possibility of error, is the norm. Paul Milvy explains that:

> A large proportion of goods and services could not be produced if the one-in-a-million standard considered acceptable for the entire society were also to be applied to those discrete and very small populations that are uniquely at risk. Were we not to exceed the level of exposures implied by this level of risk, to cite a few examples, cooks could not cook (benzo(a)pyrene and other "indoor" carcinogens), roads could not be paved (hot asphalt and products of incomplete combustion), dentists could not x-ray (x-rays), anesthesiologists could not anesthetise (halothane), and stone masons (thorium), plumbers (lead, fumes), painters (solvents, epoxies), carpenters (wood dusts), and farmers (UV from sunlight) could not work. Whole industries would cease to function (e.g., steel, chromium, nickel, trucking, agriculture, and woodworking). Other industries and other economic activities would probably adjust to the strict risk guidelines: production would fall and/or prices would rise. The very nature of specialization in an industrial society implies that the constraints on individual risk and the risk to small discrete groups must be relaxed from the more stringent safety requirements applicable to society at large.[2]

But someone will get hurt. Assuredly. For if the axiom of connectedness holds, there is no way to choose so as to do no harm: the safety we seek is bound up in the danger that accompanies it.

The only way to avoid harming any one is to harm everyone. Consider the food we eat. Eliminating every substance that has harm in it would eliminate most if not all food.[3] How could any plant life have passed through the process of evolution without developing poisons to ward off predators? And how can we eat a sufficiently balanced diet without ingesting part of these poisons? The damage from such toxins has to be balanced against the nutrients we need.

Instead of contesting the contrary-to-fact position that health has declined along with the rise of technology, I consider a more reasonable argument—life is not as safe as it could be if unsafe things were regulated. No doubt, improvement is possible. But the assumptions required to accomplish this through anticipatory regulation are impossible to meet. The first such assumption is that the safety benefits of trial and error would be maintained while only its harms would be eliminated. While the desire to pick the eyes out of the potato of life is understandable, it is not achievable. For a second assumption requires that society, acting through government, can know in advance the difference between actions that will increase or decrease safety, and can allow the good to go on while stopping the bad. Since society cannot thus predict, and government is unlikely so to act, harm will be done to more people by preventing actions that might have made life somewhat safer.

The implications of viewing safety as a process rather than as a condition are profound. Evolution, for example, does not guarantee optimization. According to Darwin, sources of variation produce alternatives that are then tested through competition. Only if all of the best possible variations are produced and tried, Herbert Simon argues, would it be possible to say that anything like a global maximum had been achieved. Inability to attain or even specify what a maximum ecological condition would be like leads to what might be called the paradox of improvement without optimization: though we do not know exactly what we are looking for, nor could we tell when we have found it, the process of search can make things better. In defense of this position, Simon states that:

> One important kind of evidence that evolution does not lead to optimization and stability was introduced by Darwin himself, although he introduced it for a very different reason. He referred to the many known instances in which an alien species, introduced into a new island or continent, has run riot thanks to its superior fitness in the new environment and has eliminated native species. He took these instances to be evidence—as they are—of the power of the forces of natural selection. They are equally evidence of the nonoptimal and nonequilibrium state of the world of evolving organisms. If, for example, the North American biota had reached an optimum of fitness prior to the introduction of the English sparrow, the sparrow could not have found a niche. Its invention, as it were, would have been anticipated.

The success of introduced species, then, is strong evidence for the incompleteness of the evolutionary generator and the consequent inability of the system to reach an optimum. In a relative sense, the *fitter* survive, but there is no reason to suppose that they are the *fittest* in any absolute sense, or that we can even define what we mean by maximum fitness.[4]

Because there is no stable optimum, there is always room for improvement in safety through the generation and testing of new combinations. What Simon says of the evolutionary process, I would apply to the safety process: there is no fixed destination, "only a process of searching and ameliorating. Searching is the end."[5] Indeed, if search is stopped or significantly slowed (as in much anticipatory behavior), the level of safety already achieved could well decline.

Safety Degrades, *or*, The Godfather Knows Best

Life could be both safer and more dangerous than it is. There is room at the top and at the bottom. Therefore, constant effort is required to keep safety from deteriorating and to take advantage of as yet unknown opportunities for improvement. Just as there are risks from new trials of products, so there are opportunity benefits to be lost by having failed to do things that might have reduced existing harms.

Safety degrades; it, too, has a half-life. Why can't we take for granted whatever level of safety that has been attained? Because unless safety is continuously reaccomplished, it will decline, though this may not be known until it is too late. When we speak of having achieved some degree of safety—assuming that we know what we are talking about—we are referring to some level of well-being under certain conditions not all of which can be specified, if only because they have not yet occurred.

Safety is relative; being safer than we used to be, the historical standard, does not mean necessarily being as safe as we might be. There are always alternative arrangements that over a range of conditions might make us better off. For this reason I have paid particular attention to the benefits that might have been gained had opportunities been taken to reduce existing harms—ones that, knowing no better, we take for granted.

In the fullness of time, however, new dangers arise. Yet our alertness declines precisely because of past successes. Recently, for instance, the Prime Minister of Sweden (I write this in Uppsala) was shot on a Stockholm street while returning from a movie with his wife and son. It is not so much that precautions were not taken, for Swedes may well prefer to run some risks rather than live with armed guards, but rather that the police failed to take "obvious" measures, such as shutting off exits from the city after the deed had been done, that has excited negative comment. Since such a terrible thing had not occurred for several centuries, it is understandable that the reflexes acquired by police forces elsewhere, where public figures make constant targets, had been dulled in Sweden. But that is exactly the point.

No doubt the Stockholm police might have tried the equivalent of fire drills by imagining that their public servants would be under attack. Such exercises tend to become pro forma. They are inconvenient, perhaps costly. Officials may object to being followed or restricted in their movements. Worse still, the test is likely to differ in critical ways from the reality. That is why, while recognizing the limited utility of preparing for "expected surprises," I have regarded such "fire drills" as offering insufficient protection.

For another kind of advice in avoiding and/or coping with surprise, let us turn to an expert. In Mario Puzo's novel, the Godfather explains why he works so hard at doing favors, though he expects no immediate return, nor necessarily any return at all. The Godfather wishes to have others beholden to him in diverse and unspecified ways precisely because he knows that he won't know in advance who he will need or when or for what purpose. Hostages to a precarious future, these random credits increase the odds that when the Godfather needs something he can't do for himself, there will be a coffin maker-cum-tailor-tinker-soldier who will be obligated to do it for him. A social ecologist, the Godfather is fulfilling his need for resilience.

From the literature on ecology we learn that organisms well adapted to a narrow niche thrive so long as favorable circumstances continue. When the environment suddenly changes, however, such organisms may be wiped out or subject to catastrophic loss. Organisms that are more frequently perturbed do less well in any single environmental band but can survive in a number of bands. The resilience they gain from constantly coping with adversity diminishes the kinds of episodes they find surprising and also enables them to bounce back when systemic shocks occur.

Yet it is doubtful whether most human organizations would willingly expose themselves to shocks. Their tendency is to reduce, not increase, uncertainty. When Ronald Heiner argues that animals follow simpler, instinctive, even imprinted strategies to compensate for living in an environment of relatively greater uncertainty, we can take his point: regularity in human affairs stems from efforts to mitigate uncertainties.[6] Risk aversion is the normal condition of organizational life. The question is: Should society reinforce this tendency?

In an essay on "The Self-Evaluating Organization,"[7] I sought to explain why organizations ordinarily do not subject themselves to continuous change in pursuit of solutions to the latest studies that tell them they are falling short of previously announced objectives. For one thing, such studies may well be mistaken. For another, the instability created by perpetual change may render the organization incapable or less capable of performing essential tasks. Departing from past practice opens organizations up to the unanticipated consequence of new moves. Hence, they are reluctant to change. Since risk aversion is the normal state of most hierarchical organizations, I ask, why should we reinforce this hesitance to adapt in the name of safety?

Now we come to the nub of the matter: safety decays because products and practices that once were helpful become harmful under altered circumstances. Nor do we need to look far for examples. Conservation practices have much to commend them. How were we to know, however, when reacting to the known evils of huge oil price increases and polluting effects of burning coal, that making our houses more energy efficient through extensive insulation would also increase the danger of radon (internal radiation)?

Nor need we limit our observations to technology. The movement to decrease child abuse is aimed at an acknowledged evil; no one, so far as I know, defends beating children. Yet the intrusion of government into family life does have negative effects. Were it possible to optimize child welfare by limiting intervention to only the most egregious cases, all would be well. But it isn't. Public authorities are faced with the usual problem of what kind of error to make—allowing parents to go on abusing children because there is some doubt, or resolving all but the most clear-cut cases in favor of removing the child from its family. Since children are hurt by such separation (especially when it is unjustified), and since alternative living arrangements could well be worse, the choice is not easy.[8]

There is also another possible source of harm to which thinking about risk has made me more sensitive than I otherwise would be. Because child abuse also has been linked to sexual exploitation, not only parents but everyone else who comes into contact with children on a regular basis—teachers, group leaders, family friends—have become aware that overt displays of affection may be misinterpreted and may subject them to severe sanction. Hence, there has been (or so I think from observation) a shrinking from spontaneous display. How do we compare the severe harm prevented when a relatively few children are shielded from abuse, with the smaller harm (but critical deprivation) done to much larger numbers of children cut off from the warmth of benign physical contact?

One good way to keep safety from deteriorating is to arrange random perturbations that will either improve the situation through the discovery of something better, or will teach us how to bounce back faster. All this is accomplished, need I say, by decentralizing processes of trial and error, and it is accomplished, moreover, in an incremental and hence more manageable manner. Such a strategy is by no means perfect. Some harm comes of it. But the overall result of increasing resilience is not only maintenance but steady improvement in safety.

We must have been doing something right because, since the Industrial Revolution, human safety has constantly improved. Whether out of preference for progress or because it came anyway, our artifacts, processes, and organizations have been subject to competition. At the minimum, continuous and haphazard change has kept our existing mechanisms alert. The level of safety has been maintained by the need to cope with a stream of small surprises. While the "creative destruction" of which Joseph Schumpeter wrote[9] has sometimes gone awry, as with the too early abandonment of streetcars in certain major cities, it has prevented complacency. At the same time as this progress produced more unanticipated as well as desired change, it also created even more general global resources to clean up after itself. (After all, Superfund is itself funded by a tax on industry profits.) Resilience has outpaced risk.

Health is Not the Only Kind of Safety

It is easy to see that protecting people in one way may result in harming them in others. All of us, for example, benefit from federal deposit insurance. We are made more secure by knowing that our savings, up to a considerable amount, are protected against bank failure. The negative side of this protection, however, is the increasing difficulty in finding constituencies whose interest it is to keep banks from taking excessive risks. The increasing rate of bank failures, which is harmful to society, is one of the prices we pay for enhancing the security of depositors.

Our interest in protecting identifiable human beings from grave harm, to take another relevant example, has understandably led to an interest in hostages held by terrorists. Yet we are coming to understand that giving money or arms or otherwise acceding to terrorists' demands encourages terrorists to harm a larger number of people.

It is more difficult to see that the kind of safety discussed in this book—the damage versus the improvement to individual health stemming from technology—may be achieved at the expense of other values and, therefore, other senses of safety people hold dear. Improvements in personal health could be achieved at the expense of liberty, although a trip to the Gulag is not usually recommended for such a purpose. Risk aversion may put democracies at a disadvantage to dictatorships. Persuaded as I am that health is not heaven and that, indeed, there may be a "safe" way to a variety of hells, I can plead only that the subject undertaken here, while it by no means exhausts the subject of safety, is sufficient for a single volume.

The wealth that is related to human health may have a devastating impact on other valued aspects of human life. To the extent that "safe" is "soft," the survival training that comes with living amidst harsher circumstances may better fit societies for adversity. Whether the decline of societies has something to do with moral rot stemming from material indulgence has been a subject of much inconclusive speculation, but there may be truth to it.

Without going into the murky waters of hypotheses about decadence, there are undoubtedly important social factors in the development of resilience. Though I hope to have shown the importance of general resources, like knowledge and wealth, the willingness and ability to deploy them may well be a function of different types of social relations. Technology is no one-way street. It can hurt as well as help. Imagine the social upheavals stemming from easily available technologies to choose the gender of children during conception and the consequent disruption of the basic statistical foundation of all human societies, the moral consequences of human cloning, and similar possibilities. Concentrating as it does on physical health, this book necessarily omits much that is relevant both to technology and to human life.

Turning back to the relationship between technology and human health, the nagging feeling that there are more dangers around nowadays may be a product of misplaced nostalgia. Though cars may pollute more than other forms of transportation, they are a lot cleaner and safer than horses. True, there are more dangerous objects about, like autos and toxic chemicals, but the very same things help make us safer in new ways, with something left over. And that something increases resilience because the extra resources can be used for diverse purposes. The process increases alertness and the product increases resilience. Whatever it is that has made us safer than our predecessors must be understood if we are to try to do better—or, not mistakenly to do worse by eliminating that which has helped us.

But What About the Future?

Though my approach has the virtue of attempting to explain what actually has occurred, namely, immense improvement in safety, the past and present cannot guarantee the future. The admitted gains of the last 200 years might have been purchased at the cost of future losses in safety. If the universe is running down, if the ozone layer is being permanently depleted, if cancer-causing chemicals (whose full effect may not be known for many years) spread throughout the environment, or if irreplaceable resources are being lost, so that no amount of ingenuity will replace them, our global position will decline and, with it, at least some of the gains in life expectancy and reduction of disease and injury.

"The most crucial knowledge of all," Kenneth Boulding asserts (in a passage with which I would like to associate myself), "leads to the release of resources for the pursuit of knowledge." He sees knowledge as central because it does not behave like most other commodities, in that it is not consumed by use. On the contrary, this "peculiar commodity"—created, exchanged, priced, yet apparently inexhaustible—can expand through use. For, as Boulding goes on to say, "Its first peculiarity is that it does not obey the law of conservation.... When a teacher teaches class, at the end of the hour the pupils know more and the teacher truly knows more too."[10] That another's use need not diminish my own may explain why there appears to be an ever-increasing fund upon which to draw: "This self-multiplicative property of knowledge, by which it serves to transgress the fundamental law of conservation, may be the base explanation, not only of phenomena like economic development, but even of the whole evolutionary process."[11]

When the average age at death is low, Boulding argues, a large part of society's resources go just to replacing the lost knowledge. As life expectancy grows, say, from thirty to sixty years, and the proportion in the population of fifteen-year olds doubles, more time and energy are available for increasing the store of knowledge. The less the energy expended merely in keeping a society alive, the more is available for change, "for every increase in knowledge permits the release of resources to develop a further increase in knowledge."[12] Knowledge increases wealth and wealth releases resources to gain knowledge, the one generalizable resource enhancing the other.

Suppose there are limits to resources, including human ingenuity, so that at some point global resources would be fixed. Would a different set of safety strategies then be desirable? For the most part, I think the answer is "no." Even if it is not possible for the level of global resources to increase indefinitely, it is still possible for it to shrink. With less wealth, knowledge, and the rest, there will be poorer health. Hence, it will still be necessary to search for the combinations of resources that would maintain the level of global resources. It will still be necessary to calculate the adverse effects of safety measures on global resources and to keep them as small as possible. Trial and error will still be preferable to trial without error because society will be in still greater need of opportunity benefits.

As the world population grows, the specter of mass starvation is often cited as a sign of resource depletion. Yet world production of food per capita keeps rising. New knowlege keeps pushing forward the frontiers of agricultural productivity. Dennis Avery provides us with a convenient list:

The first genetically engineered vaccines. One prevents a major form of malaria, the other is the first fully safe weapon against foot-and-mouth disease. Both vaccines are made from the protein coatings of the disease organism, which triggers the immune reaction without risk of infection.

The first viral insecticide, which attacks only the *Heliothis* genus of insects (corn earworm, tomato hornworm, tobacco budworm, soybean podworm). The spores of the virus remain in the field after the worms have been killed, and attack any succeeding generations.

A weed, *Stylosanthes capitata*, turned into a high-yielding forage legume for the huge acid savannas of Latin America. The plant outyields the best previous forage crops in the region by 25 percent.

Isoacids, a new class of feed additives for dairy cows. They increase bacterial action and protein synthesis in bovine stomachs, raising milk production or reducing feed requirements. The product is already being test-marketed.

Embryo transplant operations to boost the genetic impact of top-quality dairy cows. The cows are given fertility drugs to induce multiple ovulation, and the fertilized eggs are then transplanted into the ovaries of average cows for gestation. The supercow can thus produce dozens of calves per year instead of just one. Thousands of such operations are now being performed each year.

Short-season hybrids that have extended corn production 250 miles nearer to the earth's poles in the past decade. The grain is now being grown as far north as central Manitoba. East Germany has developed a corn hybrid and plans to shift its hog feed from imported shelled corn to a domestically produced mix of corn and cobs.

The first practical hybrids for wheat, rice, and cotton. Hybrid alfalfa and rapeseed are at the field test stage. Triticale has recently outyielded the best wheats under difficult conditions, such as cool temperatures and acid soils.[13]

So far, everyone who predicted declining or only stable agricultural productivity has been proved wrong. Even the more reasonable prediction, that agriculture would face sharp discontinuities with which it would not be able to cope, has not yet come true. So far, knowledge has overcome adversity. More than that cannot be said.[14]

Different models of resource growth and depletion are held by people Cotgrove evocatively labels "cornucopians" and "catastrophists." Cornucopians view resources as manipulable by mankind; they expect mankind's creativity to make the world a continuously richer and, therefore, a safer place. Catastrophists see danger lurking in depletion of nonrenewable resources as well as in ignorant assaults upon the natural environment of whose interconnections we know little. Unless we mend our ways, catastrophists envisage ecological disasters deeply damaging to human life.[15] These views, as Cotgrove demonstrates, are rooted in rival conceptions of desirable social relations—catastrophists rejecting capitalism, and therefore predicting doom, cornucopians accepting capitalism, and therefore exuding optimism. Now this book is not about subjective preferences for ways of life, but rather about the objective consequences of different strategies for securing safety. How, then, based on evidence that can draw only on past and present, can we decide which theory of the future is likely to be most accurate?

Of course, nature cannot speak for itself; we impose our prejudices and preferences upon it. I am no different. I count myself a modified cornucopian in regard to the consequences of technological progress for human safety: life can get safer, but presently unsuspected threats to human safety may well occur. Starting from this point—no guarantees against massive surprise—what can be said about the rival strategies for securing safety?

We are not without guidance. The uncertainty principle tells us that the consequences of and interactions among past and present acts must, to a great degree, remain unknown. Hence surprise—not merely a change in the quantity but also in the quality of events, a change that is genuinely unexpected—is a real possibility. Being alert to the advantages of surprise and being capable of coping with it after it occurs are prime requisites. These requirements enhance the desirability of accumulating general, global resources that can be diverted to emergency uses. The importance for safety of convertible resources gives a new dimension to processes that create and expand wealth: these aid in the search for safety by maintaining a redundancy of means and a varied repertoire of responses to unpleasant surprises.

To the question—how can the present generation justify taking risks that impose hazards on future populations?—I reply: since danger is ever-present, any action on our part will inevitably leave the future less safe than it would have been had we discovered even better ways of doing things. Insofar as we today should consider the welfare of future generations, our duty lies not in leaving them exactly the social and environmental life we think they ought to have, but rather in making it possible for them to inherit a climate of open choices—that is, in leaving behind a larger level of general, global resources to be redirected as they, not we, will see fit.

Since safety is a discovery process, and the rule of risk applies to that process, the parts of the system being considered must vary if the whole is to be stabilized. To the extent that various parts can stabilize themselves, the whole, when faced with disturbances, will become more unstable. If the safety of the whole is to be given priority, therefore—that is, if the individuals that make up the whole are to have a chance to improve their safety—risks must be shared. This denial of risk shedding is not equivalent to the sacrifice of the individual to the collective. The overall level of safety depends on each part doing its share of risk taking.

Rights or Special Interests

When one hears, as the reader has throughout this book, that individuals must take chances if the safety of society is to improve, it may appear that individual rights are being sacrificed on the altar of public welfare. This charge is plausible but misguided. To the contrary, the consequences of chosen actions must be considered part of their moral merits. Hence, if the thesis argued here is roughly correct—no safety without risk—nearly the reverse is true: rejection of risk would lessen the ability of most individuals to carry out their plans. Fortunately, I myself do not have to make up an argument about rights and risks because this has already been done elegantly by Christopher H. Schroeder.[16] Elementary considerations of equity, writes Professor Schroeder, appear to make it "delightfully self-evident" that since individuals have rights, no one ought to be able to invade them.[17] Should an act be such that a particular individual would, with near certainty, be harmed, courts may grant injunctions against it. Suppose, however, as usually happens, that such a person belongs to a much larger group or society whose chances may be adversely affected by acts justified in the name of some greater good. This understandable conjecture of events, which leaves potential sufferers at the mercy of claims by others, has led, Schroeder observes, to "the anxiety to preserve some fundamental place for the individual that cannot be overrun by larger social considerations...."[18] A fine idea. Finding and defending such a place is the problem.

Theorists in the rights tradition wish to carve out criteria of risk prevention "defined independently of the benefits flowing from risk creation."[19] They want to abandon utilitarian notions of comparing costs and benefits so as to establish that there are certain things one cannot do to some individuals no matter how many others would receive how much benefit. This idea—"nonconsensual risks are violations of 'individual entitlements to personal security and autonomy'"[20]—has widespread appeal. But what about the rights of the other members of society?

The law of large numbers makes it "virtually certain" that many feared harms will eventually overtake someone who has not directly consented to them. Why not, then, if the contemplated harm is serious, stop the action through law rather than wait for it to occur? Schroeder replies that:

> When carried to its logical extreme, this argument can raise questions about even very ordinary actions. Many, perhaps all, common actions generate

some risk of serious harm to others. Driving a car down the street might lead to a fatal third-party accident; mowing a lawn might kick up a rock that kills a neighbor; pushing a child on a swing might result in another child's death if the swing clips the back of his head. As individual acts, these are common, but somewhat risky actions. When they are amalgamated into a set of like actions, the set becomes virtually certain to produce the feared harm. Once one begins thinking this way...every risky action that *might* be an action that really will cause harm becomes a candidate for regulation.[21]

Although Schroeder wants to preserve a strong sphere of individual autonomy, he demonstrates (to my satisfaction, at least) that, of the major theorists in the rights tradition (he discusses Ronald Dworkin, Richard Epstein, Charles Fried, and John Rawls), "none support government protection of rights against risks regardless of the adverse consequences."[22]

We would all agree, presumably, "that there must be some actions that are wrong even if social welfare would be increased by them, just because an individual would be wronged by them."[23] Are there, then, criteria of choice that will protect individual rights without having to take into account adverse consequences for others? Not, Schroeder argues, in the usual cases involving risk. One could invoke rights against being affected by a substance that helped many others, but then what happens to their rights not to be hurt against their will? Saying that the basic health of each individual cannot be affected, moreover, "is quite likely to exhaust resources totally, so that according bodily integrity absolute status would virtually threaten to enslave everyone in the service of that single objective."[24] Making the prolongation of human life or some such criterion into the only or overriding objective, besides its authoritarian implications, would become a kind of moral monomania. According to Schroeder,

> Beyond this obsession, such an absolute norm also leads to contradiction. Searching for innocent victims in order to prevent their harm will necessitate action, and any action carries with it some possibilities of injuring someone else. An innocent-victim inspector may hit a pedestrian on his way to an inspection site, or he might trip and fall while snooping around a suspected injury location, knocking into someone else in the process. If the norm truly applies absolutely, the very actions that are required to obey it must be avoided because they also carry the possibility, perhaps the statistical certainty, of violating it. Such a categorical norm is contradictory and incoherent. These difficulties suggest why absolutist systems are greatly preoccupied with drawing a sharp distinction between action and nonaction: to avoid contradiction one needs a safe haven from the absolute demands of the norm, and the realm of nondoing may supply such a haven.[25]

Stopping trials so as to avoid error, we know, may also do much harm even though those who are being hurt may not realize it.

I agree entirely that:

> Some may be moved by these remarks and yet still resist them on the ground it is callous or offensive to announce a principle that authorizes risks to human life and, inevitably, the death of some of those exposed....
>
> But why is such a confession callous or immoral, if it comes as the result of thoughtful and sensitive reflection upon the clash of legitimate values? Implicit in the suggestion that it is may be a mistaken opinion about the necessary structure of moral judgments, namely that the "bottom line" conclusion of any moral claim says all that is morally relevant about the situation.... One can speak of valid moral claims or points of view that, all things considered, have not been found to be sufficiently persuasive to dictate choice, and yet continue to revere such values and both express and experience regret over the necessity that they cannot be totally vindicated because of a conflict with other valid interests and claims. This structure supplies the appropriate way to conceive of the issues that risk regulation raises.[26]

Because the safety we wish to promote and the harm we wish to mitigate are bound together, to talk as if one person's "rights" to safety could be upheld without denigrating the rights of others falsifies most risk situations. Acting as if the two could be clearly separated, so that the individual could claim one part without having to share in the other, I would add, is not establishing what ought to be a "right" but, rather, is an effort to cloak a special interest in the language of rights. Attempting to seize the benefits while refusing to pay the costs is not the usual justification for invoking rights.

I would also like to expand upon Schroeder's assertion that "'do no harm' is an appropriate goal for a system of justice but not an appropriate standard to judge specific behavior.... "[27] In one sense, even this distinction collapses. Were it required that no system of justice could ever miscarry—never imprison the innocent or allow the guilty to go free—there could be no acceptable justice. In the sense that criteria applied to processes and institutions should be different from those for individuals, however, we have a distinction that opens up new horizons for the student of risk. After all, it is not the proclivities of individual scientists on which we rely to reduce elements of personal bias in scientific research but, rather, elaborate institutional devices for regulating competition.[28] "The Republic of Science," as Polanyi calls it in his famous essay,[29] is an example of a system that is more reliable than its parts. It is possible to improve the safety of the system precisely because all of its parts are not required to be equally safe. Granting rights to some people so that others must pay the price of change is not a benevolent act. At a minimum, Schroeder's principle—"a commitment to treat protection from harm associated with candidate rules [criteria of choice] and the adverse consequences of those rules as legitimate, valid interests"[30]—is essential for thinking about safety. As soon as the adverse consequences of rules for securing safety become a legitimate subject of debate, moreover, a strategy of preventing harms from occurring becomes suspect. How, after all, would we know which ones are likely to occur?

Anticipation Versus Resilience Redux

Totally unexpected risks are by no means rare. No one anticipated the disaster of thalidomide, which resulted from the fact that primates have an unusual teratologic sensitivity toward thalidomide undetectable in the standard test species then in use for detecting birth defects—rats, mice, dogs. No one anticipated Legionnaire's disease; and no one could possibly have anticipated the outbreak of AIDS, a form of infectious immune deficiency that had never before been seen in humans. How can society prepare itself to cope with harms whose specific nature is unpredictable and, thus, against which specific defenses cannot be raised in advance? Clearly, some resources must be retained in a sufficiently flexible form to be shifted around and brought to bear wherever needed, once unanticipated harm becomes manifest. Evidently, there is some, as yet unknown, optimal point between sinking resources into specific defenses against particular anticipated risks and retaining resources in a form sufficiently flexible—storable, convertible, malleable—to cope with whatever unanticipated harms might emerge. Too great an advance expenditure of society's resources against known hazards—given that hypothesized hazards are limitless while realized hazards are finite—can therefore increase society's vulnerability to truly unanticipated dangers.

The argument in favor of increasing global resources is strengthened if, as detailed elsewhere in this book, a relation does exist between a society's general level of economic well-being and the damage suffered by members of that society. Resources used up in order to lower hypothetical future risks are thus not available for attaining other social goals, which indirectly may also lower risks. Making a society poorer than it would have been through too great a level of expenditures to reduce hypothesized risks is likely, because of the reduction in wealth, to cause a rise in the overall level of damage from realized risks.

The fact that hypothetical harms are limitless is what makes great expenditures on them dangerous. After the fact, it is easy to say that whatever happened should have been prevented. But it is easy also to forget how many dangers that were predicted never came to pass.

One way to deal with the possibility of unexpected dangers, moreover, is to generate economic growth and technical progress, in the expectation, based on experience, that the accrued benefits will make society less vulnerable to whatever unanticipated risk may crop up.

We are in an enormously more favorable position to deal with AIDS now than we would have been 20 years ago, as an unanticipated consequence of the tremendous progress in molecular biological understanding (particularly in the study of genetics, viruses, and the immune system) that has occurred in this time period. Had the progress of molecular biology been stifled in the 1960s—as it may have been in the 1980s by concern over the creation of new genetic organisms—we would now be at a loss in searching for a cure for AIDS. Once again, a potentially tremendous cost of delaying progress is that knowledge will not have been gained that could have been, knowledge that would make possible an informed, prompt, and effective response to an unforeseen risk.

A strategy of resilience does not mean waiting for a disease to strike before trying to respond to it. Rather, it means preparing for the inevitable—the appearance of a new, surprising disease—by expanding general knowledge and technical facility, and generalized command over resources. Knowledge also grows by responding to diseases as they develop, which knowledge can be used in unanticipated ways to combat newer threats. Solutions, as well as problems, are difficult to anticipate. Attempting to predict both a disease and its cure is less likely to increase safety than the ability to use generalized and specific knowledge in unexpected ways. If this knowledge were to be sought in a deliberate effort to anticipate particular diseases, a good guess would make the knowledge supremely useful but, far more likely, a bad one would be useless against the unexpected.

There is a role for anticipation, however, a very vital one, namely, protection against risks whose potential for realization is substantial. No one, at least in the West, argued against containment buildings for nuclear power reactors, or advocated turning off all major safety devices. Where risks are highly predictable and verifiable, and remedies are relatively safe, anticipation makes sense; most vaccines fit this criterion of efficient anticipation. Where risks are highly uncertain and speculative, and remedies do harm, however, resilience makes more sense because we cannot know which possible risks will actually become manifest. The risk-averse argument is that there should be fewer experiments (less trial and error). The advice this book gives is to proceed incrementally with trial and error so that society can try out innovations on a small scale, thus enabling it to better sample the unknown and to assess the risks.

Discovering Safety

How should technological danger be treated so as to improve human health and safety? In a global context. It is well to begin by ascertaining whether and to what extent the alleged risk is real. Deciding that there is a potential for danger is just the beginning. The next step is to ask, "Compared to what?" For if the harm is tiny compared to others we already face, we may wish to accept it rather than turn our attention away from others that are probably more dangerous. Since society cannot attend to many things simultaneously, setting too low a threshold on the limits of intervention is likely to strain our capacities so that more serious matters are neglected. Once we consider removing or diminishing a danger, society's representatives should ask whether the remedy might itself be more dangerous. When asked, "How is your husband?" the old joke goes, the woman answers in the Yiddish manner with a question: "Compared to who?" Abolition of a product or practice may lead to the substitution of others even more dangerous. It does not appear to be asking too much to find out whether available substitutes are known to be more healthful: but, as the bans of cyclamates and EDB (among numerous other examples) show, failure to ask this elementary question happens all too often.

Yet the question of benefits—How much good is being done by a dangerous technology?—has not yet been raised. When many more lives or injuries could be saved than lost, a technology that may harm some people may nevertheless be the safest alternative. This is not a deliberate choice to do harm, for harm already is being done. Inaction is a sure strategy for allowing more people to remain hurt who by trial and error would have been helped. The courage to take a chance is the only way—not of playing it safe, for that is impossible—to play it safer.

Still to be answered is the most complex, because the most indirect, question about safety—"Will the danger we know be replaced or displaced by others that are far worse in ways we do not now expect?" Since it is impossible to predict which dangers actually will confront us, it is wise both to probe the environment for clues and to develop a variety of potential responses; this capacity is called resilience. Ultimately, the debate over risk comes down to what is the best response to these unknowable dangers. My vote goes to the resilience that comes from passing many trials and learning from many errors so that (1) the defects of society's limited current imagination are constantly being balanced by continuously larger amounts of local knowledge, and (2) there is growth of general resources that can be converted into meeting future dangers.

Asking a question implies that there ought to be an answer. The optimal amount of risk or safety is.... To expect this sort of an answer, in turn, implies that someone or some government already knows the answer. Safety, in this conception, is not the cumulative result of activities carried on for many societal purposes—pleasure, material gain, aesthetic appreciation, even altruism—but is a condition that presumably can be achieved only by central design. Because it is also presumed that safety is within our grasp, if only government would reach for it, the search for safety is over before it has fairly begun. Whether to take risks is not a useful question, I claim, because there is no choice: both risk taking and risk aversion are potentially dangerous.

Think of the Constitution of the United States. Self-government is a risky enterprise. How were the risks apportioned? Without free institutions dependent upon public support, there could be no self-government. Yet the very existence of central institutions empowered to exert coercive authority over individuals—the crucial difference between the Articles of Confederation and the Constitution—opened up the possibility of abuse. How, then, to rate the risks?

Every institutional actor is considered risky, i.e., prone to abuse. That is why powers are separated. But these powers are shared not merely to prevent abuse; they are also dispersed to encourage innovation in the form of a multiple approach to problems. The framers felt able to anticipate a few major problems, such as war and debasement of the currency. For these they created as strong a central authority as consent of the governed would permit. For the rest, expecting that life would reveal difficulties of which they and their successors might well remain unaware, they dispersed the capacity to consider the unknown as widely as possible. The residual police power to secure the general welfare was left with the states.

The glittering generalities for which the Constitution is famous constitute a rejection of the view that central authority knows best. Otherwise, a long list of specific dangers to be avoided would have been followed by an even longer list of policy prescriptions for avoiding them. Rejecting this, the framers instead set up a House of Representatives based on population, a Senate elected by state legislatures, and a President presumably chosen by local elites with national reputations. These elements were placed in partly cooperative and partly conflicting relationships and then superimposed upon a federal structure so that diverse views of dangers (geographical, social, philosophical) would be considered. It was in the system as a whole, rather than in the sanctity of its parts, that such safety as is given to human beings was thought to reside.[31]

Just as the resilience of their political institutions has served Americans reasonably well in overcoming the vicissitudes of fortune, so would searching for safety by multitudes of individuals give us as good a chance of overcoming adversity as is given to mortal beings. But can we expect government in our time to rely on resilience instead of anticipation?

The Politics of Anticipation

What is the relation among predicting hazards, specialized protections, centralization, and detailed standards—all identified with anticipation? Or among trial and error, general capacities, and decentralization—all identified with resilience? Is there more than one independent dimension? Investing resources to avoid predicted hazards implies using specialized protections, whereas relying on trial and error keeps resources invested in general capacities. But what about centralization?

The governmental bias toward anticipatory measures is monumental. No one gets credit for improvements that take place without him. Everyone is subject to blame for not intervening. Former FDA Commissioner Schmidt describes the reasons FDA tends to err on the side of caution:

> For example, in all of FDA's history, I am unable to find a single instance where a congressional committee investigated the failure of FDA to approve a new drug. But, the times when hearings have been held to criticize our approval of new drugs have been so frequent that we aren't able to count them.... The message to FDA staff could not be clearer. Whenever a controversy over a new drug is resolved by its approval, the agency and the individuals involved likely will be investigated. Whenever such a drug is disapproved, no inquiry will be made. The congressional pressure for our negative action on new drug applications is, therefore, intense.[32]

Central agencies are able to engage in repeated, large-scale anticipatory efforts. They are tempted to do so, moreover, because their experts think they can outguess the future and because their ability to claim credit is tied to visible projects.

When cries of disaster are heard, it is difficult for government to act in a discriminating manner. Thus, William Ruckelshaus, ruminating on his second tour of duty as EPA administrator, observes that nationwide, uniform environmental standards fail to take into account local differences that affect the risk a given level of pollution presents to a population.

> For example, the Clean Air Act requires EPA to impose expensive automobile inspection and maintenance programs in communities where certain pollutant criteria have been exceeded twice a year. EPA must do this even though the violations may be a consequence of the placement of the air-quality monitoring devices and may not reflect the general quality of the air, even though there is no discernible health effect, and even though the people in the community strongly oppose the action. The law does not allow the federal government to distinguish between (for example) Los Angeles and Spokane, Washington, in this regard—a restriction that defies common sense. In the same way, we cannot distinguish between a plant discharging pollutants into a highly stressed river in Connecticut and one discharging into Alaskan waters that bear no other pollutant burden. In other words, the law does not permit us to act sensibly.[33]

Government should be allowed to make mistakes. It does not seem scandalous that the government acted on a judgment, later proved incorrect, that we would be better off drinking saccharine than cyclamate, or that adding TRIS to children's pajamas would make them safer. The scandal occurs when these errors are not corrected, or if they occur so often that the totality of regulation does more harm than good. Why, in sum, can't we have trial and error in regulation?

Whose trials and errors are we talking about? Sweeping regulations, say, efforts to control fluids in all dry cleaning establishments, are not easy to turn on and off; they are not readily reversible. Room for learning is much reduced when one practices on large populations.

Implying that we do not (perhaps cannot) know our destination, the process of searching for safety implies both blind alleys and blunders. The inevitability of blind alleys suggests that society be cautious about putting too many resources into each trial. A market economy does that pretty well. The ubiquity of blunders suggests again that trials be kept small and also that general, global resources be accumulated to cope with the aftereffects. Technological and economic progress—learning how to do more with less—helps provide this capacity for resilient response.

The Fear of Regret[34]

A strategy of anticipation is based on a fear of regret. Rejection of "trial and error" in favor of "trial without error" enables those so disposed to claim that they have done all that conceivably could be done. No errors of omission remain; no catastrophes can be laid at their door.

Once having started on the path of minimizing regret (because one believes that is safer, because one doesn't trust institutions to act appropriately, whatever the reasons), its internal dynamic is self-reinforcing. We can know that no matter how many trials we have run, we can always do more. So we can know that we never have done everything. And if the problem not yet identified lies in the still unexplored residuum, we won't have found it. And if it is a problem that would have made us change our mind about proceeding, had we only known about it, we would then regret we had proceeded. To avoid the possibility of maximum regret, the path is clear: don't allow others to act unless they can prove safety in advance. Ergo, without trials enough is known to enforce prohibitions. The criterion for decision seems evident, for the anticipatory position does imply that avoiding regret is indeed all one cares about. But, after all, every action we take is ripe with varied and numerous opportunities for regret—choosing to get married, choosing to have children, choosing an occupation, or, to make things even, choosing just the opposite or differently.

The hidden anticipatory assumption is that the regrets we knowingly avoid are more worth avoiding than the regrets we implicitly don't know how to avoid or have gotten accustomed to. If we invent a new drug, we may regret the side effects knowingly caused for hundreds of people; if we don't invent it (or market it), we don't have to regret an inaction that led to the death or morbidity of anonymous thousands. The fear of regret rationalizes acts of omission. The adage—out of sight, out of mind—applies particularly well to opportunity benefits.

The attractiveness of avoiding regret is illustrated by the popularity of John Rawls's maximin theory of preferences: not knowing what your future would be like, choose as if you would end up in the worst possible position.[35] The possibility of doing better is here sacrificed on the altar of not doing worse. But the only way not to do worse, I have argued, is to take risks to do better. Otherwise, static arrangements to secure safety will decay: progress is not only necessary to get ahead, it is indispensable to stand still.

Anticipatory strategies, justified by fear of regret, have an outstanding rhetorical advantage: their proponents can claim that they are aiming directly at safety by seeking to prevent expected harm from taking place. Adherents of resilience face a corresponding rhetorical disadvantage: by encouraging risk taking they are apparently opposed to safety, offering mainly indirect capacities to cope with the unexpected. Though neither side can offer guarantees against ultimate catastrophe, the making of direct claims to prevent the worst—malformation or diseases born of genetic engineering, ultraviolet deaths from ozone destruction, poisoning the earth by repeated nuclear meltdowns, epidemics of latent cancers from chemical pollution—appears to give the anticipator a moral upper hand.

In response to this, any talk about trade-offs among risks seems anemic. Accepting certain risks in order to be prepared for uncertain ones appears problematic. The benefits of missed opportunities are just that, missed; as it is said, "you don't miss what you don't know."

Actually, the part played by experience has been misassessed. What we do know is that life has gotten progressively safer as resilience has grown; what remains speculative is whether more uniform and stringent application of anticipatory measures will do any better. Static societies do not look as well as progressive ones when we see—and wonder why—each generation has been safer than its predecessors. Guarding against innovation has not shaped up as a superior strategy to encouraging it.

Societies that rely on the price mechanism in competitive markets, though they have their share of ill health, do far better in the economic growth and, hence, the safety sweepstakes than societies operating on the basis of central command. Where does the crucial difference lie? I have eschewed the argument that market prices quickly come to embody all that is known about the risks of a process or product (e.g., costs rise to cover legal liability) and thus that businesses should be induced to act in a safe manner. Maybe they do and maybe they do not. Evidence on compensation for hazardous occupations is inconclusive.[36] The exact sequence of steps through which safety has been secured, if indeed it has, remains unknown.

Rather than take this direct route—comforting though it might be ("See, I'm traveling the royal road to safety too!")—I have chosen to emphasize the dependence of safety on search. Search is essential because uncertainty is ever present, because the safe and dangerous are intertwined, and because protecting the parts endangers the whole. Thus, safety remains a condition for which we have to search without knowing ahead of time what we will find.

The most dangerous fear is fear of regret, because it restricts this search for safety. Just as breakdowns occur in all sorts of unexpected ways—"The problem," Perrow tells us, "is just something that never occurred to the designers. Next time they will put in an extra alarm and fire suppressor, but who knows, that might just allow three more unexpected interactions among inevitable failures"[37]—so, too, many developments that improve safety have come to do so in ways that were unknown in advance. Trial and error works to increase the resilience that improves safety because it is the most vigorous search procedure in existence. Markets overcome defects to enhance overall safety not because "they" know the answer, but precisely because they don't; convinced that better bargains can always be struck, markets are based on the principle of incessant search. The more decentralized, dispersed, variegated, and, need I add, competitive markets become, the more likely it is that there will be more different kinds of search and, therefore, more safety, especially against the unforeseen.

Searching Versus Scooping: Safety as a Process of Discovery

We used to make fun of the idea that there was gold in the streets of America, and all one had to do was reach down and pick it up. If we treat safety as if it were there for the taking, how much better are our ideas about this?

Since there are no objects or processes wholly safe under all conditions, and since there is always room for improvement, it is crucial to discover better combinations. That is why searching for safety (as distinguished from just picking it up) is so important. What is more, only experience, which may differ from time to time and place to place, may give us genuine insight into the more desirable combinations. For if we do not already know how to combine resources to make life safer, then figuring out how to look for it is a better bet than assuming that all we have to do is scoop it up.

My objection to current discussions of risk and safety is that they are one-sided, focusing almost entirely on the dangers of risk taking while neglecting, to the detriment of our common safety, opportunity benefits that would be lost by risk aversion. Improving safety over time does not depend on the good will or perspicacity of individuals any more than the social benefits of free elections or scientific advance depend on uniformly good motives among the individual participants. On the contrary, safety that improves is a quality of institutions that encourage a search so vigorous that no one can be said either to have designed or controlled it.

Safety is not a hothouse plant that can survive only in a carefully controlled environment. Nor is safety a ripe fruit waiting only to be plucked. (Human history might well have been different, and duller, if Eve had been able to choose between two clearly labeled apples, respectively marked Danger and Safety. Indeed, her presumption of divinity was that she professed to know the difference beforehand.) Safety results from a process of discovery. Attempting to short-circuit this competitive, evolutionary, trial and error process by wishing the end—safety—without providing the means—decentralized search—is bound to be self-defeating. Conceiving of safety without risk is like seeking love without courting the danger of rejection.

Notes

Introduction

1. My view of the subjective aspects of safety conceived as the variable perception of danger is found in Mary Douglas and Aaron Wildavsky, *Risk and Safety* (Berkeley: University of California Press, 1982). On political feasibility, see, inter alia, my *Speaking Truth to Power* (Boston: Little, Brown, 1979; 2nd ed., New Brunswick, NJ: Transaction Press, 1987).
2. E. Sidall, "Risk, Fear and Public Safety," Atomic Energy of Canada Limited, April 1980.
3. In the economic literature, following Frank Knight, risk was used to denote measurable certainty, while uncertainty was nonmeasurable. If one knew the probability of consequences but not the outcome, that was certainty; if one did not even know the probabilities, that was uncertainty. Frank H. Knight, *Risk, Uncertainty and Profit* (Boston/New York: Houghton Mifflin, 1921). Thinking that further distinctions would be helpful, I shall return to kinds and degrees of uncertainty in the chapter on anticipation versus resilience.
4. William D. Rowe, "Evaluation of Risks Involving Rare Events," typescript, nd., p. 3.
5. The four definitions of risk presented by Charles Vlek and Pieter-Jan Stallen reveal the different considerations involved as the scope of the subject increases:

   (1) *'Risk' is the probability of loss.* This definition...implies that possible losses can be distinguished beforehand. It is useful to the extent that probabilities of differing losses can be transformed into probabilities of a standard loss, e.g. the death of one person during one hour of involvement in a risky activity.
   (2) *'Risk' is the size of (credible) loss....* This definition implicitly underlies safety regulations whereby limits are imposed upon the "maximum credible accident."
   (3) *'Risk' is expected loss,* i.e., the product of the probability and the (dis)utility of the possible loss.
   (4) *'Risk' is the variance of the probability distribution* over the utilities of *all* possible consequences.... This definition takes losses *and* gains into account, and it does not require an *a priori* discrimination of desired and undesired consequences.

   I prefer the fourth definition. Charles Vlek and Pieter-Jan Stallen, "Rational and Personal Aspects of Risk," *Acta Psychologica*, vol. 45 (1980), pp. 273-300.
6. Kenneth Boulding, "Irreducible Uncertainties," *Society,* vol. 20, no. 1 (Nov./ Dec. 1982), pp. 15-17.

7. The uncertainty principle in physics contains an echo of the axiom of connectedness. According to Dietrick E. Thomsen:

> As the new quantum mechanics developed, it forced physicists to radical departures from their previous ideas about the nature of things.
> Contrary states of being seemed somehow—could one say hypostatically?—united in the same object. A thing is both a particle and a wave. A particle is something with a well-defined and relatively small extent in space—it is localizable. A wave cannot be localized. In principle it can extend from infinity to infinity. Classical physics can easily answer the question: Where is the planet Jupiter now? Quantum mechanics has no answer to the question: Where is the electron now?
> From this conjunction of opposites follows the so-called uncertainty principle. The physical characteristics of objects come in pairs indissolubly linked together—for example, position and momentum, energy and time. The better you know one member of these pairs, the worse you know the other.

"Going Bohr's Way in Physics," a Symposium Report in *Bulletin* of the American Academy of Arts and Sciences, vol. 39, no. 7 (April 1986), pp. 6-7; reprinted from *Science News,* January 11, 1986.
8. Burton Klein, "The Role of Feedback in a Dynamically Stable Economic System," Social Science Working Paper 305, Calif. Inst. of Technology, Feb. 1980. See also his *Dynamic Economics* (Cambridge, MA: Harvard Univ. Press, 1977).
9. The best moral argument in favor of restricting new, risky things to be done is Leon Kass, *Toward a More Natural Science: Biology and Human Affairs* (New York: Free Press, 1985).
10. Book review by Peter Franken of *Rem Khokhlov* by V.I. Grigoryev, *Science,* vol. 233 (July 11, 1986), p. 232.
11. Ronald A. Heiner, "The Origin of Predictable Behavior," *American Economic Review,* vol. 13, no. 4 (Sept. 1983), pp. 560-595.
12. Stephen Jay Gould, "Darwinism and the Expansion of Evolutionary Theory," *Science,* vol. 216 (April 23, 1982), pp. 380-387.
13. Gerald A. Rosenthal, "The Chemical Defenses of Higher Plants," *Scientific American,* vol. 254, no. 1 (January 1986), pp. 94-99; quote on p. 98.
14. *ibid.*
15. *ibid.*
16. Michael Novak, "Crime and Character," *This World,* no. 14 (Spring/Summer 1986), p. 26.
17. David S. Siscovick, et al., "The Incidence of Primary Cardiac Arrest During Vigorous Exercise," *The New England Journal of Medicine,* vol. 311, no. 14 (October 4, 1984), pp. 874-877. See also an earlier article by Paul D. Thompson, Eric J. Funk, Richard Carleton, and William Q. Sturner, "Incidence of Death During Jogging in Rhode Island from 1975 through 1980," *Journal of the American Medical Association,* vol. 247, no. 18 (May 14, 1982), pp. 2535-2538.

Chapter 1

1. Joseph Morone and Edward Woodhouse, *Averting Catastrophe: Strategies for Regulating Risky Techologies,* typescript, April 1985, p. 230.

2. Charles E. Lindblom, "Who Needs What Social Research for Policy Making?," paper for the New York Education Policy Seminar, Albany, New York, May 1984.

3. David W. Pearce, "The Preconditions for Achieving Consensus in the Context of Technological Risk," Meinolf Dierkes, Sam Edwards, and Rob Coppock, eds., *Technological Risk: Its Perception and Handling in the European Community* (Cambridge, MA: Oelgeschlager, Gunn & Hain, Publishers; and Konigstein/Ts: Berlag Anton Hain, 1980), p. 58.

4. *The Journal of Gas Lighting, Water Supply, and Sanitary Improvement* (November 14, 1865), p. 807.

5. Pearce, "The Preconditions," p. 63.

6. Robert E. Goodin, "No Moral Nukes," *Ethics*, vol. 90 (April 1980), pp. 418-419.

7. Maurice Richter, Jr., *Technology and Social Complexity* (Albany, NY: State University of New York Press, 1982), p. 97.

8. Goodin, "No Moral Nukes," p. 418.

9. *ibid.,* p. 421.

10. Morone and Woodhouse, *Averting Catastrophe*, p. 14.

11. *ibid.,* p. 215.

12. See James Whorton, *Before Silent Spring: Pesticides and Public Health in Pre-DDT America* (Princeton, NJ: Princeton University Press, 1974).

13. R. Shep Melnick, *Regulation and the Courts: The Case of the Clean Air Act* (Washington, DC: The Brookings Institution, 1983).

14. *Inside the Administration,* January 2, 1986.

15. Peter N. Nemetz and Aiden R. Vining, "The Biology-Policy Interface: Theories of Pathogenesis, Benefit Valuation and Public Policy Formation," *Policy Sciences,* vol. 13, no. 2 (April 1981), pp. 125-138; quote on page 137.

16. Efforts have been made to distinguish natural from man-made chemicals on the grounds that we could stop or limit use of the latter while nothing much can be done about the former. True, but not, I think, the most important truth. Sometimes it is suggested that human beings have grown up with natural carcinogens and have thus somehow adjusted to them while this is not true at all or to the same extent of man-made chemicals. Yet no evidence whatsoever exists to show that the body distinguishes differences between the sources of chemicals. Furthermore, were it true, this argument would lead us to expect that rats and mice would not get cancer from natural foods. But, like human beings, rats and mice can get cancer from any number of natural foods. Of course, there could be synergistic effects of two or more chemicals interacting that would increase their potency and hence their danger. So far as is known, however, which is not far, such synergy is as likely to reduce as to increase cancer-causing agents. See Bruce Ames, "Dietary Carcinogens and Anticarcinogens," *Science,* vol. 221, no. 4617 (Sept. 23, 1983), pp. 1256-1264; Edith Efron, *The Apocalyptics* (New York: Simon & Schuster, 1984); and William R. Havender and Kathleen A. Meister, "Does Nature Know Best?," a Report by the American Council on Science and Health, October 1985, pp. 28-30.

17. 29 CFR 1990.144(a) *Federal Register,* January 22, 1980, p. 5287.

18. John Mendeloff, "Overregulation and Underregulation: Standard Setting for Toxic Chemicals," unpublished book manuscript, 1986, p. 24.

19. Jon Elster, "Risk, Uncertainty, and Nuclear Power," *Social Science Information,* vol. 18, no. 3 (1979), pp. 371-400.

20. *ibid.*
21. Jacqueline Verrett and Jean Carper, *Eating May Be Hazardous to Your Health* (Garden City, NY: Anchor/Doubleday, 1975), pp. 148-149, cited in Efron, *The Apocalyptics,* p. 91.
22. Marvin Schneiderman, "Extrapolating Animal and Microbiological Tests to Human," Urban Environment Conference, p. 10, cited in Efron, *The Apocalyptics,* p. 76.
23. See the extensive discussion in *ibid.,* pp. 88-92 and pp. 335-344.
24. *ibid.,* inter alia.
25. See Karl Popper, *The Open Society and Its Enemies* (Princeton, NJ: Princeton Univ. Press, 1971).
26. See Aaron Wildavsky, *The Politics of the Budgetary Process,* 3rd ed. (Boston: Little, Brown, 1979), and M.A.H. Dempster and Aaron Wildavsky, "On Change... or, There is No Magic Size for an Increment," *Political Studies,* vol. 27, no. 3 (Sept. 1979), pp. 371-389. See also Charles E. Lindblom, "The Science of 'Muddling Through'," *Public Administration Review,* vol. 19 (1959), pp. 78-88, and his reservations, "Still Muddling: Not Yet Through," *Public Administration Review,* vol. 6 (1979).
27. See Ian Lustick, "Explaining the Variable Utility of Disjointed Incrementalism: Four Propositions," *American Political Science Review* (June 1980), pp. 342-353.
28. See Aaron Wildavsky, *The Politics of the Budgetary Process* (Boston: Little, Brown and Company, 1964), and David Braybrooke and Charles E. Lindblom, *A Strategy of Decision: Policy Evolution as a Survival Process* (London: The Free Press, 1963).
29. Popper, *The Open Society.*
30. Jack H. Knott, "Incremental Theory and the Regulation of Risk," paper presented to the American Political Science Association Annual Meeting, September 1982, pp. 1-2.
31. *ibid.,* p. 2-3. The work referred to is Martin Landau, "On the Concept of a Self-Correcting Organization," *Public Administration Review,* vol. 33, no. 6 (Nov./Dec. 1973), pp. 533-542.
32. Cf. Martin Landau, *ibid.*; John Steinbrunner, *A Cybernetic Theory of Decision* (Princeton, NJ: Princeton Univ. Press, 1974); James Thompson and Arthur Tuden, "Strategies, Structures, and Processes of Organizational Decision," Thompson, et al., eds., *Comparative Studies in Administration* (Pittsburgh: Univ. of Pittsburgh Press, 1959); and many other works.
33. Knowledge might grow even more by the invention of new and broader hypotheses that then were subjected to screening through results. See Peter Munz, *Our Knowledge of the Growth of Knowledge: Popper or Wittgenstein?* (London: Routledge & Kegan Paul, 1985). But it is not easy to develop new and fruitful hypotheses on command or to subject them to test when avoidance of trial and error is part of public policy.
34. Letter from Lewis Dexter to the author, July 12, 1986.
35. Examples abound. For traditional pollution problems where the effluent is obvious, Talbot Page contends, an incremental approach may well be useful in avoiding overly abrupt changes. "But for environmental risk the process of incremental reaction is not self-correcting. Because of latency, an effect is irreversibly determined before it is clearly observed.... Rather than relying...upon the perception of past failures, adequate control of environmental risks re-

quires institutions that anticipate the risks" (Talbot Page, "A Generic View of Toxic Chemicals and Similar Risks," *Ecology Law Quarterly,* vol. 7, no. 2 (1978), pp. 207-242; quote on p. 242).

Bryan Norton likens incremental choices on the diversity of species to the alcholic's choice of whether to take a single drink. The one drink here is not a small matter but, rather, a prelude to catastrophe. "These arguments imply," he concludes, "that...almost all costs of preserving a species should be considered 'reasonable'...." (Bryan Norton, "On the Inherent Dangers of Undervaluing Species," Working Paper PS-3, Center for Philosophy and Public Policy, Univ. of Maryland, p. 22). On this ground, any act, however small in and of itself, could be prohibited on the grounds that it will hammer the last nail into society's coffin.

36. H.L. Lewis, "Technological Risk," typescript, pp. 23-24.
37. *ibid.,* p. 30.
38. *ibid.*
39. Albert L. Nichols and Richard S. Zeckhauser, "The Dangers of Caution: Conservatism in Assessment and the Mismanagement of Risk," Discussion Paper Series E-85-11, Energy and Environmental Policy Center, John F. Kennedy School of Government, Harvard University, November 1985, pp. 1-3; published as "The Perils of Prudence," *Regulation* (Nov./Dec. 1986), pp. 13-24.
40. *Inside the Administration,* April 24, 1986, p. 4.
41. Nathan Rosenberg, "Learning by Using," Chapter 6, *Inside the Black Box: Technology and Economics* (Cambridge: Cambridge Press, 1982), pp. 121-140.
42. F.A. Hayek, "The Use of Knowledge in Society," *The American Economic Review,* vol. 35, no. 4 (September 1945), pp. 519-530.
43. David Cohen and C.E. Lindblom, *Useable Knowledge* (New Haven, CT: Yale Univ. Press, 1979).
44. Kenneth J. Arrow, "The Economic Implications of Learning by Doing," *Review of Economic Studies,* vol. 29 (June 1962), pp. 155-173.
45. Alvin M. Weinberg, "Nuclear Safety and Public Acceptance," *Nuclear News* (October 1982), pp. 54-58.
46. See Kenneth Arrow, "The Economic Implications of Learning by Doing."
47. Rosenberg, "Learning by Using."
48. *ibid.,* p. 122.
49. *ibid.,* pp. 135-138.
50. *ibid.,* p. 139.
51. Thomas J. Peters, "The Mythology of Innovation, or A Skunkworks Tale, Part I," *The Stanford Magazine,* vol. 11, no. 2 (Summer 1983), pp. 12-21.
52. John Jewkes, David Sawers, and Richard Stillerman, *The Sources of Invention* (New York: St. Martin's Press, 1959).
53. James Utterback, "The Dynamics of Product and Process Innovation in Industry," Christopher T. Hill and James M. Utterback, eds., *Technological Innovation for a Dynamic Economy* (New York: Pergamon Press, 1979), p. 48.
54. Peters, "The Mythology of Innovation, or A Skunkworks Tale, Part II," *The Stanford Magazine,* vol. 11, no. 3 (Fall 1983), pp. 10-19.
55. Eric Von Hippel, *Novel Product Concepts From Lead Users: Segmenting Users by Experience* (Cambridge, MA: Marketing Science Institute, 1984).
56. Leon R. Kass, *Toward a More Natural Science: Biology and Human Affairs* (New York: Free Press, 1985), p. 19 (emphasis in original).
57. Peter Huber, "Exorcists vs. Gatekeepers in Risk Regulation," *Regulation* (Nov./Dec. 1983), pp. 23-32.

58. *ibid.,* pp. 23-24.
59. David Foster, letter to the Editor of *Regulation* (March/April, 1984), p. 2.
60. "Screening systems," Huber continues, "...place the cost of acquiring the information needed for regulation on the regulatee; standard-setting systems place that cost on the agency. This makes all the difference when the product or process targeted for regulation is only marginally profitable. A pesticide manufacturer may have to spend $20 million on tests needed for licensing. Even if a pesticide is completely safe, it will never be submitted for review if the manufacturer stands to make only $19 million from its sale." (Huber, "Exorcists vs. Gatekeepers," pp. 25-26).
61. *ibid.,* p. 26.
62. In this regard, Huber's position comes close to Mancur Olson's thesis that nations decline because existing interest groups receive special privileges. See Mancur Olson, *The Rise and Decline of Nations: Economic Growth, Stagflation and Social Rigidities* (New Haven, CT: Yale Univ. Press, 1982).
63. Huber, "Exorcists vs. Gatekeepers," p. 27.
64. Peter Huber, "The Old-New Division in Risk Regulation," *The Virginia Law Review,* vol. 69, no. 6 (1983), pp. 1025-1107.
65. *ibid.,* p. 1063.
66. Albert O. Hirschman, "The Principle of the Hiding Hand," *The Public Interest,* no. 6 (Winter 1967), pp. 10-23.
67. See any of the recent volumes of *Accident Facts* published by the National Safety Council.
68. Bruce Ames, "Dietary Carcinogens and Anticarcinogens," *Science,* vol. 221, no. 4617 (Sept. 23, 1983), pp. 1256-1264.

Chapter 2

1. Freeman J. Dyson, "The Hidden Cost of Saying NO!," *Bulletin of the Atomic Scientists,* vol. 31, no. 5 (June 1975), p. 24.
2. "Galling Stones: Fill'er Up," *Science News,* vol. 127, no. 7 (Feb. 16, 1985), p. 104.
3. Ralph W.F. Hardy and David J. Glass, "Our Investment: What is at Stake?," *Issues in Science and Technology,* vol. 1, no. 3 (Spring 1985), pp. 69-82.
4. Jeryl Mumpower, "An Analysis of the *de minimus* Strategy for Risk Management," *Risk Analysis,* vol. 6, no. 4 (Dec. 1986), pp. 437-446; quote on p. 442.
5. *ibid.,* pp. 444-445.
6. *ibid.,* p. 444.
7. National Safety Council, *Accident Facts: 1985 Edition* (Chicago: National Safety Council, 1985), p. 21.
8. U.S. Public Health Service, National Center for Health Statistics, *Vital Statistics of the United States, 1980* (Washington, DC: Government Printing Office, 1984), vol. 2, Table 5.5.
9. U.S. Census Bureau, *Statistical Abstract of the United States, 1985 Edition,* (Washington, DC: Government Printing Office, 1985), Table 117, p. 79.
10. *ibid.*
11. *ibid.,* Table 358, p. 205.
12. *ibid.*
13. Center for Disease Control, "Tornado Disaster—Pennsylvania," *Morbidity and Mortality Weekly Report,* vol. 34, nos. 51-52 (Jan. 3, 1986), pp. 765-769.

14. U.S. Census Bureau, *Historical Abstract of the United States,* vol. 2 (Washington, DC: Government Printing Office, 1975), Series J 276-278, p. 448.
15. *World Almanac* (New York: Newspaper Enterprise Association, 1986), p. 689.
16. United Nations Disaster Relief Coordinator, *Disaster Prevention and Mitigation: A Compendium of Current Knowledge* (New York: United Nations, 1977), p. 1.
17. *ibid.,* pp. 108-109.
18. *ibid.,* p. 134.
19. *ibid.,* pp. 178-182.
20. World Health Organization, *World Health Organization Annual* (Geneva, 1985), p. 45.
21. Leonard Safir and William Safire, compilers, *Good Advice* (New York: New York Times Books, 1982), p. 72.
22. Mary Comerio, "Seismic Sanity: Somebody Else's Problem," paper for ASCE-AIA seminar on "Aspects of Seismic Risk in the New Madrid Fault Region," St. Louis, Missouri, Oct. 25-26, 1984.
23. *ibid.,* pp. 5-6.
24. "Even though a serious event such as a report of one death from treating 100,000 patients may reflect only a very low risk, this is regarded as important if the overall use of the drug is very large. In treating two million patients, the total number of deaths would be 20. A figure of this magnitude would put the authorities under pressure to remove the drug because of the general view that public action should be taken on the basis of absolute numbers and not on the basis of relative risk. No one would say that 20 deaths are not important, but I feel that they really should be seen in relation to the two million benefited, otherwise the authorities will remove many drugs carrying a very low risk simply because they are used on a large scale, which in turn is because they are effective and therefore popular among patients and doctors. We will find ourselves obliged to continue to use older remedies which may well be less effective and more dangerous." William H.W. Inman, "Risks in Medical Intervention," M.G. Cooper, ed., *Risk: Man-Made Hazards to Man* (Oxford: Clarendon Press, 1985), pp. 35-53; quote on pp. 38-39.
25. See Bernard Cohen and I.S. Lee, "A Catalogue of Risks," *Health Physics,* vol. 36 (1979). Responses to disaster that appear compassionate may encourage its continuance. Subsidized insurance or ample disaster relief may—indeed has—encouraged people to move back into the way of potential future harm. The Galveston hurricane of 1900 killed 5,000 people; better warning reduced later death tolls. Still, hurricane Alicia did $700 million damage in 1983. Today, that same area—still hurricane prone—has been rebuilt, and developers are announcing the availability of new condominiums with unrestricted views unimpeded by sea walls. In order to reduce what he calls "disaster subsidy zones," John W. Sommer suggests a simple rule of public policy: "No geographical location shall be eligible for federal disaster relief for the same kind of disaster more than once" (John W. Sommer, "Disasters Unlimited," *The Freeman,* vol. 36, no. 4 (April 1986), p. 138.
26. Bruce Ames, "Cancer Scares Over Trivia: Natural Carcinogens in Food Outweigh Traces in Our Water," *Los Angeles Times,* May 15, 1986, p. 7.
27. H.S. Eisner, "Hazard Assessment: Experience and Expectation," *Science and Public Policy,* vol. 6, no. 3 (June 1979), p. 148.
28. Robert E. Goodin, "No Moral Nukes," *Ethics,* vol. 90 (April 1980), pp. 425-426.

29. Quoted among other wrong-headed predictions by famous people (the words are attributed to Charles H. Swell, Director of the U.S. Patent Office, 1896) in the September 1985 *Wall Street Journal*, p. 3.
30. S. Weisbord, "A World Unready for its Own Hazards," *Science News*, vol. 129 (May 31, 1986), pp. 342-348.
31. *ibid.*, p. 426.
32. I am indebted to William Havender for this formulation.
33. I am not arguing the desirability of nuclear power. Perhaps nuclear power was developed too rapidly or subsidized too heavily, so that the plants were built too big, too costly, too close to population centers, and too exposed to catastrophe. A slower and smaller approach might have encouraged the development of more nearly fail-safe designs (total safety is beyond our reach), thereby ruling out the worst. I am making use of the nuclear power example partly because exponents of risk aversion use this one-armed logic of catastrophe without compensation to apply to many other fields.
34. Goodin, "No Moral Nukes," p. 426.
35. Paul R. Ehrlich, "An Economist in Wonderland," *Social Science Quarterly,* vol. 62, no. 1 (March 1981), pp. 44-48.
36. Peter Huber, "Safety and the Second Best: The Hazards of Public Risk Management in the Courts," *Columbia Law Review,* vol. 85, no. 2 (March 1985), pp. 277-337.
37. *The Economist,* vol. 297, no. 7418, p. 6.
38. Edmund W. Kitch, "Suffer the Little Children," *Wall Street Journal,* March 25, 1986, p. 30.
39. See William C. Clark, "Managing the Unknown: An Ecological View of Risk Assessment," paper prepared for the SCOPE-MAB Workshop on Identification of Environmental Hazards, held in Shrewsbury, Mass., in January 1977; and Aaron Wildavsky, "No Risk is the Highest Risk of All," *American Scientist,* vol. 67 (Jan./Feb. 1979), pp. 32-37.
40. Marjorie Sun, "The Vexing Problems of Vaccine Compensation," *Science,* vol. 227 (March 1, 1985), p. 1012.
41. *ibid.*, pp. 1013-1014.

Chapter 3

1. The most comprehensive and fair-minded discussion of these approaches that I have found is Baruch Fischhoff, Paul Slovic, and Sarah Lichtenstein, "Which Risks Are Acceptable?," *Environment,* vol. 21, no. 4 (May 1979), pp. 17-38; and Paul Slovic, Baruch Fischhoff, and Sarah Lichtenstein, "Rating the Risks," *Environment,* vol. 21, no. 3 (April 1979), pp. 14-39.
2. Clifford S. Russell, "Discounting Human Life," *Resources,* no. 82 (Winter 1986), p. 9.
3. Irma Adelman, "An Economic Analysis of Population Growth," *The American Economic Review,* vol. 53, no. 3 (June 1963), pp. 314-339; quote on p. 321.
4. Jean Daric, "Occupational and Socio-Economic Status," National Office of Vital Statistics, Special Reports, 1951, no. 10.
5. Jack Hadley and Anthony Osei, "Does Income Affect Mortality? An Analysis of the Effects of Different Types of Income on Age/Sex/Race-Specific Mortality Rates in the United States," *Medical Care,* vol. 20, no. 9 (September 1982), pp.

901-914. The Antonovsky quote is from A. Antonovsky, "Social Class, Life Expectancy and Overall Mortality," *Milbank Memorial Fund Quarterly,* vol. 48 (1967), p. 31.

6. G.H. Orcutt, et al., "Does your probability of death depend on your environment? A microanalytic study," *American Economic Review,* vol. 67 (1977), p. 260.

7. Evelyn Kitagewa and Philip Hauser, *Trends and Differentials in Mortality* (Cambridge: Harvard Univ. Press, 1973), pp. 149, 153.

8. Taken from D.K. Myers and H.B. Newcombe, "Nuclear Power and Low Level Radiation Hazards," Atomic Energy of Canada, Ltd., March 1979, AECL-6482.

9. Ernest Siddall, "Nuclear Safety in Perspective," prepared for presentation to the Canadian Nuclear Association Convention, Toronto, June 1979, p. 1.

10. Hadley and Osei, "Does Income Affect Mortality?," p. 913.

11. Peter Huber, "The Market for Risk," *Regulation* (March/April 1984), pp. 33-39; quote on p. 37.

12. LAPHA v. Veneman 349 F. Supp. 1311, 1317; quoted in Jeremy Rabkin, "Private Rights, Private Rules: The Constitutional Disorder in Public Interest Litigation," unpublished book manuscript, 1986, p. 374.

13. W. Kip Viscusi, "Phosphates and the Environmental Free Lunch," *Regulation* (Sept./Dec. 1984), pp. 53-55; quote on p. 53.

14. *ibid.,* pp. 53-54.

15. *San Francisco Chronicle,* April 6, 1984.

16. Ralph L. Keeney and Detlof von Winterfeldt, "A Methodology to Examine Health Effects Induced by the Compliance Activities and Economic Costs of Environmental Regulation of Power Plants," Draft Report, Electric Power Research Institute. For a closely related study see the authors' "Why Indirect Health Risks of Regulations Should Be Examined," *Interfaces,* vol. 16, no. 6 (Nov./Dec. 1986), pp. 13-27.

17. S.C. Black and F. Niehaus, "How Safe is Too Safe?," *International Atomic Energy Agency Bulletin,* vol. 22 (1980), pp. 40-50; National Safety Council, *Accident Facts, 1982 Edition* (Chicago: National Safety Council, 1982); and National Safety Council, *Accident Facts, 1983 Edition* (Chicago: National Safety Council, 1983).

18. S.C. Black, F. Niehaus, and D. Simpson, "Benefits and Risks of Alternative Energy Supply Systems," Technical Report, International Atomic Energy Agency, Vienna, 1978; U.S. Department of Energy, *Energy Technologies and the Environment: Environmental Information Handbook,* DOE/EP-0026 (Springfield, VA: National Technical Information Service, 1981); and L.D. Hamilton and A.S. Manne, "Health and Economic Costs of Alternative Energy Sources," *Nuclear Power and Its Fuel Cycle,* vol. 7 (Vienna: International Atomic Energy Agency, 1977).

19. Margaret W. Linn, Richard Sandifer, and Shayna Stein, "Effects of Unemployment on Mental and Physical Health," *American Journal of Public Health,* vol. 75, no. 5 (May 1985), pp. 502-506.

20. M.H. Brenner, *Mental Illness and the Economy* (Cambridge, Mass.: Harvard Univ. Press, 1973); "Personal Stability and Economic Security," *Social Policy,* vol. 8 (May/June 1977), pp. 2-4; and "Mortality and the National Economy," *Lancet* (1979), pp. 568-573.

21. M. Tabor, "The Stress of Job Loss," *Occupational Health and Safety,* vol. 51, no. 6 (June 1982), pp. 20-26.

22. Keeney and von Winterfeldt, "A Methodology to Examine Health Effects," p. 11.
23. B. McMahon, S. Johnson, and T. Pugh, "Relation of Suicide Rates to Social Conditions," *Public Health Reports,* vol. 78, no. 4 (April 1963), pp. 285-293.
24. See the review article by D. Dooley and R. Catalano, "Economic Change as a Cause of Behavioral Disorder," *Psychological Bulletin,* vol. 87, no. 3 (1980), pp. 450-468.
25. Keeney and von Winterfeldt, "A Methodology to Examine Health Effects," p. 11.
26. L.C. March, *Health and Unemployment* (New York: Oxford Univ. Press, 1933); and Brenner, "Mortality and the National Economy."
27. Dooley and Catalano, "Economic Change as a Cause of Behavioral Disorder."
28. L.D. Steinberg, R. Catalano, and D. Dooley, "Economic Antecedents of Child Abuse and Neglect," *Child Development,* vol. 52 (1981), pp. 975-985.
29. Quoted in Adelman, "An Economic Analysis of Population Growth," p. 321.
30. Lewis Thomas, "Scientific Frontiers and National Frontiers," *Foreign Affairs* (Spring 1984), pp. 980-981.
31. *ibid.,* p. 981. See also J. McKinley and S. McKinley, "The questionable contribution of medical measures to the decline of mortality in the twentieth century," *Milbank Memorial Fund Quarterly,* vol. 55 (1977), pp. 405-428.
32. *ibid.*
33. L.A. Sagan and A.A. Afifi, "Health and Economic Development II: Longevity," Research Memorandum 78-41, International Institute for Applied Systems Analysis, August 1978, p. 16.
34. Orcutt, et al., "Does your probability of death depend on your environment?"
35. Sagan and Afifi, "Health and Economic Development II," p. 18.
36. Roger Lewin, "Trial of Ironies to Parkinson's Disease," *Science,* vol. 224, no. 4653 (June 1984), p. 1083.
37. *Nature,* vol. 309, May 3, 1984, pp. 1-2.
38. Martin Landau, "Redundancy, Rationality and the Problem of Duplication and Overlap," *Public Administration Review,* vol. 29, no. 4 (July/August 1969), pp. 346-358.
39. John von Neumann, "The General and Logical Theory of Automata," Walter Buckley, ed., *Modern Systems Research for the Behavioral Scientist* (Chicago: Aldine Publishing Co., 1968), pp. 97-107. See also, W. Ross Ashby, "Variety, Constraint, and the Law of Requisite Variety," *ibid.,* pp. 129-136. Given a complex system with many parts and the assumption that all parts are equally likely to fail, a 90 percent part reliability provides a 99.5 percent system reliability. Should a system increase from 5 to 5000 steps in complexity, an increase in redundancy from three to six at each step would hold reliability to the 99.5 percent level. Robert Anthony, from whom these illustrations are taken, observes that if the parts are people, reliability may conflict with accountability because it would be difficult to determine who was responsible for a breakdown. (Robert Anthony, "Accountability and Credibility in the Management of Complex Hazardous Technology," *Policy Studies Review,* vol. 7, no. 4 [May 1982], pp. 705-715.) No principle, apparently, lives alone, or is entirely desirable in every context.
40. John Freeman and Michael T. Hannan, "The Population Ecology of Organizations," *American Journal of Sociology,* vol. 82, no. 5 (March 1977), pp. 929-964; quote on pp. 960-961.

41. M. Mitchell Waldrop, "Resolving the Star Wars Software Dilemma," *Science,* vol. 232 (May 9, 1986), p. 711.

42. Mancur Olson, *The Rise and Decline of Nations: Economic Growth, Stagflation and Social Rigidities* (Cambridge, MA: Yale Univ. Press, 1982), p. 173.

43. *ibid.*

Chapter 4

1. C.S. Holling, "Resilience and Stability of Ecological Systems," *Annual Review of Ecology and Systematics,* vol. 4 (1979), pp. 1-23.

2. *ibid.*

3. Friedrich A. Hayek, *Rules and Order,* vol. 1 of *Law, Legislation and Liberty* (Chicago: University of Chicago Press, 1973-79).

4. Michael R. Gordon, "Lehman's Navy Riding High, But Critics Question Its Strategy and Rapid Growth," *The National Journal,* vol. 17, no. 38 (Sept. 21, 1985), p. 2125.

5. John Jewkes, David Sawers, and Richard Stillerman, *The Sources of Invention* (New York: St. Martin's Press, 1959), pp. 230-231.

6. Carl-Axel S. Stael von Holstein, "An Experiment in Probabilistic Weather Forecasting," *Journal of Applied Meteorology,* vol. 10 (August 1971), pp. 635-645; and "Probabilistic Forecasting," *Organizational Behavior and Human Performance,* vol. 8 (August 1972), pp. 139-158. For a general survey, see Steve Chan, "Expert Judgments Under Uncertainty: Some Evidence and Suggestions," *Social Science Quarterly,* vol. 63, no. 3 (September 1982), pp. 428-444.

7. Richard W. Cooper, "Resource Needs Revisited," *Brookings Papers on Economic Activity,* vol. 1 (1975), pp. 238-245; William R. Cline, "Long-Term Forecasts in International Economics," *The American Economic Review,* vol. 75, no. 2 (May 1985), pp. 120-126. For further examples, see Amitai Etzioni, "Future Angst: Nine Rules for Stumbling Serenely into the Future," *NEXT* (July/August 1980), pp. 69-72.

8. John D. Graham and James W. Vaupel, "The Value of a Life: Does It Make a Difference?," *Journal of Risk Analysis,* vol. 1, no. 1 (1981), pp. 89-95.

9. Bruce Ames, Renae Magaw, and Lois Swirsky Gold, "Ranking Possible Carcinogenic Hazards," *Science,* vol. 236, no. 4759 (April 17, 1987), pp. 271-280.

10. William C. Clark, "Witches, Floods, and Wonder Drugs: Historical Perspectives on Risk Management," Richard C. Schwing and Walter A. Albers, Jr., eds., *Societal Risk Assessment: How Safe is Safe Enough?* (New York/London: Plenum Press, 1980), pp. 287-313; quote on p. 298 (emphasis added).

11. C.S. Holling, C.J. Walters, and D. Ludwig, "Myths, Time Scales and Surprise in Ecological Management," typescript, 1981.

12. *ibid.*, pp. 24-25.

13. Among the immense literature that could be cited is Richard Cyert and James March, *A Behavioral Theory of the Firm* (Englewood Cliffs, NJ: Prentice-Hall, 1963); Pendleton Herring, *The Politics of Democracy* (New York: W.W. Norton & Co. 1940); and Charles S. Hyneman, *Bureaucracy in a Democracy* (New York: Harper, 1950).

14. My sister tells of observing passengers in the early days carrying bathroom plungers on BART. Since the system was assumed to operate without error (at high speed and with powerful brakes), it was believed that trains would succeed

each other with great rapidity so no one would ever have to stand. Hence, no provision was made for straps or handles to which passengers might attach themselves. As engines and brakes burned out and the all-seeing computer lost track of trains, passengers piled up in the remaining vehicles. Alas, they could not steady themselves while standing; nothing if not resilient, however, some standees brought plungers, stuck them on the ceilings, held on, and got to their destinations in one piece.

15. Clark, "Witches, Floods, and Wonder Drugs."
16. Henry Petroski, *To Engineer is Human: The Role of Failure in Successful Design* (New York: St. Martin's Press, 1985).
17. H.W. Lewis, "Technological Risk," typescript, pp. 37-38.
18. Michele Kenzie, "Volcanoes: The Problem of Prediction," *Yale Scientific* (Spring 1986), pp. 14-17.
19. *ibid.,* p. 17.
20. *ibid.,* p. 14.
21. *ibid.,* p. 17.
22. W. Henry Lambright and Jane Heckley, "Policymaking for Emerging Technology: The Case of Earthquake Prediction," *Policy Sciences,* vol. 18, no. 3 (1985), pp. 227-240. See also Kiyoo Mogl, *Earthquake Prediction* (Orlando, FL: Academic Press, 1985).
23. Graeme Coughley, *The Deer Wars* (Auckland, New Zealand: Heinemann, 1983).
24. Elizabeth Walker Mechling and Jay Mechling, "Sweet Talk: The Moral Rhetoric of Sugar," *Central States Speech Journal,* vol. 34, no. 1 (Spring 1983), pp. 19-32; William Havender, "The Science and Politics of Cyclamates," *The Public Interest,* no. 71 (Spring 1983), pp. 17-32; and Elizabeth Whelan, *Toxic Terror* (Ottawa, IL: Jameson Books, 1985), inter alia.
25. L. Davis, "The Fructose Connection: Copper and Heart Disease," *Science News,* May 3, 1986, p. 279. See also *Science News,* June 8, 1985, p. 357.
26. Louise B. Russell, *Is Prevention Better Than Cure?* (Washington, DC: Brookings Institution, 1986), p. 7.
27. *ibid.,* p. 8.
28. *ibid.,* p. 107.
29. *ibid.,* p. 78.
30. *ibid.,* p. 108.
31. Bernard L. Cohen, "Criteria for Technology Acceptability," *Risk Analyses,* vol. 5, no. 1 (March 1985), pp. 1-3.
32. John Mendeloff, *The Dilemma of Rulemaking for Toxic Substances* (Cambridge, MA: MIT Press, forthcoming), pp. 62-63 of typescript.
33. Joseph Morone and Edward Woodhouse, "Adverting Catastrophe: Strategies for Regulating Risky Technologies," draft manuscript, 1985, p. 281; adapted from Table 6, p. 534, in E.P. O'Donnell and J.J. Mauro, "A Cost-Benefit Comparison of Nuclear and Nonnuclear Health and Safety Protective Measures and Regulations," *Nuclear Safety,* vol. 20 (Sept./Oct. 1979), pp. 525-540.
34. Mendeloff, "Overregulation and Underregulation," p. 38.
35. Dary M. Freedman, "Reasonable Certainty of No Harm: Reviving the Safety Standard for Food Additives, Color Additives, and Animal Drugs," *Ecology Law Quarterly,* vol. 7 (1978).
36. *Wall Street Journal,* September 22, 1986, p. 10.
37. Edward I. Koch, "Death and Justice," *The New Republic,* April 15, 1985, p. 14.

38. S. Weisbord, "A World Unready for Its Own Hazards," *Science News,* vol. 129, no. 22 (May 31, 1986), pp. 342-343.

39. *ibid.*

40. Qualitative surprise might more simply be called "ignorance." But I prefer to reserve that term for situations where neither the class nor the probability of consequences are known, but the ignorant do not know that they don't know. A beginning taxonomy of ignorance is provided by Robert Wolfson and Thomas Carroll:

> By ignorance we mean that state of knowledge wherein the decision maker lacks awareness of some objectively possible states of the world which he faces. We can detail three types of ignorance.
> 1. *Ignorance of actions.* There are some actions which are objective alternatives but about which the individual is unaware. We take this to mean that he is in ignorance of all outcomes attributable solely to these unknown alternatives.
> 2. *Ignorance of outcomes.* There exist some outcomes of which the decision maker is completely unaware. He believes that the *n* outcomes he has in mind constitute the full set of consequences attributable to a particular set of actions; but in fact there are *m* others.
> 3. *Ignorance of values.* There are some outcomes of which he is aware, but whose nature is a complete mystery to him. That is there are *n* possible outcomes which he knows well enough to say that if the *i*th occurs, it will benefit or disadvantage him in some imaginable manner and/or amount. There are *m* others which he knows might occur, but which he cannot describe in any such fashion. (Robert J. Wolfson and Thomas M. Carroll, "Ignorance, Error, and Information in the Classic Theory of Decision," *Behavioral Science,* vol. 21 [1976], pp. 107-115.)

41. Jerome S. Bruner, "The Conditions of Creativity," Howard E. Gruber, et al., eds., *Contemporary Approaches to Creative Thinking* (Englewood Cliffs, NJ: Prentice Hall, 1962).

42. Israel M. Kirzner, "Uncertainty, Discovery, and Human Action: A Study of the Entrepreneurial Profile in the Misesian System," Israel M. Kirzner, ed., *Method, Process, and Austrian Economics: Essays in Honor of Ludwig von Mises* (Lexington, MA: Lexington Books, 1982), p. 151.

43. In the trace gases update, Robert E. Dickenson and Ralph S. Cuerone of the National Center for Atmospheric Research write in regard to global warming that "the expected global temperature change of about 0.5°C is masked by natural climate variations" (*Environment,* vol. 28, no. 2 [March 1986], p. 2). The same journal contains a summary of a report from *Science* indicating that a "0.2 percent irradiance reduction" could bring about "a 1% cooling...that is believed to have caused the 'Little Ice Age' in Europe...." (*ibid.,* p. 23).

44. Bernard Ramberg, *Nuclear Power Plants as Weapons for the Enemy: An Unrecognized Military Peril* (Berkeley/Los Angeles, CA: University of California Press, 1984).

45. Amory R. Lovins and L. Hunter Lovins, *Brittle Power: Energy Strategy for National Security* (Andover, MA: Brick House Publishing Co., 1982), pp. 27, 178-179.

46. *ibid.,* p. 179.

47. *ibid.,* p. 181.

48. *ibid.*, p. 182.
49. *ibid.*, p. 183.
50. Amory Lovins, *Soft Energy Paths* (Harmondsworth: Penguin, 1977), p. 148.
51. Lovins and Lovins, *Brittle Power,* p. 186.
52. *ibid.*, p. 185 (emphasis in original).
53. *ibid.*
54. *ibid.*, p. 191.
55. *ibid.*, p. 188.
56. *ibid.*, p. 201.
57. I have taken this evocative phrase from a letter written to me by Robert Goodin containing a critique of my critique of his position as discussed in the first chapter.

Chapter 5

1. Barry Commoner, *The Closing Circle: Nature, Man and Technology* (New York: Knopf, 1971).
2. Clifton Lee Gass, "Biological Foundations of Surprise," typescript, n.d., p. 8.
3. Kenneth E.F. Watt and Paul Craig, "Surprise, Ecological Stability Theory, and a Reinterpretation of the Industrial Revolution," C.S. Holling, ed., *The Anatomy of Surprise* (New York: Wiley Press, forthcoming), p. 10 of typescript.
4. William Havender, "On Human Hubris," *Political Psychology,* vol. 2, no. 1 (Spring 1980), pp. 52-58. See the clarifying discussion in Herbert A. Simon, *Reason in Human Affairs* (Stanford, CA: Stanford Univ. Press, 1983), chap. 2.
5. Watt and Craig, "Surprise, Ecological Stability Theory," p. 1 of typescript.
6. Interesting discussions of stability, including some disagreement about how it might usefully be defined, may be found in W.A. Van Dobben and R.H. Lowe-McConnell, *Unifying Concepts in Ecology,* Report of the Plenary Session of the First International Congress of Ecology, Sept. 8-14, 1974 (The Hague: Dr. W. Junk B.V. Publishers, 1975).
7. I omit Watt and Craig's *potential principle* partly because it refers to physical systems and partly because the authors feel that "this principle may be revealed as all-encompassing, and including all of the others, after further theoretical research" (Watt and Craig, "Surprise, Ecological Stability Theory," p. 19).
8. *ibid.*, p. 13. (All underlining of names given to principles is added.)
9. *ibid.*, pp. 25-26.
10. *ibid.*, pp. 13-14.
11. *ibid.*, p. 26; and R.V. O'Neill, in *Ecology,* vol. 57 (1976), p. 1244.
12. Watt and Craig, p. 13.
13. *ibid.*, p. 14.
14. *ibid.*, p. 27.
15. L.R. Lawlor, "A Comment on Randomly Constructed Model Ecosystems," *American Naturalist,* vol. 112 (1978), p. 445.
16. M. Rejmanek and P. Stary, in *Nature,* vol. 280 (1979), p. 329.
17. Watt and Craig, "Surprise, Ecological Stability Theory," p. 16.
18. Martin Landau, "Redundancy, Rationality and the Problem of Duplication and Overlap," *Public Administration Review* (July/August 1969), pp. 346-358, quote from pp. 350-351.
19. W.S. McCulloch, "The Reliability of Biological Systems," M.G. Yovitz and S.

Cameron, eds., *Self-Organizing Systems* (New York: Pergamon Press, 1960), quoted in Landau, "Redundancy," p. 352.

20. Landau, "Redundancy," p. 350.
21. *ibid.,* pp. 355-356.
22. W. Ross Ashby, "Variety, Constraint, and the Law of Requisite Variety," Walter Buckley, ed., *Modern Systems Research for the Behavioral Scientist: A Sourcebook* (Chicago: Aldine, 1968), pp. 129-135.
23. Watt and Craig, "Surprise, Ecological Stability Theory," pp. 16-17.
24. *ibid.,* p. 17.
25. See Richard M. Cyert and James G. March, *A Behavioral Theory of the Firm* (Englewood Cliffs, N.J.: Prentice-Hall, 1976); and Victor A. Thompson, "Organizations as Systems," University Programs Modular Studies, General Learning Press, 1973.
26. Watt and Craig, "Surprise, Ecological Stability Theory," p. 17.
27. *ibid.,* pp. 28-29.
28. *ibid.,* pp. 17-18, 30.
29. *ibid.,* p. 19.
30. Stephen Jay Gould, "Darwinism and the Expansion of the Evolutionary Theory," *Science*, vol. 216 (April 23, 1982), pp. 380-386.
31. Watt and Craig, "Surprise, Ecological Stability Theory," pp. 19-20.
32. Stephen S. O'Brien, David E. Wildt, and Mitchell Bush, "The Cheetah in Genetic Peril," *Scientific American*, vol. 254, no 5 (May 1986), pp. 84, 89.
33. Phyllis D. Coley, John P. Breyant, and F. Stuart Chapin III, "Resource Availability and Plant Antiherbivon Defense," *Science*, vol. 230, no. 4728 (November 22, 1985), p. 896.

Chapter 6

1. Bennet Ramberg, "Learning From Chernobyl," *Foreign Affairs* (Winter 1986/87), p. 307.
2. H.W. Lewis, a review of "The Accident at Chernobyl Nuclear Power Plant and Its Consequences," by the USSR State Committee on the Utilization of Atomic Energy, *Environment*, vol. 28, no. 9 (Nov. 1986), p. 26.
3. See IE Bulletin 79-14 and revisions.
4. See IE Bulletin 79-04, and interviewee comments.
5. Office of Inspection and Enforcement, "Lessons Learned from Three Mile Island," NUREG-616, pp. 92, 152-158.
6. "Inspecting Operating Nuclear Powerplants: Shortcomings in the Nuclear Regulatory Program," Committee on Government Operations, U.S. Government Printing Office (June 12, 1981), especially the testimony of Victor Stello.
7. Edward Teller, the inventor of the hydrogen bomb, served as the first chair of the Reactor Safeguards Committee of the Atomic Energy Commission. The AEC's official historians, in their recent work on the early AEC, quote Teller at some length on this point: "We could not follow the usual method of trial and error. This method was an integral part of American industrial progress before the nuclear age, but in the nuclear age it presented intolerable risks.... The trials had to be on paper because actual errors could be catastrophic." George T. Mazuzan and J. Samuel Walker, *Controlling the Atom* (Berkeley: Univ. of California Press, 1984), p. 61.

8. There has been an effort to gain greater recognition of this particular problem through a steering committee on piping systems, under the auspices of the Pressure Vessel Research Committee of the Welding Research Council.
9. This example is taken from *NRC Issuances: Opinions and Decisions,* 12 NRC 30 (1980), p. 43ff.
10. The probable loss of power was thought to lie between 1.0 and 0.1. Over the expected forty year life of the reactor, this would mean power loss frequency would lie between a maximum of forty and a minimum of four. The 0.4 estimate agreed on would translate into sixteen such occasions over the life of the plant.
11. "Running the diesels unloaded or only lightly loaded would cause incomplete fuel combustion that would lead to varnish and gum deposits and create a risk of fire in the engine exhaust system." 12 NRC 30 (1980), p. 62.
12. "Fire Damage Data Analysis as Related to Current Testing Practice for Nuclear Power Application," Brookhaven National Laboratories, BNL-NUREG-23364, cited in 13 NRC 778 (1981).
13. Interview with section chief, February 8, 1985.
14. Interview with NRC manager, March 9, 1985.
15. Interview with section chief, February 6, 1985.
16. Interview with NRC research manager, March 8, 1985.
17. Letter from Spencer Bush to L.J. Chockie, dated August 27, 1981.
18. This is an ongoing issue. For the Vermont Yankee case, see, for example, *AEC Issuances: Opinions and Decisions,* ALAB-217, RAI-74-7 61 (July 11, 1974); ALAB-229, RAI-74-9 (September 18, 1974); AEC, CLI-74-40 (November 7, 1974). For the Sequoyah and other cases, see F.R. Myatt, "Nuclear Research Since Three Mile Island," *Science,* vol. 216, no. 4542 (April 9, 1982), p. 134.
19. Interview with NRC resident inspector, February 7, 1985.

Chapter 7

1. Quoted in John Doull, Curtis D. Klaassen, and Mary O. Andur, eds., *Casarett and Doull's Toxicology,* 2nd ed. (New York: Macmillan, 1980).
2. Michael J. Brabec and I.A. Bernstein, "Cellular, Subcellular and Molecular Targets of Foreign Compounds," Andrew L. Reeves, ed., *Toxicology: Principles and Practice,* vol. 1 (New York: Wiley, 1981).
3. Susumu Tonegawa, "The Molecules of the Immune System," *Scientific American,* vol. 253, no. 4 (October 1985), pp. 122-131.
4. See Alvin M. Weinberg and John B. Storer, "Ambiguous Carcinogens and Their Regulation," *Risk Analysis,* vol. 5, no. 2 (1985), pp. 151-156.
5. See Arthur J. Vander, James H. Sherman, and Dorothy S. Luciano, *Human Physiology* (New York: McGraw-Hill, 1975).
6. See John Langone, "Heart Attack and Cholesterol," *Discover,* vol. 5, no. 3 (March 1984), pp. 20-23.
7. M. Alice Ottoboni, *The Dose Makes the Poison* (Berkeley, CA: Vincente Books, 1984), p. 113.
8. *ibid.,* p. 108.
9. Curtis D. Klaassen and John Doull, "Evaluation of Safety: Toxicological Evaluation," John Doull, Curtis D. Klaassen, and Mary O. Amdur, eds., *Casarett and Doull's Toxicology,* 2nd ed. (New York: Macmillan, 1980), p. 22.

10. Irwin Fridovich, "Superoxide Radical: An Endogenous Toxicant," *Annual Review of Pharmacology and Toxicology,* vol. 23 (1983), pp. 239-257; quote on p. 239.

11. Ottoboni, *The Dose Makes the Poison,* p. 36.

12. *Harvard Medical School Letter,* vol. 9, no. 2 (Dec. 1983), pp. 1-2.

13. Ted R. Norton, "Metabolism of Toxic Substances," John Doull, ed., *Toxicology: The Basic Science of Poisons* (New York: Macmillan, 1975), p. 45.

14. See Brabec and Bernstein, "Cellular, Subcellular and Molecular Targets of Foreign Compounds," p. 42; and Klaassen and Doull, "Evaluation of Safety," p. 22.

15. W. Jack Miller, "Zinc in animal and human health," J. Rose, ed., *Trace Elements in Health* (London: Butterworths, 1983), pp. 182-192.

16. See Bryan E. Hainline and K.V. Rajagopalan, "Molybdenum in animal and human health," *ibid.,* pp. 150-166.

17. Ottoboni, *The Dose Makes the Poison,* pp. 37, 93.

18. R. McN. Alexander, "Optimum Strengths for Bones Liable to Fatigue or Accidental Fracture," *Journal of Theoretical Biology,* vol. 109 (1984), pp. 621-636.

19. Ottoboni, *The Dose Makes the Poison,* p. 41.

20. R.J. Richardson, "Toxicology of the Nervous System," Andrew L. Reeves, ed., *Toxicology: Principles and Practice,* vol. I (New York: Wiley, 1981), p. 115; and Stata Norton, "Toxicology of the Central Nervous System," Louis J. Casarett and John Doull, eds., *Toxicology* (New York: Macmillan, 1975), p. 151.

21. Stata Norton, "Toxicology," p. 153.

22. Curtis D. Klaassen, "Absorption, Distribution, and Excretion of Toxicants," Casarett and Doull, eds., *Toxicology,* p. 35.

23. Brabec and Bernstein, "Cellular, Subcellular and Molecular Targets," p. 45.

24. Ottoboni, *The Dose Makes the Poison,* p. 107.

25. Ted Norton, "Metabolism of Toxic Substances," p. 45.

26. Ottoboni, *The Dose Makes the Poison,* p. 59.

27. Steven B. Mizel and Peter Jaret, *In Self-Defense* (San Diego: Harcourt Brace Jovanovich, 1985), uncorrected page proofs, p. 60.

28. Bruce N. Ames and Robert L. Saul, "Oxidative DNA Damage as Related to Cancer and Aging," *Fourth International Conference of Environmental Mutagens* (New York: Alan R. Liss, 1985), p. 8; Brabec and Bernstein, "Cellular, Subcellular and Molecular Targets," pp. 46-47.

29. Brabec and Bernstein, "Cellular, Subcellular and Molecular Targets," pp. 45, 30.

30. R.J. Richardson, "Toxicology of the Nervous System," p. 115.

31. Brabec and Bernstein, "Cellular, Subcellular and Molecular Targets," p. 45.

32. Richardson, "Toxicology of the Nervous System," p. 129.

33. Ames and Saul, "Oxidative DNA Damage," p. 4. See also Barry Halliwell and John M.C. Gutteridge, "Oxygen toxicity, oxygen radicals, transition metals and disease," *Biochemical Journal,* vol. 219 (1984), pp. 1-14.

34. Ames and Saul, p. 2.

35. Martin Landau, "Redundancy, Rationality and the Problem of Duplication and Overlap," *Public Administration Review,* vol. 29, no. 4 (July/August 1969), pp. 346-358.

36. Robert I. Macey, *Human Physiology,* 2nd ed. (Englewood Cliffs, NJ: Prentice-Hall, 1975), p. 170.

37. Ted Norton, "Metabolism of Toxic Substances," p. 45.

38. Brabec and Bernstein, "Cellular, Subcellular and Molecular Targets," p. 37.
39. Howard Falk, "Defending the Human Body: The Immune System," *Biology Digest,* vol. 2, no. 1 (Sept. 1975), pp. 11-26.
40. See J.A. Miller, "Nerve Chemicals Direct Immunity," *Science News* (Dec. 8, 1984), p. 357.
41. William B. Jakoby, "Detoxification Enzymes," Jakoby, ed., *Enzymatic Basis of Detoxification,* vol. I (New York: Academic Press, 1980), pp. 4-5.
42. Macey, *Human Physiology,* p. 125.
43. Mizel and Jaret, *In Self-Defense,* p. 78.
44. Brabec and Bernstein, "Cellular, Subcellular and Molecular Targets," p. 45.
45. Falk, "Defending the Human Body," p. 13.

Chapter 8

1. G. Edward White, *Tort Law in America: An Intellectual History* (New York: Oxford Univ. Press, 1980), p. 8.
2. *ibid.,* p. 12.
3. *ibid.,* p. 13.
4. *ibid.,* p. 17.
5. *ibid.*
6. *ibid.,* p. 18.
7. This doctrine—that contributory negligence would prevent an injured person from receiving damages—was first set forth in *Butterfield v. Forrester,* an English case decided in 1809 (11 East 59, 103 Eng. Rep. 926 [K.B. 1809]) and cited in Dean Maleney, "From Contributory to Comparative Negligence: A Needed Law Reform," *University of Florida Law Review,* vol. 11 (1958), pp. 145-146.
8. For example, the California Supreme Court in 1934, *Kalash v. Los Angeles Ladder Company,* cited by Gary T. Schwartz, "Foreword: Understanding Products Liability," *California Law Review,* vol. 67, no. 3 (May 1979), p. 437.
9. John Kirkland Clark, "Let the Maker Beware," *St. John's Law Review,* vol. 19 (April 1945), pp. 85-94.
10. Noore v. Perlberg, Inc., 268 App. Div. 149, 49 N.Y.S. (2d) 460 (1944), aff'd, 294 N.Y. 680, cited in *ibid.*
11. *ibid.*
12. Edwin Duval, "Strict Liability: Responsibility of Manufacturers for Injuries From Defective Products," *California Law Review,* vol. 33 (1945), p. 637.
13. Clark, "Let the Maker Beware."
14. Escola v. Coca-Cola, 24 C. 2d 453 (p. 462).
15. M. Shapo, "Towards a Jurisprudence of Injury: The Continuing Creation of a System of Substantive Justice in American Tort Law," published in 1984 as *Report to the Amerian Bar Association,* pp. 4-60 to 4-63.
16. *Dalehite v. United States,* cited in *ibid.,* p. 4-62.
17. See Second Restatement of Torts, Section 402A, published by the American Law Institute; and Dean Prosser, "The Fall of the Citadel," *Minnesota Law Review,* vol. 50 (1966), p. 791.
18. *Cronin v. J.B.E. Olson Corp.,* cited in Schwartz, "Foreword," p. 435.
19. Shapo, "Towards a Jurisprudence of Injury," p. 4-126.
20. *ibid.,* pp. 4-128 and 4-129.
21. See, for example, *McPherson v. Buick,* 160 App. Div. 55, 145 N.Y.S. 462 (1916), affirmed 217 N.Y. 382, 111 N.E. 1050.

22. Mike Hoenig, "Resolution of 'Crashworthiness' Design Claims," *St. Johns Law Review,* vol. 55, no. 4 (Summer 1981), pp. 633-727.

23. Larsen v. General Motors Corporation, 391 F. 2d 495, 502-506 (8th cir. 1968).

24. Hoenig, "Resolution," pp. 636-637.

25. Dawson v. Chrysler Corporation, 630 F. 2d 950 (3rd cir. 1980).

26. Hoenig, "Resolution," p. 648.

27. *ibid.,* p. 643.

28. Tien and Testa, "Critical Assessment of Social and Economic Implications of Safety Cars," August 1974, cited in *ibid.,* pp. 640-641.

29. *ibid.*

30. Samuel Peltzman, *Regulation of Automobile Safety* (Washington, DC: Enterprise Institute, 1975).

31. Shapo, "Towards a Jurisprudence of Injury," pp. 6-2 and 6-3.

32. *National Journal,* July 6, 1985.

33. *California Journal* (May 1984), p. 184.

34. *ibid.*

35. *ibid.,* pp. 183-185.

36. League of California Cities, March 1985 survey.

37. *San Francisco Chronicle,* "A Town That May Vanish," July 29, 1985.

38. *Oakland Tribune,* Sept. 15, 1985, p. A-2.

39. Mark A. Peterson, *Compensation of Injuries: Civil Jury Verdicts in Cook County,* R-3011-ICJ; Audrey Chin and Mark A. Peterson, *Deep Pockets, Empty Pockets: Who Wins in Cook County Jury Trials,* R-3249-ICJ.

40. "Deep Pockets, Empty Pockets: Patterns of Bias in Civil Jury Trials," *Rand Research Review.* vol. 9, no. 2 (Summer 1985), p. 2.

41. See Douglas J. Besharov, "How One Group Found a Path Out of the Liability Jungle," *Wall Street Journal,* April 17, 1986, p. 26.

42. Frank E. James, "With Most Contraceptives Put on Hold, Couples Face Grim Birth Control Choices," *Wall Street Journal,* April 17, 1986, p. 29.

Chapter 9

1. Attributed to Neils Bohr in Dietrick E. Thomsen, "Going Bohr's Way in Physics," *Bulletin of the American Academy of Arts and Sciences,* vol. 39, no. 7 (April 1986).

2. *Newsweek,* June 17, 1985.

3. Op-Ed piece by Rep. Don Edwards of California, *New York Times,* June 19, 1985; also June 16, 1985.

4. Douglas J. Besharov, "An Overdose of Concern: Child Abuse and the Over-reporting Problem," *Regulation,* vol. 9, no. 6 (Nov./Dec. 1985), pp. 25-26.

5. See Sam Peltzman, *Regulation of Pharmaceutical Innovation: The 1962 Amendments* (Washington: American Enterprise Institute, 1974); and William M. Wardell and Louis Lasagna, *Regulation and Drug Development* (Washington: American Enterprise Institute, 1975).

6. "Irradiated Foods," American Council on Science and Health, New York, 1985.

7. *Nature,* vol. 315, May 30, 1985, pp. 358-359; *New York Times,* April 20, 1985; *Science,* vol. 228, June 7, 1985, pp. 1176-1177. This situation has now (Feb. 1986) changed. Intense pressure was brought to bear on FDA, both to grant a

compassionate exemption (pituitary dwarves can only be helped by growth hormone at the time of puberty; once this sensitive phase is over, it is too late), and to approve the genetically-engineered product. These steps have now been taken (*New York Times*, Sept. 10, 1985; *Nature*, Oct. 24-30, 1985, p. 659; *Science*, Nov. 1, 1985, p. 523). While FDA deserves credit for waiving its normal schedule and speeding approval, this is, in fact, a tacit admission that its normal approval procedures do result in drug lag. The same is true for its recent speed up in approving anti-AIDS drugs despite admitted serious side effects.

8. *Wall Street Journal*, March 8, 1985.
9. *Science*, vol. 227, March 15, 1985, p. 1321.
10. *Science*, vol. 229, July 5, 1985, pp. 34-35.
11. American Council on Science and Health, "Ethylene Dibromide (EDB)," New York, 1984. On September 19, 1985, the EPA announced its intention to ban carbon disulfide and carbon tetrachloride. The sale of such products was made illegal after Dec. 31, 1985, although existing stocks may be used until June 30, 1986. (*Federal Register*, 50, Thursday, Sept. 19, 1985, pp. 38092-38095.)
12. *New York Times*, Jan. 13, 1985.
13. American Council on Science and Health, "PCB's: Is the Cure Worth the Cost?," New York, 1985; Petr Beckmann, *Access to Energy*, March 1985.
14. *Wall Street Journal*, March 26, 1985; Michael J. Bennett, in a series of articles in the *Detroit News*, March 3, 4, 5, and 6, 1985.
15. *Science*, vol. 227, March 8, 1985, pp. 1184-1186.
16. Robert W. Crandall, "An Acid Test for Congress," *Regulation* (Sept./Oct. 1984), p. 22.
17. Milton Copoulos, "It's Effective—But Is It Safe?," *Reason* (March 1985), pp. 29-30.
18. *Wall Street Journal*, July 12, 1985.
19. *San Francisco Examiner*, June 28, 1985; *Journal of the American Medical Association*, June 28, 1985.
20. Peter Huber, "The IChing of Acid Rain," *Regulation* (Sept./Dec. 1984), p. 17.
21. *Wall Street Journal*, May 16, 1985; *Washington Post*, March 10, 1985.
22. American Council on Science and Health, "Ethylene Dibromide (EDB)"; Chris Whipple, "Redistributing Risk," *Regulation* (May/June 1985), p. 40.

Chapter 10

1. Peter Huber, "Safety and the Second Best: Risk Management in the Courts," *Columbia Law Review*, vol. 85 (1985), p. 337.
2. Paul Milvy, "A General Guideline for Management of Risk From Carcinogens," *Risk Analysis*, vol. 6, no. 1 (1986), p.70.
3. Bruce Ames, "Dietary Carcinogens and Anticarcinogens," *Science*, vol. 221, no. 4617 (September 23, 1983), pp. 1256-1264. See also Ames, et al., "Ranking Possible Carcinogenic Hazards," *Science*, vol. 236, no. 4759 (April 17, 1987).
4. Herbert A. Simon, *Reason in Human Affairs* (Stanford, CA: Stanford Univ. Press, 1983), p. 69.
5. *ibid.*, p. 70.
6. Ronald A. Heiner, "The Origin of Predictable Behavior," *American Economic Review*, vol. 13, no. 4 (Sept. 1983), pp. 560-595.
7. Aaron Wildavsky, "The Self-Evaluating Organization," *Public Administration Review*, vol. 32, no. 5 (Sept./Oct. 1972), pp. 509-520.

8. See Douglas J. Besharov, "Unfounded Allegations—A New Child Abuse Problem," *The Public Interest*, no. 83 (Spring 1986), pp. 18-34.

9. Joseph Schumpeter, *Capitalism, Socialism, and Democracy* (New York: Harper, 1942).

10. Kenneth E. Boulding, *Beyond Economics: Essays on Society, Religion, and Ethics* (Ann Arbor: Univ. of Michigan Press, 1968), pp. 142-143.

11. *ibid.*, p. 144.

12. *ibid.*, pp. 142-145.

13. Dennis Avery, "U.S. Farm Dilemma: The Global Bad News is Wrong," *Science*, vol. 230 (Oct. 25, 1985), pp. 409-410.

14. This book is about danger and safety stemming from domestic uses of technology. Nuclear or other kinds of war are not included. It is quite possible that humankind will do itself in in ways not contemplated here.

15. Stephen Cotgrove, *Catastrophe or Cornucopia: The Environment, Politics, and the Future* (New York: Wiley, 1982).

16. Christopher H. Schroeder, "Rights Against Risks," *Columbia Law Review*, vol. 86, no. 3 (April 1986), pp. 495-563. Readers should consult the original and not be content with my slim summary.

17. *ibid.*, p. 499.

18. *ibid.*, p. 508.

19. *ibid.*, p. 509.

20. *ibid.*, p. 510. The quote within a quote is from p. 499, note 19.

21. *ibid.*, p. 501.

22. *ibid.*, p. 511.

23. *ibid.*, p. 516.

24. *ibid.*, p. 519.

25. *ibid.*, pp. 527-528.

26. *ibid.*, pp. 553-555.

27. *ibid.*, p. 555.

28. Martin Landau, "The Classroom and Political Science: An Essay on Political Theory," V. Van Dyke, ed., *Teaching Political Science: The Professor and the Polity* (Atlantic Highlands, NJ: Humanities Press, 1977), pp. 71-88.

29. Michael Polanyi, "The Republic of Science: Its Political and Economic Theory," *Minerva*, vol. 1, no. 1 (Autumn 1962) pp. 54-73.

30. Schroeder, "Rights Against Risks," p. 562.

31. See Martin Landau, "Federalism, Redundancy and System Reliability," *Publius*, vol. 3 (Fall 1973).

32. A. Schmidt, "The FDA Today: Critics, Congress, and Consumerism," speech to National Press Club, (Washington, D.C., Oct. 29, 1974; cited in Henry G. Grabowski and John M. Vernon, *The Regulation of Pharmaceuticals: Balancing the Benefits and Risks* (Washington, DC: American Enterprise Institute, 1983), pp. 317-318.

33. William D. Ruckelshaus, "Risk, Science, and Democracy," *Issues in Science and Technology*, vol. 1, no. 3 (Spring 1985), pp. 19-38; quote on p. 33.

34. Eugene Bardach brought "fear of regret" to my attention.

35. John Rawls, *A Theory of Justice* (Cambridge: Harvard Univ. Press, 1971). For a critique closer to the view advanced here, see John Harsanyi, "Can the Maximin Principle Serve as a Basis for Morality? A Critique of John Rawls's Theory," *American Political Science Review*, vol. 69, no. 2 (June 1975), pp. 594-606.

36. Robert S. Smith, "Compensating Wage Differentials and Public Policy: A Review," *Industrial and Labor Relations Review,* vol. 32, no. 3 (April 1979), pp. 339-352.
37. Charles Perrow, *Normal Accidents: Living With High Risk Technologies* (New York: Basic Books, 1984), p. 4.

Index